AF698114

Differential Cryptanalysis of the Data Encryption Standard

Eli Biham
Adi Shamir

Differential Cryptanalysis of the Data Encryption Standard

With 56 Illustrations

Springer-Verlag
New York Berlin Heidelberg London Paris
Tokyo Hong Kong Barcelona Budapest

Eli Biham
Computer Science Department
Technion-Israel Institute of Technology
Haifa 32000
Israel

Adi Shamir
Department of Applied Mathematics and Computer Science
The Weizmann Institute of Science
Rehovot 76100
Israel

QA
76.9
.A25
B54
1993

Library of Congress Cataloging-in-Publication Data
Biham, Eli.
Differential cryptanalysis of the Data Encryption Standard / Eli Biham, Adi Shamir.
p. cm.
Includes bibliographical references and index.
ISBN 0-387-97930-1. --ISBN 3-540-97930-1
1. Computer – Access control. 2. Cryptography. I. Shamir, Adi. II. Title.
QA76.9.A25B54 1993
005.8'2 – dc20 92-44581

Printed on acid-free paper.

© 1993 by Springer-Verlag New York, Inc.
All rights reserved. This work may not be translated or copied in whole or in part without the written permission of the publisher (Springer-Verlag New York, Inc., 175 Fifth Avenue, New York, NY 10010, USA), except for brief excerpts in connection with reviews or scholarly analysis. Use in connection with any form of information storage and retrieval, electronic adaptation, computer software, or by similar or dissimilar methodology now known or hereafter developed is forbidden.
The use of general descriptive names, trade names, trademarks, etc., in this publication, even if the former are not especially identified, is not to be taken as a sign that such names, as understood by the Trade Marks and Merchandise Marks Act, may accordingly be used freely by anyone.

Production managed by Dimitry L. Loseff; manufacturing supervised by Vincent Scelta.
Photocomposed copy prepared using the authors' LATEX files.
Printed and bound by Edwards Brothers, Inc., Ann Arbor, MI.
Printed in the United States of America.

9 8 7 6 5 4 3 2 1

ISBN 0-387-97930-1 Springer-Verlag New York Berlin Heidelberg
ISBN 3-540-97930-1 Springer-Verlag Berlin Heidelberg New York

Preface

The security of iterated cryptosystems and hash functions has been an active research area for many years. The best known and most widely used function of this type is the Data Encryption Standard (DES). It was developed at IBM and adopted by the National Bureau of Standards in the mid 70's, and has successfully withstood all the attacks published so far in the open literature. Since the introduction of DES, many other iterated cryptosystems were developed, but their design and analysis were based on ad-hoc heuristic arguments, with no theoretical justification.

In this book, we develop a new type of cryptanalytic attack which can be successfully applied to many iterated cryptosystems and hash functions. It is primarily a chosen plaintext attack but under certain circumstances, it can also be applied as a known plaintext attack. We call it "differential cryptanalysis", since it analyzes the evolution of differences when two related plaintexts are encrypted under the same key.

Differential cryptanalysis is the first published attack which is capable of breaking the full 16-round DES in less than 2^{55} complexity. The data analysis phase computes the key by analyzing about 2^{36} ciphertexts in 2^{37} time. The 2^{36} usable ciphertexts are obtained during the data collection phase from a larger pool of 2^{47} chosen plaintexts by a simple bit repetition criteria which discards more than 99.9% of the ciphertexts as soon as they are generated.

This attack can be applied to a wide variety of DES-like substitution/ permutation cryptosystems, and it demonstrates the crucial role of each element in their design. In particular, we show that almost any structural modification of DES leads to a much weaker cryptosystem, and that DES reduced to eight rounds is so weak that it can be broken in two minutes on a personal computer. The attack is also applicable to bounded-round versions of the cryptosystems FEAL, Khafre, REDOC-II, LOKI and Lucifer, and to the hash functions Snefru and N-Hash.

We would like to use this opportunity to thank our colleagues who contributed remarks, suggestions, ideas and designs. Shoji Miyaguchi's FEAL cryptosystem motivated the first version of our attack, and Ralph Merkle's Snefru motivated its extension to hash functions. We had valuable discussions with Henry Gilbert and Matthew Kwan, who carried out related attacks on some of the cryptosystems discussed here, and we received valuable remarks from Philip Zimmermann. Don Coppersmith, Martin Hellman, and Alan Konheim sent us many helpful comments and suggestions which greatly improved the presentation of our results. Finally, the encouragement and help of our families are greatly appreciated.

Remark: Shortly before this book was sent to the publishers, Don Coppersmith (who was a member of the DES design team at IBM in the early 70's) revealed that his team was aware of differential cryptanalysis back in 1974, and designed the S boxes and the permutation in order to optimally defeat it. They had to keep this information secret for 18 years for national security reasons since it was such a potent form of cryptanalysis, but decided to break the silence after we rediscovered and published it. In response to our question, Don refused to reveal whether this is the strongest attack on the DES that his team was aware of, but reiterated his belief that the DES is still viable.

Contents

1

Introduction

Iterated cryptosystems are a family of cryptographically strong functions based on iterating a weaker function n times. Each iteration is called a *round* and the cryptosystem is called an *n-round cryptosystem*. The *round-function* is a function of the output of the previous round and of a *subkey* which is a key dependent value calculated via a *key scheduling algorithm*. The round-function is usually based on lookup tables (also known as substitutions or *S boxes*), bit permutations, arithmetic operations and the exclusive-or (denoted by $\oplus$ and XOR) operation. In most applications the encryption algorithm is assumed to be known and the secrecy of the data depends only on the secrecy of the randomly chosen key.

An early proposal for an iterated cryptosystem was Lucifer[15], which was designed at IBM to resolve the growing need for data security in its products. The round-function of Lucifer has a combination of non-linear S boxes and a bit permutation. The input bits are divided into groups of four consecutive bits. Each group is translated by a reversible S box giving a four bit result. The output bits of all the S boxes are permuted in order to mix them when they become the input to the following round. In Lucifer only two fixed S boxes (S_0 and S_1) were chosen. Each S box can be used at any S box location and the choice is key dependent. For a block size of 128 bits and a 16-round cryptosystem there are 512 S box entries for which 512 key bits are needed (for the eight-round variants 256 key bits are needed). A key expansion algorithm that repeats each key bit four times reduces the key size to 128 bits. Decryption is accomplished by running the data backwards using the inverse of each S box. Another variant of Lucifer is described in [37].

The Data Encryption Standard (DES)[28] is an improved version of Lucifer. It was developed at IBM and adopted by the U.S. National Bureau of Standards (NBS) as the standard cryptosystem for sensitive but unclassified data (such as financial transactions and email messages). DES has become a well known and widely used cryptosystem. The key size of DES is 56 bits and the block size is 64 bits. This block is divided into two halves of 32 bits each. The main part of the round function is the *F function*, which works on the right half of the data using a subkey of 48 bits and eight (six-bit to four-bit) S boxes. The 32 output bits of the F function are XORed with the left half of the data and the two halves are exchanged. The complete specification of the DES algorithm appears in Appendix A and in [28].

An extensive cryptanalytic literature on DES was published since its adoption in 1977. Yet, no short-cuts which can reduce the complexity of cryptanalysis to less than half of exhaustive search were ever reported in the open literature.

The 50% reduction[18] is based on the complementation property of DES. If the encryption of a plaintext P under a key K produces the ciphertext T:

$$T = \mathrm{DES}(P, K)$$

then the encryption of $\bar{P}$ under $\bar{K}$ produces $\bar{T}$:

$$\bar{T} = \mathrm{DES}(\bar{P}, \bar{K})$$

where $\bar{X}$ denotes the bit by bit complementation of X. Cryptanalysis can exploit this symmetry if two plaintext/ciphertext pairs (P_1, T_1) and (P_2, T_2) are available with $P_1 = \bar{P}_2$ (or similarly $T_1 = \bar{T}_2$). The attacker encrypts P_1 under all the 2^{55} keys K whose least significant bit is zero. If such a ciphertext T is equal to T_1 then the corresponding key K is likely to be the real key. If $T = \bar{T}_2$ then $\bar{K}$ is likely to be the real key. Otherwise neither K nor $\bar{K}$ can be the real key. Since testing whether $T = \bar{T}_2$ is much faster than a trial encryption, the computational saving is very close to 50%. This 50% reduction is achievable not only under a chosen plaintext attack, but also under a known plaintext attack, since any collection of 2^{33} random plaintexts is likely to contain a complementary pair of plaintexts by the birthday paradox.

Diffie and Hellman[14] analyzed the performance of an exhaustive search of the entire key space on a parallel machine. They estimated that a VLSI chip may be built which can search one key every microsecond. By building a search machine with a million such chips, all searching in parallel, 10^{12} keys can be searched per second. The entire key space contains about $7 \cdot 10^{16}$ keys and it can be searched in 10^5 seconds which is about a day. They estimated the cost of this machine to be $20-million and the cost per solution to be $5000.

Hellman[17] presented a time memory tradeoff under a chosen plaintext attack which can also be used under some circumstances under a known plaintext attack. This attack requires mt words of memory and t^2 operations provided that mt^2 equals the number of possible keys (2^{56} for DES). A special case ($m = t$) of this method requires about 2^{38} time and 2^{38}

Number of Rounds	Reduction Factor
4	2^{19}
5	2^9
6	2^2
7	–

Table 1.1. The key search reduction factor in Chaum and Evertse's attack.

memory, with a 2^{56} preprocessing time. Hellman suggested a special purpose machine which produces 100 solutions per day with an average wait of one day. He estimated that the cost of the machine was about $4-million and that the cost per solution was between $1–100. The preprocessing was estimated to take 2.3 years on the same machine.

The *Method of Formal Coding*, in which the formal expression of each bit in the ciphertext is found as a XOR sum of products of the bits of the plaintext and the key, was suggested in [18]. The formal manipulations of these expressions may decrease the key search effort. Schaumuller-Bichl[31, 32] studied this method and concluded that it requires an enormous amount of computer memory which makes the whole approach impractical.

There has been a considerable controversy about the key size of 56 bits in DES. Some researchers have proposed to strengthen DES by increasing the key size[2,18] or even making all the subkeys independent. However, these modifications were not adopted by the NBS.

In 1985 Chaum and Evertse[7] showed that a meet in the middle attack can reduce the key search for variants of DES with a small number of rounds by the factors shown in Table 1.1. They also showed that a slightly modified version of DES reduced to seven rounds can be solved with a reduction factor of 2. However, they proved that a meet in the middle attack of this kind is not applicable to DES reduced to eight or more rounds.

In their method they look for a set of data bits (J) in a middle round and a set of key bits (I) for which any change of the values of the I bits cannot change the value of the J bits in either directions. Knowing those fixed sets and given several plaintext/ciphertext pairs the following algorithm is used:

1. Try all the keys in which all the key bits in I are zero. Partially encrypt and decrypt a plaintext/ciphertext pair to get the data in the middle round.
2. Discard the keys for which the J bits are not the same under partial encryption/decryption.

3. For the remaining keys try all the possible values of the key bits in I.

This algorithm requires about $2^{56-|I|}+2^{|I|}$ encryption/decryption attempts.

In 1987 Davies[9] described a known plaintext cryptanalytic attack on DES. Given sufficient data, it could yield 16 linear relationships among key bits, thus reducing the size of a subsequent key search to 2^{40}. It exploited the correlation between the outputs of adjacent S boxes, due to their inputs being derived from, among other things, a pair of identical bits produced by the bit expansion operation. This correlation could reveal a linear relationship among the four bits of key used to modify these S box input bits. The two 32-bit halves of the DES result (ignoring IP) receive these outputs independently, so each pair of adjacent S boxes could be exploited twice, yielding 16 bits of key information.

The analysis does not require the plaintext P or ciphertext T but uses the quantity $P \oplus T$ and requires a huge number of random inputs. The S box pairs vary in the extent of correlation they produce so that, for example, the pair S7/S8 needs about 10^{17} samples but pair S2/S3 needs about 10^{21}. With about 10^{23} samples, all but the pair S3/S4 should give results (i.e., a total of 14 bits of key information). To exploit all pairs the cryptanalyst needs about 10^{26} samples. The S boxes do not appear to have been designed to minimize the correlation but they are somewhat better than a random choice in this respect. Since the number of samples is larger than the 2^{64} size of the sample space, this attack is purely theoretical, and cannot be carried out. However, for DES reduced to eight rounds the sample size of 10^{12} or 10^{13} (about 2^{40}) is on the verge of practicality. Therefore, Davies' analysis had penetrated more rounds than previously reported attacks.

During the last decade several cryptosystems which are variants of DES were suggested. Schaumuller-Bichl suggested three such cryptosystems [31, 33]. Two of them (called C80 and C82) are based on the DES structure with the replacement of the F function by nonreversible functions. The third one, called The Generalized DES Scheme (GDES), is an attempt to speed up DES. GDES has 16 rounds with the original DES F function but with a larger block size which is divided into more than two parts. She claimed that GDES increases the encryption speed of DES without decreasing its security.

Another variant is the Fast Data Encryption Algorithm (FEAL). FEAL was designed to be efficiently implementable on an eight-bit microprocessor. The structure of FEAL is similar to that of DES with a new F function and new initial and final transformations. The basic operations of FEAL are exclusive-or, byte additions and byte rotations. The first version of

FEAL[36], called FEAL-4, has four rounds. FEAL-4 was broken by Den-Boer[12] using a chosen plaintext attack with 100–10000 encryptions. The designers of FEAL reacted by introducing a new version with eight rounds, called FEAL-8[35,26]. Both versions were described as cryptographically better than DES in several aspects. Later, two new versions were added to the family: FEAL-N[23] with any even number of rounds and FEAL-NX[24] with extended 128-bit keys.

Recently, several new attacks on FEAL were published. One of them analyzes FEAL-8 using 10000 chosen plaintexts[16]. This attack was partially derived from the attack developed in this book. Another attack analyzes FEAL-4 using 20 chosen plaintexts[27]. We have devised[3] a non-differential attack using about 100000 known plaintexts, but later a much better attack was published[20] which analyzes FEAL-4 using five known plaintexts and analyzes FEAL-8 with 2^{15} known plaintexts faster than exhaustive search.

Khufu and Khafre[22] are fast software oriented cryptosystems suggested by Merkle whose round-functions are based on one eight-bit to 32-bit S box. Although the number of rounds is not specified, the designer expects that almost all applications will use 16, 24 or 32 rounds.

REDOC-II[38,8] is a high speed confusion/diffusion/arithmetic cryptosystem suggested by Cryptech Inc. REDOC-II has ten rounds, but even the one-round variant is claimed to be sufficiently strong since the round-function is very complicated. A reward of $5000 was offered for the best theoretical attack performed on the one-round variant and a reward of $20000 was offered for a practical known plaintext attack on the two-round variant.

LOKI[6] is a 64-bit key/64-bit block cryptosystem similar to DES which uses one twelve-bit to eight-bit S box based on irreducible polynomials in four S box entries. Two new modes of operation which convert LOKI into a hash function are defined.

Functions which map arbitrarily long messages into fixed length values are called *hash functions*. A hash function is called *cryptographically strong* if it is difficult to find any message that maps to a given value or any pair of messages that map to the same value. Many cryptographic hash functions are designed using the same building blocks as iterated cryptosystems, like the XOR operation, S boxes and iteration of a simple round-function many times. A universal attack on hash functions can be derived from the birthday paradox: Given about $2^{m/2}$ random messages where m is the size of the hash value, there is a high probability that two of the messages hash to the same value. The complexity of this attack is the standard tool to compare the strength of hash functions.

Snefru[21] is a hash function suggested by Merkle as the Xerox secure hash function. In March 1990 a $1000 reward was offered to the first person to break the two-pass variant of Snefru by finding two messages which hash to the same value. A similar reward was later announced for breaking the four-pass variant of Snefru.

Another hash function is N-Hash[25] which was suggested by the designers of FEAL as a cryptographically strong hash function. The round-function of N-Hash is based on the F function of FEAL, and is iterated eight times.

The open cryptographic literature contains very few examples of universal methods of cryptanalysis, which can be successfully applied to a wide variety of encryption and hash functions. This book describes a powerful new technique of this type, which we call *differential cryptanalysis.* It is a chosen plaintext attack which can often be converted into a known plaintext attack. The basic tool of the attack is the *ciphertext pair* which is a pair of ciphertexts whose plaintexts have particular differences. The two plaintexts can be chosen at random, as long as they satisfy a certain difference condition, and the cryptanalyst does not have to know their values.

The structure of this book is as follows: Chapter 2 contains a brief description of the major results. Chapter 3 formally introduces the notion of differential cryptanalysis. The application of differential cryptanalysis to variants of DES is described in Chapter 4, while the attack on the full 16-round DES is described in Chapter 5. The application of differential cryptanalysis to FEAL is described in Chapter 6. Chapter 7 describes the differential cryptanalysis of Khafre, REDOC-II, LOKI and Lucifer. In Chapter 8 differential cryptanalysis is applied to the hash functions Snefru and N-Hash. Chapter 9 describes several new non-differential attacks on the functions considered in this book. Finally, a technical description of DES and the difference distribution tables of its S boxes are given in the appendices.

2

Results

In this chapter we summarize the complexities of the major attacks described in this book. In the data collection phase, many pairs are encrypted under the unknown key on the target machine. The resultant ciphertexts are then fed into a data analysis algorithm, whose goal is to find the key. The complexities are quoted in terms of the number of encryptions needed to create all the necessary pairs in the data collection phase, since the data analysis algorithm is usually faster and uses fewer and simpler operations. These complexities are calculated for the electronic code book (ECB) mode of operation; however, the quoted known plaintext complexities hold even when the cipher block chaining (CBC) mode, the cipher feedback (CFB) mode, or the output feedback (OFB) mode are used.

The results of the attacks on variants of DES with reduced numbers of rounds are as follows. DES reduced to six rounds can be broken by a chosen plaintext attack in less than 0.3 seconds on a personal computer using 240 ciphertexts. Its known plaintext variant needs about 2^{36} ciphertexts. DES reduced to eight rounds can be broken by a chosen plaintext attack in less than two minutes on a computer by analyzing about 2^{14} ciphertexts. Its conversion to a known plaintext attack needs about 2^{39} ciphertexts. Any reduced variant of DES is breakable by a chosen plaintext attack faster than via exhaustive search. The known plaintext variants of the attacks are faster than exhaustive search for up to 14 rounds. A summary of these results appears in Table 2.1.

An advanced form of differential cryptanalysis can also break the full 16-round DES. The data analysis phase requires 2^{37} time and negligible space by analyzing 2^{36} ciphertexts obtained from a larger pool of 2^{47} chosen plaintexts. An interesting feature of the new attack is that it can be applied with the same complexity and success probability even if the key is frequently changed and thus the collected ciphertexts are derived from many different keys. The attack can be carried out incrementally, and one of the keys can be computed in real time while it is still valid. This is particularly important in attacks on bank authentication schemes, in which the opponent needs only one opportunity to forge a multi-million dollar wire transfer, but has to act quickly before the next key changeover invalidates

No. of Rounds	Dependent Key		Independent Key	
	Chosen Plaintexts	Known Plaintexts	Chosen Plaintexts	Known Plaintexts
4	2^{3}	2^{33}	2^{4}	2^{33}
6	2^{8}	2^{36}	2^{8}	2^{36}
8	2^{14}	2^{38}	2^{16}	2^{40}
9	2^{24}	2^{44}	2^{26}	2^{45}
10	2^{24}	2^{43}	2^{35}	2^{49}
11	2^{31}	2^{47}	2^{36}	2^{50}
12	2^{31}	2^{47}	2^{43}	2^{53}
13	2^{39}	2^{52}	2^{44}	2^{54}
14	2^{39}	2^{51}	2^{51}	2^{57}
15	2^{47}	2^{56}	2^{52}	2^{58}
16	2^{47}	2^{55}	2^{60}	2^{61}

Table 2.1. Summary of the cryptanalysis of DES: The number of operations and plaintexts required to break the specified number of rounds.

his message. This is the first published attack which is capable of breaking the full DES in less than the complexity of exhaustive search of 2^{55} keys.

Some researchers have proposed to strengthen DES by making all the subkeys Ki independent (or at least to derive them in a more complicated way from a longer actual key K). Our attack can be carried out even in this case, and thus the additional margin of safety achieved by this modification may be smaller than anticipated. DES reduced to eight rounds with independent subkeys (i.e., with $8 \cdot 48 = 384$ independent key bits which are not compatible with the key scheduling algorithm) can be broken by a chosen plaintext attack in less than two minutes by analyzing 15000 ciphertexts chosen from a pool of 50000 candidate ciphertexts. The known plaintext variant needs about 2^{40} ciphertexts. The full DES with independent subkeys (i.e., with $16 \cdot 48 = 768$ independent key bits) is breakable by either a chosen plaintext attack or a known plaintext attack with up to 2^{61} steps.

Our attacks on DES reduced to 10–16 rounds are not affected by the choice of the P permutation, and thus the replacement of the P permutation by any other permutation cannot make DES stronger, but many replaced permutations would allow even much faster attacks on the resultant cryptosystems. Even the replacement of the order of the eight DES S boxes (without changing their values) can make DES much weaker: DES with 16 rounds with a particular replaced order is breakable using about 2^{38} chosen plaintexts. The replacement of the XOR operation by the more complex addition operation makes this cryptosystem much weaker. DES with random S boxes is shown to be very easy to break. Even a minimal

No. of Rounds	Chosen Plaintexts	Known Plaintexts
4	8	2^{34}
8	128	2^{36}
12	2^{21}	2^{42}
16	2^{29}	2^{46}
20	2^{37}	2^{50}
24	2^{45}	2^{54}
28	2^{56}	2^{60}
30	2^{60}	2^{62}
31	2^{63}	2^{63}

Table 2.2. Summary of the cryptanalysis of FEAL: The number of operations and plaintexts required to break the specified number of rounds.

change of one entry in one of the DES S boxes can make DES easier to break. A generalized version of DES (called GDES) is shown to be trivially breakable by a chosen plaintext attack with six encryptions in less than 0.2 seconds, while GDES with independent subkeys is breakable with 16 encryptions in less than 3 seconds.

The FEAL-8 cryptosystem can be broken with about 128 chosen plaintexts or with about 2^{36} known plaintexts. As a reaction to our attack on FEAL-8, two new versions were introduced: FEAL-N[23], with any even number of rounds and FEAL-NX[24] with a key size extended to 128 bits. Nevertheless, FEAL-N and FEAL-NX can be broken for any $N \leq 31$ rounds faster than exhaustive search by either a chosen plaintext attack or a known plaintext attack. A summary of the differential cryptanalytic results on FEAL with various numbers of rounds appears in Table 2.2.

Khafre with 16 rounds is breakable by a differential cryptanalytic chosen plaintext attack using about 1500 encryptions within about an hour on a personal computer. By a differential cryptanalytic known plaintext attack it is breakable using about 2^{38} encryptions. Khafre with 24 rounds is breakable by a chosen plaintext attack using about 2^{53} encryptions and using a differential cryptanalytic known plaintext attack it is breakable using about 2^{59} encryptions.

REDOC-II with one round is breakable by a differential cryptanalytic chosen plaintext attack using about 2300 encryptions within less than a minute on a personal computer. For REDOC-II with up to four rounds it is possible to find three bytes of the masks (created by 1280 byte key tables) faster than via exhaustive search of the key. The three masks can even be found by a known plaintext attack.

LOKI with up to eleven rounds is breakable faster than via exhaustive search by a differential cryptanalytic attack. We further show that every key of LOKI has 15 equivalent keys due to a key complementation property and thus the complexity of a known plaintext attack on the full 16-round version can be reduced to 2^{60}. Another complementation property can reduce the complexity of a chosen plaintext attack by another factor of 16 to 2^{56}.

Lucifer with eight rounds is breakable within 2^{21} steps using 24 ciphertext pairs. The other variant of Lucifer reduced to eight rounds is even weaker.

Our results on hash functions are as follows: Two-pass Snefru is easily breakable within three minutes on a personal computer. Our attack can find many pairs which hash to the same values and can even find several messages hashing to the same hashed value as a given message. The attack is also applicable to three-pass and four-pass Snefru with complexities which are much better than the birthday attack. The attack is independent of the actual choice of the S boxes and one of its variants can even be used as a black box attack in which the choice of the S boxes is not known to the attacker.

Variants of N-Hash with up to 12 rounds (rather than eight rounds) can be broken faster than via the birthday paradox, but for technical reasons we can apply this attack only when the number of rounds is divisible by three.

The two hash function modes of LOKI are shown to be insecure.

3

Introduction to Differential Cryptanalysis

Differential cryptanalysis is a method which analyzes the effect of particular differences in plaintext pairs on the differences of the resultant ciphertext pairs. These differences can be used to assign probabilities to the possible keys and to locate the most probable key. This method usually works on many pairs of plaintexts with the same particular difference using the resultant ciphertext pairs. For DES and many other DES like cryptosystems the difference is chosen as a fixed XORed value of the two plaintexts. In this introduction we show how these differences can be analyzed and exploited. Due to its importance, we use DES as the canonical example of an iterated cryptosystem, but try to make the definitions and theorems applicable to other cryptosystems as well.

3.1 Notations and Definitions

We first introduce the following notations:

The numbers: An hexadecimal number n is denoted with the subscript x as n_x (e.g., $10_x = 16$). Decimal numbers are denoted without subscripts.

The plaintext: The plaintext is denoted by P. In the discussion on DES, we ignore the existence of the initial permutation of DES, and thus P is the value after the initial permutation which is entered directly into the first round. In differential cryptanalytic attacks the plaintexts are used in pairs. The other plaintext in the pair is denoted by P^* and the difference of the two plaintexts is denoted by $P' = P \oplus P^*$ and is called the *plaintext XOR*. The left and the right halves of the plaintext P are denoted by P_L and P_R respectively (i.e., $P = (P_L, P_R)$).

The ciphertext: The ciphertext is denoted by T. Since we ignore the existence of the initial permutation of DES, T is the value before the inverse initial permutation IP^{-1}. The ciphertext of the second plaintext P^* is denoted by T^* and the difference of the two ciphertexts $T' = T \oplus T^*$ is called the *ciphertext XOR*. The left and the right halves of the ciphertext T are denoted by T_L and T_R respectively (i.e., $T = (T_L, T_R)$). We denote the ciphertext by T, rather than by the usual notation C, since we reserve C for other purposes.

The difference: At any intermediate point during the encryption of pairs of plaintexts, if X denotes a value during the encryption of the first plaintext, X^* denotes the corresponding value during the encryption of the second plaintext. The *difference* of these values is denoted by X'. For DES-like cryptosystems we define $X' = X \oplus X^*$. Since the difference is usually the XOR of the two values, we call the difference of the two plaintexts the *plaintext XOR*, the difference of the two ciphertexts the *ciphertext XOR*, the difference of some two inputs the *input XOR* and the difference of some two outputs the *output XOR*.

The inputs and the outputs of the F function: The 32-bit inputs of the F function in the various rounds are denoted by the lowercase letters a, b, ..., j. The corresponding 32-bit outputs of the F function in the various rounds are denoted by the uppercase letters A, B, ..., J. Therefore, the input of the first round is denoted by a (in DES $a = P_R$) and the output of the first round is denoted by A, the input of the second round is denoted by b and the output of the second round is denoted by B, and so on. See Figure 3.1 for more details.

The subkeys: The F function of each round has a unique key dependent input, called the *subkey*. The subkeys are calculated from the key by a *key scheduling algorithm*. The subkeys are named Ki, where i indicates the round to which they enter.

The following notations are specific to DES:

The initial permutation: The initial permutation of DES is denoted by $IP(X)$. In this book the existence of the initial permutation IP and the inverse initial permutation IP^{-1} of DES are ignored, since they have no cryptanalytic significance in our attack. In many other cryptosystems (such as FEAL) the initial permutation is replaced by a more complex initial transformation which can also XOR the data with subkeys.

The subkeys: DES iterates the round-function 16 times and uses 16 subkeys, named K1, K2, ..., K16. All the bits of the subkeys are chosen by the key scheduling algorithm of DES by duplicating each bit of the 56-bit key into about 14 out of the 16 48-bit subkeys.

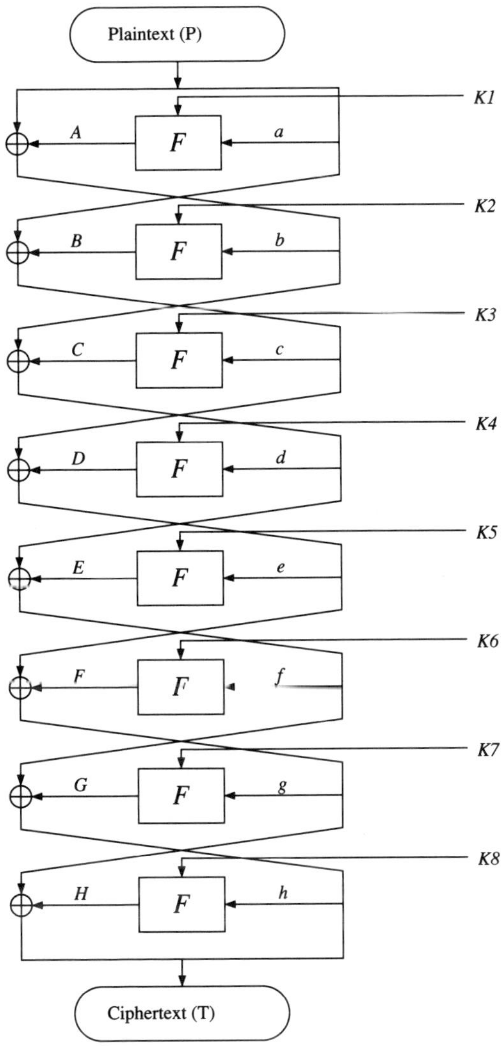

Figure 3.1. DES reduced to eight rounds.

The P permutation: The P permutation of DES is denoted by $P(X)$. Note that P as a variable denotes the plaintext.

The E expansion: The E expansion of DES is denoted by $E(X)$.

The S boxes: The S boxes of DES are S1, S2, ..., S8. The input of the S box Si in the round whose input letter is X ($X \in \{a, \ldots, j\}$) is denoted by Si_{IX}. The corresponding output of Si is denoted by Si_{OX}. The value of the six bits of the subkey entering the S box Si after they are

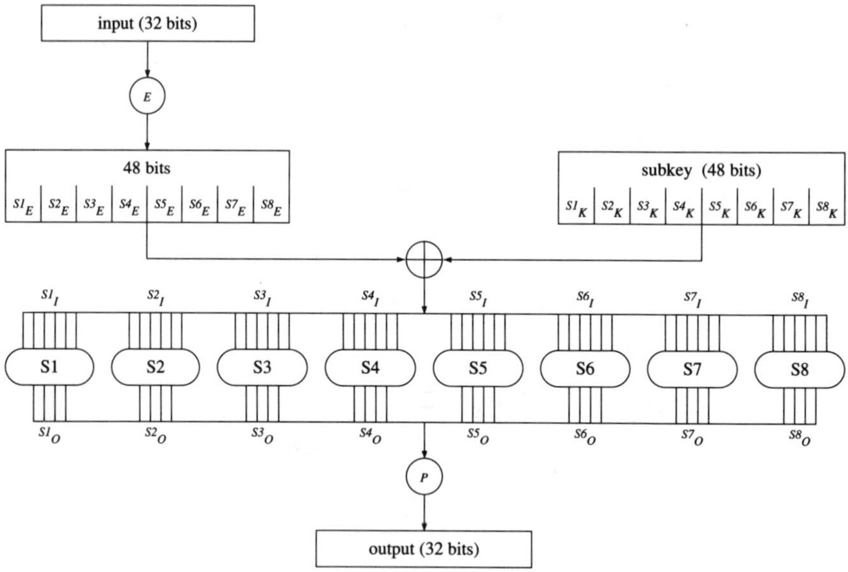

Figure 3.2. The F function of DES.

XORed with the expanded data is denoted by Si_{KX} and the value of the six input bits of the expanded data (E(X)) which are XORed with Si_{KX} to form Si_{IX} is denoted by Si_{EX}. In these notations, the S box number i and the round marker X are optional. For example $S1_{Ea}$ denotes the first six bits of $E(a)$. $S1_{Ka}$ denotes the first six bits of the subkey K1. $S1_{Ia}$ denotes the input of the S box S1 which is $S1_{Ia} = S1_{Ea} \oplus S1_{Ka}$. $S1_{Oa}$ denotes the output of S1 which is $S1_{Oa} = S1(S1_{Ia})$. See Figure 3.2 for more details.

Definition 3.1 An *independent key* is a list of subkeys which is not necessarily derivable from some key via the key scheduling algorithm.

Example 3.1 DES has $2^{16\cdot 48} = 2^{768}$ possible independent keys, but only 2^{56} possible dependent keys. Note that every dependent key can be viewed as a special type of an independent key.

Remark To simplify the mathematical analysis of our attacks, we assume that all the subkeys are independent. Attacks on DES with dependent subkeys were experimentally shown to have the same probability of success, but the theoretical analysis of the probability is much harder.

3.2 Overview

The F function of DES takes a 32-bit input and a 48-bit key. The input is expanded (by the E expansion) to 48 bits and XORed with the key (see Figure 3.2). The result is fed into the S boxes and the resultant bits are permuted.

Our goal is to analyze the differential behavior of this function. Given the XOR value of an input pair to the F function it is easy to determine its XOR value after the expansion by the formula:

$$E(X) \oplus E(X^*) = E(X \oplus X^*).$$

The XOR with the key does not change the XOR value in the pair, i.e., the expanded XOR stays valid even after the XOR with the key, by the formula:

$$(X \oplus K) \oplus (X^* \oplus K) = X \oplus X^*.$$

The output of the S boxes is mixed by the P permutation and the output XOR of the P permutation is the permuted value of its input XOR, by the formula:

$$P(X) \oplus P(X^*) = P(X \oplus X^*).$$

The output XOR of the F function is linear in the XOR operation that connects the different rounds:

$$(X \oplus Y) \oplus (X^* \oplus Y^*) = (X \oplus X^*) \oplus (Y \oplus Y^*).$$

The XOR of pairs is thus invariant in the key and is linear in the E expansion, the P permutation and the XOR operation.

The S boxes are known to be non-linear. Knowledge of the XOR of the input pairs cannot guarantee knowledge of the XOR of the output pairs. Usually several output XORs are possible. A special case arises when both inputs are equal, in which case both outputs must be equal too. However, a crucial observation is that for any particular input XOR not all the output XORs are possible, the possible ones do not appear uniformly, and some XORed values appear much more frequently than others.

Before we proceed we want to mention the known design rules of the S boxes[4]:

1. No S box is a linear or affine function of its input.
2. Changing one input bit to an S box results in changing at least two output bits.

14	4	13	1	2	15	11	8	3	10	6	12	5	9	0	7
0	15	7	4	14	2	13	1	10	6	12	11	9	5	3	8
4	1	14	8	13	6	2	11	15	12	9	7	3	10	5	0
15	12	8	2	4	9	1	7	5	11	3	14	10	0	6	13

Table 3.1. S box S1.

3. $S(X)$ and $S(X \oplus 001100)$ must differ in at least two bits.
4. $S(X) \neq S(X \oplus 11ef00)$ for any choice of e and f.
5. The S boxes were chosen to minimize the differences between the number of 1's and 0's in any S box output when any single bit is kept constant.

In DES any S box has $64 \cdot 64$ possible input pairs, and each one of them has an input XOR and an output XOR. There are only $64 \cdot 16$ possible tuples of input and output XORs. Therefore, each tuple results in average from four pairs. However, not all the tuples exist as a result of a pair, and the existing ones do not have a uniform distribution. Very important properties of the S boxes are derived from the analysis of the tables that summarize this distribution:

Definition 3.2 A table that shows the distribution of the input XORs and output XORs of all the possible pairs of an S box is called the *difference distribution table of the S box.* In this table each row corresponds to a particular input XOR, each column corresponds to a particular output XOR and the entries themselves count the number of possible pairs with such an input XOR and an output XOR.

Each line in a difference distribution table contains 64 possible pairs in 16 different entries. Thus in each line in the table the average of the entries is exactly four.

Example 3.2 In Table 3.1 the S box S1 of DES is described. The difference distribution table of S1[1] is given in Table 3.2.

Example 3.3 The first line of Table 3.2 shows that for the zero input XOR, the output XOR must be zero too, as we noticed above. Also, the different lines in the table have different output XOR distributions.

---

[1]See Appendix A for the description of all the S boxes and their interpretation. The difference distribution tables of all the S boxes appear in Appendix B.

Input	Output XOR															
XOR	0_x	1_x	2_x	3_x	4_x	5_x	6_x	7_x	8_x	9_x	A_x	B_x	C_x	D_x	E_x	F_x
0_x	64	0	0	0	0	0	0	0	0	0	0	0	0	0	0	0
1_x	0	0	0	6	0	2	4	4	0	10	12	4	10	6	2	4
2_x	0	0	0	8	0	4	4	4	0	6	8	6	12	6	4	2
3_x	14	4	2	2	10	6	4	2	6	4	4	0	2	2	2	0
4_x	0	0	0	6	0	10	10	6	0	4	6	4	2	8	6	2
5_x	4	8	6	2	2	4	4	2	0	4	4	0	12	2	4	6
6_x	0	4	2	4	8	2	6	2	8	4	4	2	4	2	0	12
7_x	2	4	10	4	0	4	8	4	2	4	8	2	2	2	4	4
8_x	0	0	0	12	0	8	8	4	0	6	2	8	8	2	2	4
9_x	10	2	4	0	2	4	6	0	2	2	8	0	10	0	2	12
A_x	0	8	6	2	2	8	6	0	6	4	6	0	4	0	2	10
B_x	2	4	0	10	2	2	4	0	2	6	2	6	6	4	2	12
C_x	0	0	0	8	0	6	6	0	0	6	6	4	6	6	14	2
D_x	6	6	4	8	4	8	2	6	0	6	4	6	0	2	0	2
E_x	0	4	8	8	6	6	4	0	6	6	4	0	0	4	0	8
F_x	2	0	2	4	4	6	4	2	4	8	2	2	2	6	8	8
10_x	0	0	0	0	0	0	2	14	0	6	6	12	4	6	8	6
11_x	6	8	2	4	6	4	8	6	4	0	6	6	0	4	0	0
12_x	0	8	4	2	6	6	4	6	6	4	2	6	6	0	4	0
13_x	2	4	4	6	2	0	4	6	2	0	6	8	4	6	4	6
14_x	0	8	8	0	10	0	4	2	8	2	2	4	4	8	4	0
15_x	0	4	6	4	2	2	4	10	6	2	0	10	0	4	6	4
16_x	0	8	10	8	0	2	2	6	10	2	0	2	0	6	2	6
17_x	4	4	6	0	10	6	0	2	4	4	4	6	6	6	2	0
18_x	0	6	6	0	8	4	2	2	2	4	6	8	6	6	2	2
19_x	2	6	2	4	0	8	4	6	10	4	0	4	2	8	4	0
$1A_x$	0	6	4	0	4	6	6	6	6	2	2	0	4	4	6	8
$1B_x$	4	4	2	4	10	6	6	4	6	2	2	4	2	2	4	2
$1C_x$	0	10	10	6	6	0	0	12	6	4	0	0	2	4	4	0
$1D_x$	4	2	4	0	8	0	0	2	10	0	2	6	6	6	14	0
$1E_x$	0	2	6	0	14	2	0	0	6	4	10	8	2	2	6	2
$1F_x$	2	4	10	6	2	2	2	8	6	8	0	0	0	4	6	4
20_x	0	0	0	10	0	12	8	2	0	6	4	4	4	2	0	12
21_x	0	4	2	4	4	8	10	0	4	4	10	0	4	0	2	8
22_x	10	4	6	2	2	8	2	2	2	2	6	0	4	0	4	10
23_x	0	4	4	8	0	2	6	0	6	6	2	10	2	4	0	10
24_x	12	0	0	2	2	2	2	0	14	14	2	0	2	6	2	4
25_x	6	4	4	12	4	4	4	10	2	2	2	0	4	2	2	2
26_x	0	0	4	10	10	10	2	4	0	4	6	4	4	4	2	0
27_x	10	4	2	0	2	4	2	0	4	8	0	4	8	8	4	4
28_x	12	2	2	8	2	6	12	0	0	2	6	0	4	0	6	2
29_x	4	2	2	10	0	2	4	0	0	14	10	2	4	6	0	4
$2A_x$	4	2	4	6	0	2	8	2	2	14	2	6	2	6	2	2
$2B_x$	12	2	2	2	4	6	6	2	0	2	6	2	6	0	8	4
$2C_x$	4	2	2	4	0	2	10	4	2	2	4	8	8	4	2	6
$2D_x$	6	2	6	2	8	4	4	4	2	4	6	0	8	2	0	6
$2E_x$	6	6	2	2	0	2	4	6	4	0	6	2	12	2	6	4
$2F_x$	2	2	2	2	2	6	8	8	2	4	4	6	8	2	4	2
30_x	0	4	6	0	12	6	2	2	8	2	4	4	6	2	2	4
31_x	4	8	2	10	2	2	2	2	6	0	0	2	2	4	10	8
32_x	4	2	6	4	4	2	2	4	6	6	4	8	2	2	8	0
33_x	4	4	6	2	10	8	4	2	4	0	2	2	4	6	2	4
34_x	0	8	16	6	2	0	0	12	6	0	0	0	0	8	0	6
35_x	2	2	4	0	8	0	0	0	14	4	6	8	0	2	14	0
36_x	2	6	2	2	8	0	2	2	4	2	6	8	6	4	10	0
37_x	2	2	12	4	2	4	4	10	4	4	2	6	0	2	2	4
38_x	0	6	2	2	2	0	2	2	4	6	4	4	4	6	10	10
39_x	6	2	2	4	12	6	4	8	4	0	2	4	2	4	4	0
$3A_x$	6	4	6	4	6	8	0	6	2	2	6	2	2	6	4	0
$3B_x$	2	6	4	0	0	2	4	6	4	6	8	6	4	4	6	2
$3C_x$	0	10	4	0	12	0	4	2	6	0	4	12	4	4	2	0
$3D_x$	0	8	6	2	2	6	0	8	4	4	0	4	0	12	4	4
$3E_x$	4	8	2	2	2	4	4	14	4	2	0	2	0	8	4	4
$3F_x$	4	8	4	2	4	0	2	4	4	2	4	8	8	6	2	2

Table 3.2. The difference distribution table of S1.

The following definition deals with difference distribution tables:

Definition 3.3 Let X and Y be two values (representing potential input and output XORs of an S box, respectively). We say that X *may cause* Y *by the S box* if there is a pair in which the input XOR of the S box equals X and the output XOR of the S box equals Y. If there is such a pair we write $X \rightarrow Y$, and if there is no such pair we say that X *may not cause* Y *by the S box* and write $X \not\rightarrow Y$.

Example 3.4 Consider the input XOR $S1'_I = 34_x$. It has only eight possible output XORs, while the other eight entries are impossible. The possible output XORs $S1'_O$ are 1_x, 2_x, 3_x, 4_x, 7_x, 8_x, D_x and F_x. Therefore, the input XOR $S1'_I = 34_x$ may cause output XOR $S1'_O = 1_x$ ($34_x \rightarrow 1_x$). Also $34_x \rightarrow 2_x$ and $34_x \rightarrow F_x$. On the other hand, $34_x \not\rightarrow 0_x$ and $34_x \not\rightarrow 9_x$.

Examples 3.3 and 3.4 demonstrate that for a fixed input XOR, the possible output XORs do not have a uniform distribution. The following Definition extends Definition 3.3 with probabilities.

Definition 3.4 We say that X *may cause* Y *with probability* p *by an S box* if for a fraction p of the pairs in which the input XOR of the S box equals X, the output XOR equals Y.

Example 3.5 $34_x \rightarrow 2_x$ results from 16 out of the 64 pairs of S1, i.e., with probability $\frac{1}{4}$. $34_x \rightarrow 4_x$ results only from two out of the 64 pairs of S1, i.e., with probability $\frac{1}{32}$.

Different distributions appear in different lines of the table. In total between 70% and 80% of the entries are possible and between 20% and 30% are impossible. The exact percentage for each S box is shown in Table 3.3. In various formulas in this book we approximate the percentage of the possible entries by 80%.

The difference distribution tables let us find the possible input and output values of pairs given their input and output XORs. The following example shows a simple case:

Example 3.6 Consider the entry $34_x \rightarrow 4_x$ in the difference distribution table of S1. Since the entry $34_x \rightarrow 4_x$ has value 2, only two pairs satisfy these XORs. These pairs are duals. If the first pair is $S1_I$, $S1^*_I$ then the other pair is $S1^*_I$, $S1_I$. By looking at Table 3.4 we see that these inputs must be 13_x and 27_x, whose corresponding outputs are 6_x and 2_x respectively.

Next we show how to find the key bits using known input pairs and output XORs of an S box in the F function.

S box	Percentage
S1	79.4
S2	78.6
S3	79.6
S4	68.5
S5	76.5
S6	80.4
S7	77.2
S8	77.1

Table 3.3. Percentage of the possible entries in the various difference distribution tables.

Output XOR ($S1'_O$)	Possible Inputs ($S1_I$)
1	03, 0F, 1E, 1F, 2A, 2B, 37, 3B
2	04, 05, 0E, 11, 12, 14, 1A, 1B, 20, 25, 26, 2E, 2F, 30, 31, 3A
3	01, 02, 15, 21, 35, 36
4	13, 27
7	00, 08, 0D, 17, 18, 1D, 23, 29, 2C, 34, 39, 3C
8	09, 0C, 19, 2D, 38, 3D
D	06, 10, 16, 1C, 22, 24, 28, 32
F	07, 0A, 0B, 33, 3E, 3F

Table 3.4. Possible input values for the input XOR $S1'_I = 34_x$ by the output XOR (in hexadecimal).

Example 3.7 Assume we know that $S1_E = 1_x$, $S1^*_E = 35_x$ and $S1'_O = D_x$ and we want to find the key value $S1_K$. The input XOR is $S1'_E = S1'_I = 34_x$ regardless of the actual value of $S1_K$. By consulting Table 3.2 we can see that the input to the S box has eight possibilities. These eight possibilities make eight possibilities for the key (by $S_K = S_E \oplus S_I$) as described in Table 3.5. Each line in the table describes two pairs with the same two inputs but with the opposite order. Each pair leads to one key, so each line leads to two keys (which are $S_E \oplus S_I$ and $S_E \oplus S^*_I$). The right key value $S1_K$ must occur in this table.

Using additional pairs we can get additional candidates for $S1_K$. Assume that we get an input pair $S1_E = 21_x$, $S1^*_E = 15_x$ whose output XOR is $S1'_O = 3_x$. The possible inputs to the S box where $34_x \rightarrow 3_x$ and the corresponding possible keys are described in Table 3.6. The right key must occur in both tables. The only common key values in Tables 3.5 and 3.6 are 17_x and 23_x. These two values are indistinguishable with this input XOR

S box input	Possible Keys
06, 32	07, 33
10, 24	11, 25
16, 22	17, 23
1C, 28	1D, 29

Table 3.5. Possible keys for $34_x \rightarrow D_x$ by S1 with input $1_x, 35_x$ (in hexadecimal).

S box input	Possible Keys
01, 35	20, 14
02, 36	23, 17
15, 21	34, 00

Table 3.6. Possible keys for $34_x \rightarrow 3_x$ by S1 with input $21_x, 15_x$ (in hexadecimal).

since $17_x \oplus 23_x = 34_x = S1'_E$, but may become distinguishable by using a pair with a different input XOR value ($S1'_E \neq 34_x$).

The following example extends this technique to a three-round cryptosystem.

Example 3.8 Assume we have a ciphertext pair whose plaintext XOR is known and the values of the six bits 64, 33, ..., 37 of the plaintext XOR are zero. The input XOR of the first round is zero in all the bits entering S1 ($S1'_{Ea} = S1'_{Ia} = 0$) and thus the output XOR of S1 in the first round must be zero ($S1'_{Oa} = 0$). The left half of the ciphertext is calculated as the XOR value of the left half of the plaintext, the output of the first round and the output of the third round ($T_L = P_L \oplus A \oplus C$). Since the plaintext XOR and the ciphertext XOR are known and the output XOR of S1 in the first round is known as well, the values of P'_L and T'_L and the bits of A' which correspond to the output of S1 are known. Therefore, the output XOR of S1 in the third round can be calculated by extracting the bits which correspond to the output of S1 in $C' = P'_L \oplus T'_L \oplus A'$. The input pair $S1_{Ec}$, $S1^*_{Ec}$ in the third round is easily extractable from the ciphertext pair.

If the input pair of S1 in the third round is $S1_{Ec} = 1_x$, $S1^*_{Ec} = 35_x$ and the output XOR is $S1'_{Oc} = D_x$ then the value of $S1_{Kc}$ can be found as in Example 3.7 and it must appear in Table 3.5. Using additional pairs we can discard some of the possible values till we get a unique value of $S1_{Kc}$. Since $S1'_{Ec}$ is not constant, there should not be any indistinguishable values of the subkey.

The following definition extends Definitions 3.3 and 3.4 for use with the F function:

Definition 3.5 Let X and Y be two values (representing potential input and output XOR values of the F function). We say that X *may cause* Y *with probability* p *by the* F *function* if for a fraction p of all the possible input pairs encrypted by all the possible subkey values in which the input XOR of the F function equals X, the output XOR equals Y. If $p > 0$ we denote this possibility by $X \rightarrow Y$.

Lemma 3.1 In DES, if $X \rightarrow Y$ with probability p by the F function then every fixed input pair Z, Z^* with $Z' = Z \oplus Z^* = X$ causes the F function output XOR to be Y by the same fraction p of the possible subkey values.

Proof To prove the lemma it suffices to show the property for each of the S boxes. For each input XOR of the data S'_E there is $S'_I = S'_E$ regardless of S_K. If there are k possible input pairs to the S box with this input XOR that may cause a given output XOR, we can choose precisely k key values $S_K = S_E \oplus S_I$, each taking the fixed input pair S_E, S^*_E to one of the possible input pairs S_I, S^*_I of the S box and thus causing the given output XOR. Thus, the fraction p is held constant for all the input pairs, and therefore equals the average over all the input pairs. ∎

In other iterated cryptosystems this lemma does not necessarily hold. However, we assume that the fraction is very close to p, which is usually the case.

Corollary 3.1 The probability p of $X \rightarrow Y$ by the F function is the product of p_i in which $X_i \rightarrow Y_i$ by the S boxes S_i ($i \in \{1, \ldots, 8\}$) where $X_1X_2X_3X_4X_5X_6X_7X_8 = E(X)$ and $Y_1Y_2Y_3Y_4Y_5Y_6Y_7Y_8 = P^{-1}(Y)$.

The above discussion about finding the key bits entering S boxes can be extended to find the subkey entering the F function. The method is as follows:

1. Choose an appropriate plaintext XOR.
2. Create an appropriate number of plaintext pairs with the chosen plaintext XOR, encrypt them and keep only the resultant ciphertext pairs.
3. For each pair derive the expected output XOR of as many S boxes in the last round as possible from the plaintext XOR and the ciphertext pair. (Note that the input pair of the last round is known since it appears as part of the ciphertext pair).

4. For each possible key value, count the number of pairs that result with the expected output XOR using this key value in the last round.
5. The right key value is the (hopefully unique) key value suggested by all the pairs.

3.3 Characteristics

We are left with the problem of pushing the knowledge of the XORs of the plaintext pairs as many rounds as possible (in Step 3) without making them all zeroes. When the XORs of the pairs are zero, i.e., both texts are equal, the outputs are equal too, which makes all the keys equally likely. The pushing mechanism is a statistical characteristic of the cryptosystem which is an extension of the single round analysis. Before we define it formally we give an informal definition and three examples.

Definition 3.6 (informal) Associated with any pair of encryptions are the XOR value of its two plaintexts, the XOR of its ciphertexts, the XORs of the inputs of each round in the two executions and the XORs of the outputs of each round in the two executions. These XOR values form an *n-round characteristic*. A characteristic has a probability, which is the probability that a random pair with the chosen plaintext XOR has the round and ciphertext XORs specified in the characteristic. We denote the plaintext XOR of a characteristic by Ω_P and its ciphertext XOR by Ω_T.

The following example describes a one-round characteristic with probability 1. This is the only one-round characteristic with probability greater than $\frac{1}{4}$. This characteristic is very useful and is applicable in any DES-like cryptosystem.

Example 3.9 A one-round characteristic with probability 1 is (for any L'):

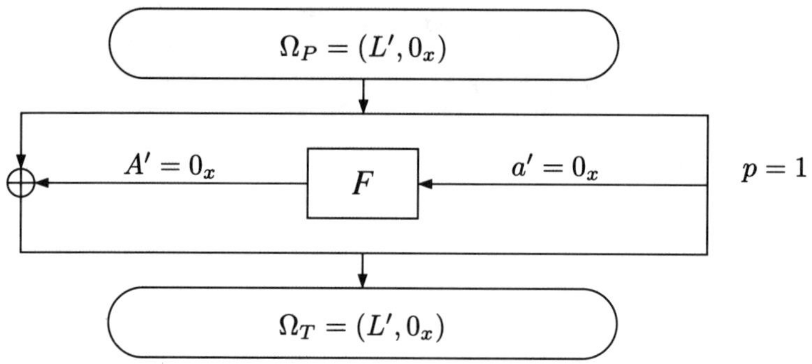

The following example describes a simple one-round characteristic with probability $\frac{14}{64}$.

Example 3.10 In this one-round characteristic the input XORs of seven S boxes are zero. The input XOR of the eighth S box is not zero, and is chosen to maximize the probability that the input XOR may cause the output XOR. Since there are several input bits that enter two neighboring S boxes by the E expansion we have to ensure that the XORs of these bits are zero. There are only two private bits entering each S box. These bits can have non-zero XOR values. The best such probability for S1 is $\frac{14}{64}$ (i.e., there is an entry that contains 14 pairs that does not cause the input of the neighboring S2 or S8 to be non-zero). Thus, it is easy to get a one-round characteristic with probability $\frac{14}{64}$ which is:

$$S1: \quad 0C_x \rightarrow E_x \qquad \text{with probability } \tfrac{14}{64}$$
$$S2,\ldots,S8: \quad 00_x \rightarrow 0_x \qquad \text{with probability } 1.$$

This characteristic can also be written (for any L') as:

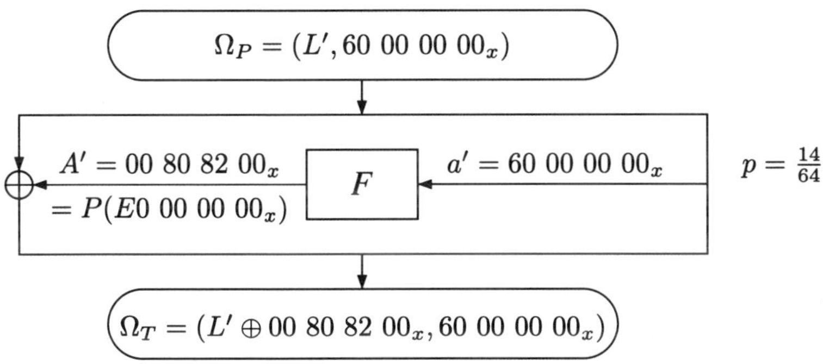

One-round characteristics with probability $\frac{1}{4}$ are possible using non-zero input XORs in S2 or S6.

The following example describes a two-round characteristic which is easily obtained by concatenating the two one-round characteristics described in Examples 3.10 and 3.9:

Example 3.11 A two-round characteristic with probability $\frac{14}{64}$:

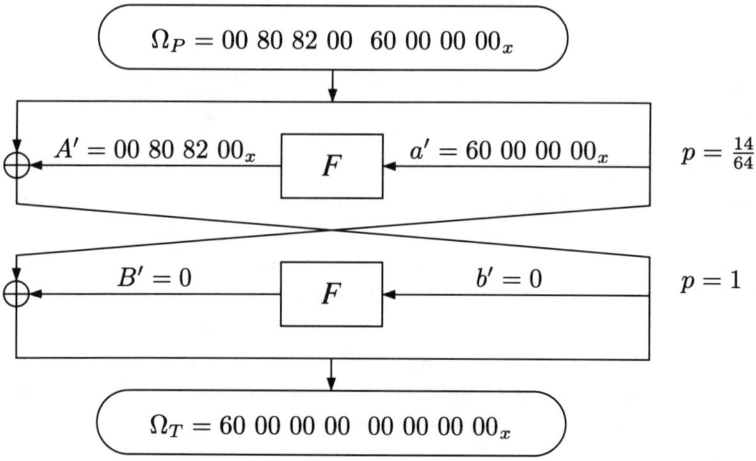

We can now formulate the exact definition of a characteristic:

Definition 3.7 An *n-round characteristic* is a tuple $\Omega = (\Omega_P, \Omega_\Lambda, \Omega_T)$ where Ω_P and Ω_T are m bit numbers and Ω_Λ is a list of n elements $\Omega_\Lambda = (\Lambda_1, \Lambda_2, \ldots, \Lambda_n)$, each of which is a pair of the form $\Lambda_i = (\lambda_I^i, \lambda_O^i)$ where λ_I^i and λ_O^i are $m/2$ bit numbers and m is the block size of the cryptosystem. A characteristic satisfies the following requirements:

$$\begin{aligned}
\lambda_I^1 &= \text{the right half of } \Omega_P \\
\lambda_I^2 &= \text{the left half of } \Omega_P \oplus \lambda_O^1 \\
\lambda_I^n &= \text{the right half of } \Omega_T \\
\lambda_I^{n-1} &= \text{the left half of } \Omega_T \oplus \lambda_O^n
\end{aligned}$$

and for every i such that $2 \le i \le n-1$:

$$\lambda_O^i = \lambda_I^{i-1} \oplus \lambda_I^{i+1}.$$

Definition 3.8 A *right pair with respect to an n-round characteristic* $\Omega = (\Omega_P, \Omega_\Lambda, \Omega_T)$ *and an independent key* K is a pair for which $P' = \Omega_P$ and for each round i of the first n rounds of the encryption of the pair using the independent key K the input XOR of the ith round equals λ_I^i and the output XOR of the F function equals λ_O^i. Every pair which is not a right pair with respect to the characteristic and the independent key is called a *wrong pair with respect to the characteristic and the independent key.* Throughout this book we refer them shortly by *right pair* and *wrong pair.*

Definition 3.9 An n-round characteristic $\Omega^1 = (\Omega_P^1, \Omega_\Lambda^1, \Omega_T^1)$ *can be concatenated with* an m-round characteristic $\Omega^2 = (\Omega_P^2, \Omega_\Lambda^2, \Omega_T^2)$ if Ω_T^1 equals the swapped value of the two halves of Ω_P^2. The *concatenation* of the characteristics Ω^1 and Ω^2 (if they can be concatenated) is the characteristic $\Omega = (\Omega_P^1, \Omega_\Lambda, \Omega_T^2)$ where Ω_Λ is the concatenation of the lists Ω_Λ^1 and Ω_Λ^2.

The following definitions and theorem deal with the probability of characteristics:

Definition 3.10 *Round i of a characteristic Ω has probability p_i^Ω* if $\lambda_I^i \rightarrow \lambda_O^i$ with probability p_i^Ω by the F function.

Definition 3.11 *An n-round characteristic Ω has probability p^Ω* if p^Ω is the product of the probabilities of its n rounds:

$$p^\Omega = \prod_{i=1}^{n} p_i^\Omega.$$

Note that by Definitions 3.9 and 3.11 the probability of a characteristic Ω which is the concatenation of the characteristic Ω^1 with the characteristic Ω^2 is the product of their probabilities: $p^\Omega = p^{\Omega^1} \cdot p^{\Omega^2}$. As a result, every n-round characteristic can be described as the concatenation of n one-round characteristics with probability which is the product of the one-round probabilities.

Theorem 3.1 The formally defined probability of a characteristic $\Omega = (\Omega_P, \Omega_\Lambda, \Omega_T)$ is the actual probability that any fixed plaintext pair satisfying $P' = \Omega_P$ is a right pair when random independent keys are used.

Proof The probability of any fixed plaintext pair satisfying $P' = \Omega_P$ to be a right pair is the probability that at all the rounds i: $\lambda_I^i \rightarrow \lambda_O^i$. The probability at each round is independent of its exact input (as proved in Lemma 3.1) and independent of the action of the previous rounds (since the independent keys completely randomize the inputs to each S box, leaving only the XOR value fixed). Therefore, the probability of a pair to be a right pair is the product of the probabilities of $\lambda_I^i \rightarrow \lambda_O^i$, which was defined above as the probability of the characteristic. ■

For practical purposes, the significant probability with respect to a characteristic is the probability that a pair whose plaintext XOR equals the characteristic's plaintext XOR is a right pair using a fixed key (the one we try to find). As shown in the next chapter, this probability is not constant for all the keys, but we can assume that for randomly chosen key it is well approximated by the probability of the characteristic.

The characteristics are defined here in terms of DES-like cryptosystems. They can be generalized to be applicable to many other round-functions. In this case we base the definition of the characteristics on one-round characteristics (rather than on the specific structure of the round as we do for DES) and conclude all the other results on the characteristics from their concatenation to n-round characteristics by the corresponding concatenation criteria. For several applications it is also advantageous to consider only partially specified output XORs in order to get a better probability. Such an extended characteristic can be viewed formally as a union of several characteristics.

After this formal discussion we show a three-round characteristic:

Example 3.12 An extension to three rounds of the characteristic described in Example 3.11 can be achieved by concatenating it again with the characteristic of Example 3.10. Thus a three-round characteristic with probability $\left(\frac{14}{64}\right)^2 \approx 0.05$ is:

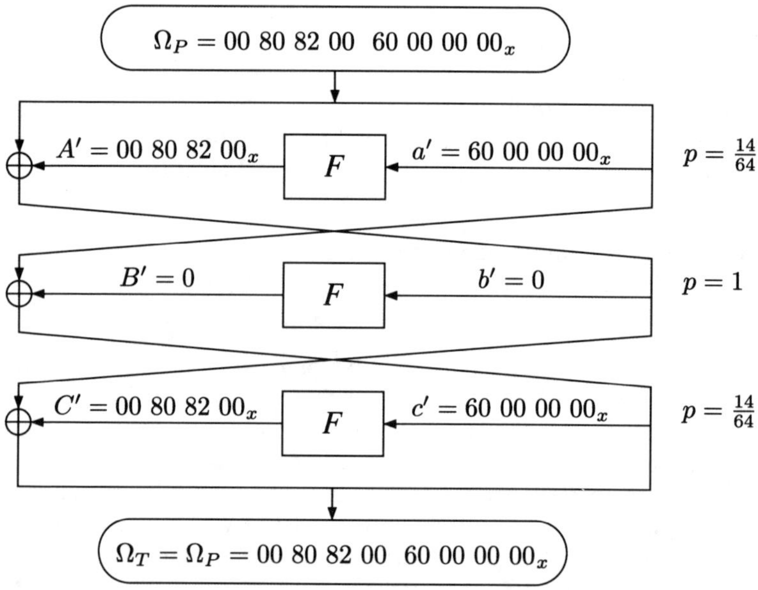

where in the fourth round (if added) $d' = 00\ 80\ 82\ 00$. We see that when the plaintexts differ in the five specified bit locations, with probability about 0.05 there is a difference of only three bits at the input of the fourth round.

This structure of three rounds with a zero input XOR in the middle round is very useful and forms the best possible probability for three-round characteristics[2]. A similar structure can be used in five-round characteristics. The middle round has zero input and output XORs and there is a symmetry around it, i.e.,

---

[2]Since less than two differing S boxes are impossible and there are characteristics of this structure with two differing S boxes, each with the best possible probability $(\frac{1}{4})$.

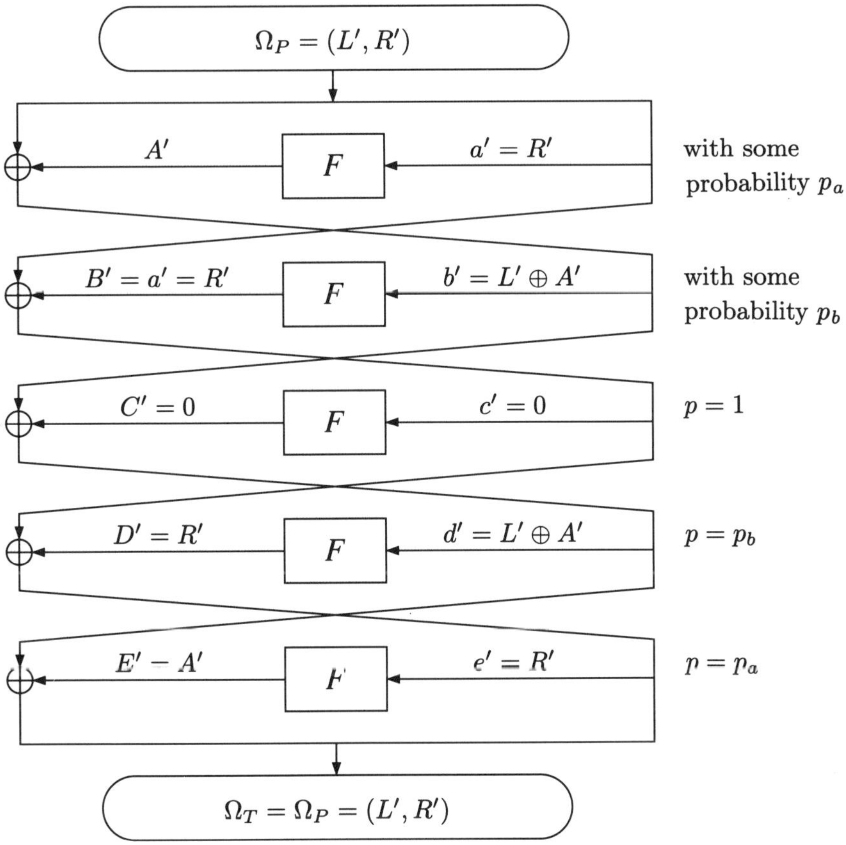

where in the sixth round (if added) $f' = L'$. The existence of a string $b' \rightarrow a' \rightarrow A'$ ensures the existence of such a five-round characteristic. The characteristic's probability is quite low since three S box inputs must differ in both rounds $b' \rightarrow a'$ and $a' \rightarrow A'$, and six in the whole five-round characteristic (due to the design rules of the S boxes mentioned earlier). The best probability for an S box is $\frac{16}{64} = \frac{1}{4}$. This limits the five-round characteristic's probability to be lower than or equal to $\left(\frac{1}{4}\right)^6 = \frac{1}{4096}$. In fact, the best known five-round characteristic has probability about $\frac{1}{10486}$.

Among the most useful characteristics are those that can be iterated.

Definition 3.12 A characteristic $\Omega = (\Omega_P, \Omega_\Lambda, \Omega_T)$ is called an *iterative characteristic* if it can be concatenated with itself.

We can concatenate an iterative characteristic to itself any number of times and can get characteristics with an arbitrary number of rounds. The advantage of iterative characteristics is that we can build an n-round characteristic for any large n with a fixed reduction rate of the probability for each additional round, while in non-iterative characteristics the reduction rate of the probability usually increases due to the avalanche effect.

There are several kinds of iterative characteristics, but the simplest ones are the most useful. These characteristics are based on a non-zero input XOR to the F function that may cause a zero output XOR (i.e., two different inputs yield the same output). This is possible in DES if at least three neighboring S boxes differ in the pair (this phenomena is also described in [4,13]). The structure of these characteristics is described in the following example.

Example 3.13 If the input XOR of the F function is marked by ψ, such that $\psi \rightarrow 0$, then we have the following iterative characteristic:

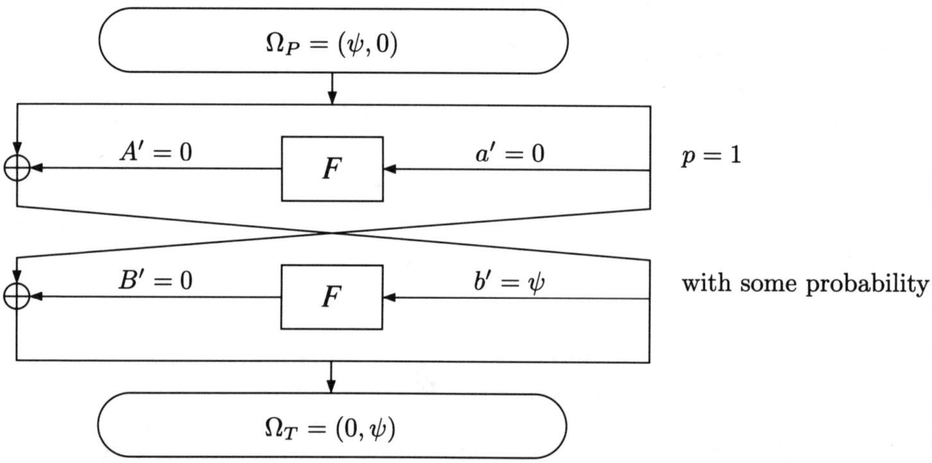

The best such characteristic has probability about $\frac{1}{234}$. A five-round characteristic based on this iterative characteristic iterated two and a half times has probability about $\left(\frac{1}{234}\right)^2 \approx \frac{1}{55000}$ (since the first half of this characteristic which consists of the single round in which $a' = 0$ and $A' = 0$ has probability 1).

All the characteristics described in this book were found manually. We wrote a heuristic program which searched for the best DES characteristics which satisfy certain plausible structural constraints. Although we believe that we have found the best DES characteristics, we have no proof that better characteristics do not exist.

3.4 The Signal to Noise Ratio

This section and the following ones deal with more advanced tools and techniques that are not necessary in order to understand the fundamental principles of the differential cryptanalytic attacks and may not be clear to the first-time reader. We suggest that such a reader should continue directly to the next chapter.

The statistical behavior of most characteristics does not allow us to look for the intersection of all the keys suggested by the various pairs as we did in Example 3.7, since when the characteristics are shorter than the cryptosystem, it is impossible to identify the right pairs and thus the intersection of the suggested keys is usually empty: the wrong pairs do not necessarily list the right key as a possible value. However, we know that the right key value should result from all the right pairs which occur (approximately) with the characteristic's probability. All the other possible key values are fairly randomly distributed: the expected XOR value (which is usually not the real value in the pair) with the known ciphertext pair can cause any key value to be possible, and even the wrong key values suggested by the right pairs are quite random. Consequently, the right key appears with the characteristic's probability (from right pairs) plus other random occurrences (from wrong pairs). To find the key we just have to count the number of occurrences of each of the suggested keys. The right key is likely to be the one that occurs most often.

Each characteristic lets us look simultaneously for a particular number of bits in the subkey of the last round of the cryptosystem (all the bits that enter some particular S boxes). The most useful characteristics are those which have a maximal probability and a maximal number of subkey bits whose occurrences can be counted. It is not necessary to count on a large number of subkey bits simultaneously, but the advantages of counting on all the possible subkey bits simultaneously are the good identification of the right key values and the small amount of data needed. On the other hand, counting the number of occurrences of all the possible values of a large number of bits usually demands huge memory which can make the attack impractical. We can count on a smaller number of subkey bits entering a smaller number of S boxes, and use all the other S boxes only to identify and discard those wrong pairs in which the input XORs in such S boxes cannot cause the expected output XORs. Since about 20% of the entries in the difference distribution tables of the S boxes are impossible, about 20% of the wrong pairs can be discarded by each S box before they are actually counted.

The following definition gives us a tool to evaluate the usability of a counting scheme based on a characteristic:

Definition 3.13 The ratio between the number of right pairs and the average count of the incorrect subkeys in a counting scheme is called the *signal to noise ratio of the counting scheme* and is denoted by S/N.

To find the right key in a counting scheme we need a high probability characteristic and sufficiently many ciphertext pairs to guarantee the existence of several right pairs. This means that for a characteristic with probability $\frac{1}{10000}$ we need several tens of thousands of pairs. How many pairs we need depends on the probability of the characteristic p, the number k of simultaneous key bits that we count on, the average count α per analyzed pair (excluding the wrong pairs that can be discarded before the counting), and the fraction β of the analyzed pairs among all the pairs. If we are looking for k key bits then we count the number of occurrences of 2^k possible key values in 2^k counters. The counters contain an average count of $\frac{m \cdot \alpha \cdot \beta}{2^k}$ counts where m is the number of the created pairs ($m \cdot \beta$ is the expected number of the analyzed pairs). The right key value is counted about $m \cdot p$ times by the right pairs, plus the random counts estimated above for all the possible keys. The signal to noise ratio of a counting scheme is therefore:

$$S/N = \frac{m \cdot p}{m \cdot \alpha \cdot \beta / 2^k} = \frac{2^k \cdot p}{\alpha \cdot \beta}.$$

In practice, the calculation of the average number of counted keys per pair $\alpha \cdot \beta$ is often simpler to estimate than the separate values of α and β.

A simple corollary of this formula is that the signal to noise ratio of a counting scheme is independent of the number of pairs used in the scheme. Another corollary is that different counting schemes based on the same characteristic but with a different number of subkey bits have different signal to noise ratio.

Usually we relate the number of pairs needed by a counting scheme to the number of the right pairs needed. The number of right pairs needed is mainly a function of the signal to noise ratio. When the signal to noise ratio is high enough, only a few occurrences of right pairs are needed to uniquely identify the right value of the subkey bits. We observed experimentally that when the signal to noise ratio is about 1–2, about 20–40 occurrences of right pairs are sufficient. When the signal to noise ratio is much higher even 3–4 right pairs are usually enough. When the signal to noise ratio is much smaller the identification of the right value of the subkey bits requires an unreasonably large number of pairs.

The applicability of a differential cryptanalytic attack is determined by comparing the number of encryptions needed by the attack to the size of the key space and the size of the plaintext space. If the number of encryptions is larger than the size of the key space, the expected encryption time of the chosen plaintexts is larger than the time needed to search for the key exhaustively. If the number of encryptions is larger than the size of the plaintext space, the attack cannot be carried out at all.

3.5 Known Plaintext Attacks

The differential cryptanalytic attacks described so far are chosen plaintext attacks in which the plaintext pairs can be chosen at random as long as they satisfy the plaintext XOR condition. Unlike other chosen plaintext attacks, differential cryptanalytic attacks can be easily converted to known plaintext attacks by the following observation.

Assume that the differential cryptanalytic chosen plaintext attack needs m pairs, and that we are given $2^{32} \cdot \sqrt{2m}$ random known plaintexts and their corresponding ciphertexts. Consider all the $\frac{(2^{32} \cdot \sqrt{2m})^2}{2} = 2^{64} \cdot m$ possible pairs of plaintexts they can form. Each pair has a plaintext XOR which can be easily calculated. Since the block size is 64 bits, there are only 2^{64} possible plaintext XOR values, and thus there are about $\frac{2^{64} m}{2^{64}} = m$ pairs creating each plaintext XOR value. In particular, with high probability there are about m pairs with each one of the several plaintext XOR values needed for differential cryptanalysis.

The known plaintext attack is not limited to the electronic code book (ECB) mode of operation, but is also applicable to the cipher block chaining (CBC) mode, the 64-bit cipher feedback (CFB) mode, and the 64-bit output feedback (OFB) mode[3], since it is easy to calculate the real inputs of the encryption function when the plaintexts and the ciphertexts are known.

3.6 Structures

In many attacks we use several simultaneous characteristics. In the known plaintext attacks we get the pairs of all the additional characteristics for

[3]The Output feedback mode with less than 64-bit blocks is not vulnerable to this known plaintext attack. However, its use is not advisable[10] since it contains cycles of size about 2^{32}.

free. In order to minimize the number of ciphertexts needed by the chosen plaintext attack, we can pack them into more economical structures.

Definition 3.14 A *quartet* is a structure of four ciphertexts that simultaneously contains two ciphertext pairs of one characteristic and two ciphertext pairs of a second characteristic. An *octet* is a structure of eight ciphertexts that simultaneously contains four ciphertext pairs of each of three characteristics.

Example 3.14 The following four plaintexts form a quartet (where Ω_P^1 and Ω_P^2 are the plaintext XORs of the characteristics):

1. A random plaintext P.
2. $P \oplus \Omega_P^1$.
3. $P \oplus \Omega_P^2$.
4. $P \oplus \Omega_P^1 \oplus \Omega_P^2$.

The two pairs of the first characteristic are the pairs labelled (1, 2) and (3, 4) and the two pairs of the second characteristic are the pairs labelled (1, 3) and (2, 4).

We can use these structures in two ways. When an attack uses n pairs of each one of two characteristics we can use $n/2$ quartets which contain the same information as each of the n pairs of each characteristic. Thus, we save half the data. Using octets we can save 2/3 of the data. The other approach is used when an attack can simultaneously use several alternative characteristics and count on the same key bits. We can again have the same factors by using structures of ciphertexts which simultaneously count according to the various characteristics.

4

Differential Cryptanalysis of DES Variants

In this chapter we attack several variants of DES: variants of DES with fewer than 16 rounds, variants with independent keys, variants with modified internal operations and S boxes, and the GDES variant.

4.1 DES Reduced to Four Rounds

In Chapter 3 we defined the notions of pairs and characteristics. In this section we describe how it can be used to cryptanalyze DES reduced to four rounds. This cryptanalysis is quite simple since it uses a characteristic with probability 1, but it serves as a good introductory example to the method of differential cryptanalysis.

In this attack we use the following one-round characteristic Ω^1 with probability 1, which is an instance of the characteristic described in Example 3.9:

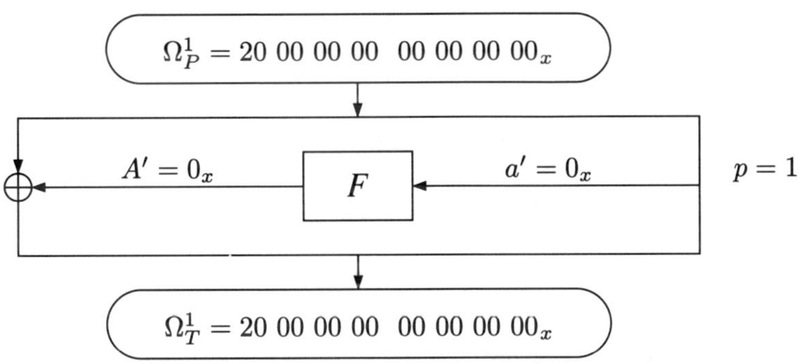

where in the second round (if added) $b' = 20\ 00\ 00\ 00_x$.

In the first round the characteristic has $a' = 0 \to A' = 0$ with probability 1. The single bit difference between the two plaintexts starts to play a

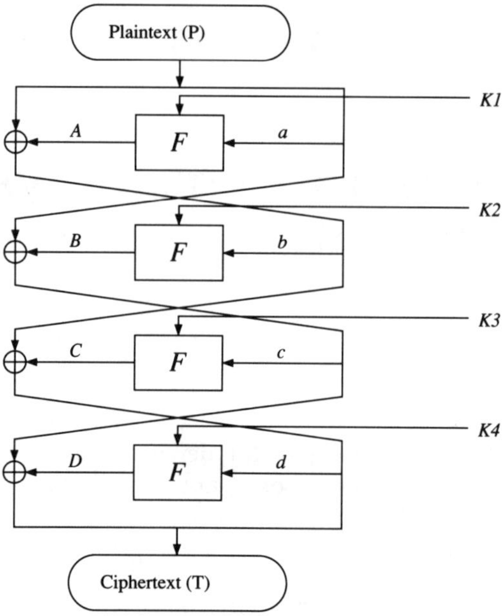

Figure 4.1. DES reduced to four rounds.

role in the second round in S1. Since the inputs to S1 differ only in one bit, at least two output bits must differ. Typically such two bits enter three S boxes in the third round ($c' = a' \oplus B' = B'$), where there is a difference of one bit in each S box input. Thus, about six output bits differ at the third round. These bits are XORed with the known difference of the input of S1 in the second round ($d' = b' \oplus C'$), making a difference of about seven bits in the input of the fourth round and about 11 bits after the E expansion. Such an avalanche makes it very likely that the input of all the S boxes differ at the fourth round. Even if an input of an S box does not differ in one pair, it can differ in another pair and the exact value of d' is usually different for every pair.

The 28 output XOR bits of S2, ..., S8 in B' must be zero, since their input XORs are zero. The value of D' can be derived from a', B' and T'_L by the equation (see Figure 4.1)

$$D' = a' \oplus B' \oplus T'_L. \tag{4.1}$$

When the ciphertext pair values T and T^* are known then d and d^* are known to be their right halves (by $d = T_R$). Since a', T'_L and the 28 bits of B' are known, the corresponding 28 bits of D' are known as well by Equation 4.1. These 28 bits are the output XORs of the S boxes S2, ..., S8. Thus, we know the values S_{Ed}, S^*_{Ed} and S'_{Od} of seven S boxes in the fourth round.

Given four encrypted pairs we use a separate counting procedure for each one of the seven S boxes in the fourth round. We try all the 64 possible values of S_{Kd} and check whether

$$S(S_{Ed} \oplus S_{Kd}) \oplus S(S^*_{Ed} \oplus S_{Kd}) = S'_{Od}.$$

For each key we count the number of pairs for which the test succeeds. The right key value is suggested by all the pairs since we use a characteristic with probability 1, for which all the pairs are right pairs. The other 63 key values may occur in some of the pairs. It is unlikely that a value occurs in all the pairs, which have various values of S'_E and S'_O. In rare cases when more than one key value is suggested by all the pairs a few additional pairs can be tried, or the analysis of the other key bits can be done in parallel for all the surviving candidates.

So far we have found $7 \cdot 6 = 42$ bits of the subkey of the last round (K4). If the subkeys are calculated via the key scheduling algorithm of DES, these are 42 actual key bits out of the 56 key bits, and thus 14 key bits are still missing. One can now try all the 2^{14} possibilities of the missing bits and decrypt the given ciphertexts using the resulting keys. The right key should satisfy the known plaintext XOR value for all the pairs, but the other $2^{14} - 1$ values have only probability 2^{-64} to satisfy this condition.

Some researchers have proposed to strengthen DES by making all the subkeys Ki independent (or at least to derive them in a more complicated way from a longer actual key K [2,18]). Our attack can be carried out even in this case. To find the six missing bits of K4 and to find K3 we use another plaintext XOR value with the following characteristic Ω^2:

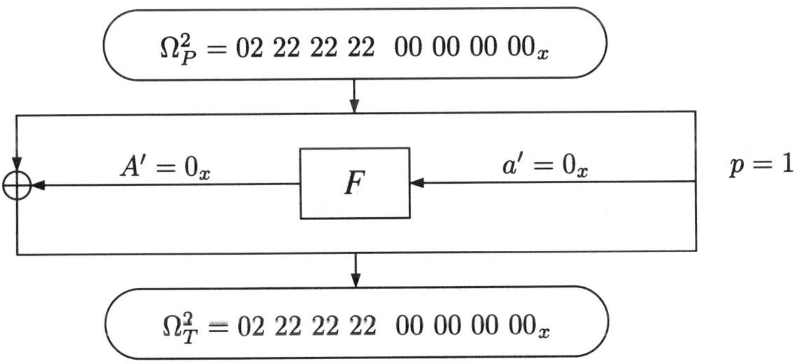

where in the second round (if added) $b' = 02\ 22\ 22\ 22_x$.

The value of $S1'_{Eb}$ is zero. Thus, $S1'_{Ob} = 0$. As above we find $S1'_{Od}$ using Equation 4.1 and similarly we can find the corresponding six key bits $S1_{Kd}$.

Now we know the complete fourth round subkey K4. Using K4 we partially decrypt all the given ciphertexts by "peeling off" the effect of the last round. As a result we remain with ciphertexts of a three-round cryptosystem. In this cryptosystem, we can use the characteristic Ω^2 again to calculate the subkey of the third round (K3). The inputs to the third round c and c^* are known as halves of the ciphertexts of the three-round cryptosystem. The input XOR c' is easily calculated. The output XOR C' is calculated by $C' = b' \oplus d'$ where b' equals the left half of Ω_P^2 and d' equals the right half of the ciphertext XOR (T'_R). The counting method is used to count the number of occurrences of the possible keys of all the eight S boxes at the third round. The values that are counted for all the pairs are likely to be the right key values. As a result the complete K3 is found with high probability.

The plaintext XORs of these characteristics do not suffice to find a unique value for K2, since the values of S'_{Eb} are constant for all the pairs, and thus the right key values are indistinguishable from the alternative key values obtained by XORing them with S'_{Eb}. Although we can find these two possibilities for each S box, i.e., 2^8 possibilities for K2, we cannot use these characteristics to find K1, since in both plaintext XORs the right halves are zero, and thus $a' = 0$ and $A' = 0$. Note that regardless of the subkey, if $a' = 0$ then all the possible values of K1 are equally likely. To solve this problem we have to use additional plaintext XORs which have non-zero input XORs for all the S boxes of the first round. In addition we want to be able to distinguish the key values of all the S boxes, so we choose two plaintext XORs P'_3 and P'_4. These plaintext XORs can be chosen arbitrarily under the following two conditions:

- $S'_{Ea} \neq 0$ for all the S boxes using either P'_3 or P'_4.
- The value of S'_{Ea} derived from P'_3 is different from the value of S'_{Ea} derived from P'_4, for every S box.

Then b and b^* are known by decryption of the third round and B' is known by $B' = a' \oplus c' = P'_R \oplus c'$. The counting method is used to find K2. This time it has to use the appropriate P'_R value for each pair. Now a, a^* and a' are known by decryption of the second round and A' is known by $A' = P'_L \oplus b'$. The counting method finds K1. Using K1, K2, K3 and K4 we can decrypt the original ciphertexts to get the corresponding plaintexts and then verify their plaintext XOR values. If we find only one possibility for all the subkeys the verification must succeed. If several possibilities are found then only one of them is likely to be verified successfully, and thus the right key can be identified.

Typically, 16 chosen plaintexts are required for this attack. These 16 plaintexts contain eight pairs of the characteristic Ω^1, eight pairs of Ω^2, four pairs with the plaintext XOR P'_3 and four pairs with the plaintext

XOR P'_4. In order not to increase the amount of data needed, we use two octets which give rise to four pairs of each of three plaintext XORs. The known plaintext variant of the attack needs about $2^{33.5}$ known plaintexts (see Section 3.5 for the conversion to known plaintext attacks).

4.2 DES Reduced to Six Rounds

The cryptanalysis of DES reduced to six rounds is more complex than the cryptanalysis of the four-round version. We use two characteristics with probability $\frac{1}{16}$, and choose the key value that is counted most often. Each one of the two characteristics lets us find the 30 key bits of K6 which enter five S boxes in the sixth round, but three of the S boxes are common so the total number of key bits found by the two characteristics is 42. The other 14 key bits can be found later by means of exhaustive search or by a more careful counting on the key bits entering the eighth S box in the sixth round.

The first characteristic Ω^1 is:

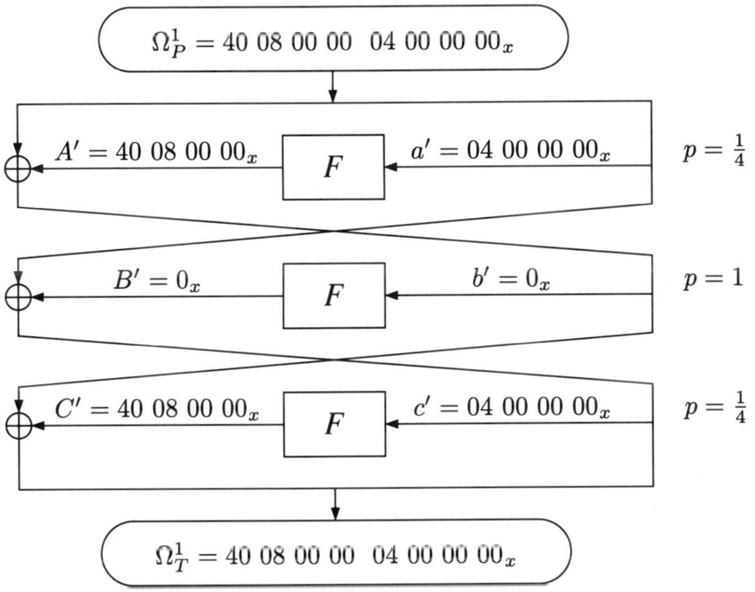

where in the fourth round (if added) $d' = 40\ 08\ 00\ 00_x$.

Five S boxes in the fourth round (S2, S5, ..., S8) have zero input XORs ($S'_{Ed} = 0$) and thus their output XORs are zero ($S'_{Od} = 0$). The corresponding output XORs in the sixth round can be found by $F' = c' \oplus D' \oplus T'_L$.

Since the right key value is not suggested by all the pairs (due to the probabilistic nature of the characteristic), we cannot use a separate counting procedure for the subkey bits entering each S box. In order to increase the signal to noise ratio we should simultaneously count on subkey bits entering several S boxes. The best approach is to count on all the 30 countable subkey bits together, which maximizes the probability that the right key value is the one counted most often. A straightforward implementation of this method requires 2^{30} counters, which is impractical on most computers. However, the improved counting procedure described at the end of this section achieves exactly the same result with much smaller memory.

The same efficient algorithm is used to find the 30 key bits of S1, S2, S4, S5 and S6 using the second characteristic Ω^2 which is:

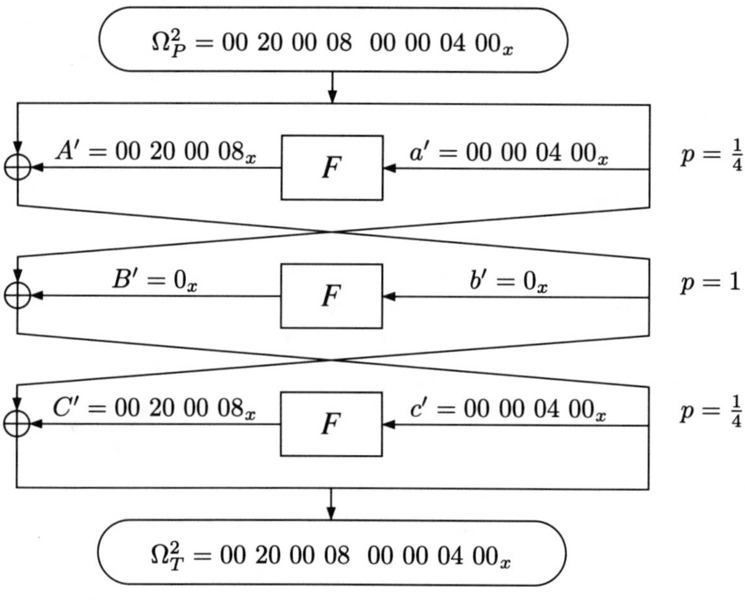

where in the fourth round (if added) $d' = 00\ 20\ 00\ 08_x$.

Again, five S boxes in the fourth round (S1, S2, S4, S5 and S6) have zero input XORs. The computed key values of the common S boxes S2, S5 and S6 should be the same in both calculations (otherwise we should analyze more pairs or consider additional candidate keys with almost maximal counts). If this test is successful, we have probably found 42 bits of K6.

DES has 56 key bits, of which 14 bits are still unknown. The simplest way to find them is to search all the 2^{14} possibilities for the expected plaintext XOR value of the decrypted ciphertexts. A faster way is to start looking for the six missing bits of K6 which enter S3 (the other eight key bits occur

Into S box number	e bits S_{Ee}	Key bits S_{Ke}
S1	++++++	3+..++
S2	++3+++	+3+333
S3	++++++	++++++
S4	++++3+	++..++
S5	3+++++	+++.++
S6	++++3+	+.+.++
S7	3+++++	+++.++
S8	++3+++	++++++

Table 4.1. Known bits at the fifth round.

only in other subkeys). At first we use our partial knowledge of the key to discard wrong pairs. For each pair we check if at the five S boxes having $S'_{Ed} = 0$ by the characteristic, the value of S'_{Of} obtained by f and f^* and the known key bits form the expected value from $F' = c' \oplus D' \oplus T'_L$. If not, this cannot be a right pair. Otherwise it is almost certainly a right pair (since the condition can be satisfied accidentally only with probability 2^{-20}). For the remainder of the cryptanalysis we use only the (roughly) $\frac{1}{16}$ of the pairs which are believed to be the right pairs. This filtration greatly improves the signal to noise ratio of the following scheme, which otherwise would be impractical.

Table 4.1 describes the known bits of the input of the F function and of the subkey at the fifth round, assuming we know the 42 key bits. The digit '3' means that the bit depends on the exact value of the missing key bits that enter S3 in the sixth round. '+' means that it depends only on known key bits. The eight key bits which are not used at all in the subkey K6 are marked by '.'. This table shows that by guessing the six missing bits of K6 we can verify its correctness by calculating e and e^* for each right pair by a single round decryption with K6 and by verifying that the values of $S2'_{Oe}$, $S3'_{Oe}$ and $S8'_{Oe}$ (for which all the input and key bits are known) are as expected by $E' = d' \oplus f'$. Furthermore, for the five other S boxes we can verify that there are values of the missing key bits which are not used in K6, such that the output XORs are as expected. The verification of most of the 64 possibilities of the six missing bits of K6 should fail, and with high probability only one possibility survives. This value completes K6. Only eight key bits are missing now. They can be found by trying all the 256 possibilities, or by applying a similar analysis to key bits that enter S boxes in the fifth round.

How much data is needed? The signal to noise ratio of the first part of the algorithm (which finds 30 key bits) is

$$S/N = \frac{2^{30} \cdot \frac{1}{16}}{4^5} = 2^{30-4-10} = 2^{16}.$$

The signal to noise ratio is high and thus only 7–8 right pairs of each characteristic are needed. Since the characteristics' probability is $\frac{1}{16}$, we need about 120 pairs of each characteristic for the analysis. The signal to noise ratio of the later part is

$$S/N = \frac{2^6 \cdot 1}{4} = 16.$$

This is lower, but we do not care since we can almost certainly identify and use only the 7–8 right pairs from the first part (while eliminating most of the noise) and intersect the sets of possible key values. To reduce the number of ciphertexts needed we use quartets which combine the two characteristics. As a result only 240 ciphertexts (representing 120 pairs of each characteristic) are needed for the complete cryptanalysis. The conversion of this attack to a known plaintext attack needs about 2^{36} known plaintexts.

In order to decrease the amount of memory needed in the first part of this attack we devised an equivalent but faster counting algorithm that uses negligible memory and can count on all the countable subkey bits simultaneously. This algorithm can be used in any counting scheme that requires a huge memory but analyzes a relatively small number of pairs (after filtering out all the identifiable wrong pairs). The idea behind this algorithm is to describe the pairs and the possible key values by a graph. In this graph each pair is a vertex and every two pairs which suggest a common key value have a connecting edge labelled by this value. Thus, each key value forms a clique which contains all its suggesting pairs. The largest clique corresponds to the key value which is counted by the largest number of pairs. In our implementation, for each of the five S boxes which we count on we keep a bit mask of 64 bits, one bit for each possible value of S_K. Given the values of S_E, S_E^* and S'_O we set the bits of the key masks that correspond to possible values. Each pair has five such key masks, one for every S box. A clique is defined as a set of pairs for which for each of the five key masks there is a common bit set in all the pairs in the set (i.e., the binary "and" operation is non-zero for all the five key masks). Finding the largest clique can be done in the following way: first compare the key masks of every pair with all the following pairs in the pairs list. At each comparison there is usually at least one key mask without any common bit set. For the remaining possibilities we try to "and" the result with third pairs, fourth pairs and so on until no more pairs can be added to the clique. Given the largest clique we can easily compute the corresponding key bits by looking at each key mask for the key value that it represents.

Using the clique method with 240 ciphertexts it takes about 0.3 seconds on a personal computer to find the key in 95% of the tests conducted on DES reduced to six rounds. When 320 ciphertexts are used the program succeeds in almost all the cases. The program uses about 100K bytes of memory, most of which is devoted to various preprocessed tables used to speed up the algorithm. A known plaintext attack needs about 2^{36} known plaintexts.

4.3 DES Reduced to Eight Rounds

DES reduced to eight rounds can be broken using about 25000 ciphertext pairs for which the plaintext XOR is $P' = 40\ 5C\ 00\ 00\ 04\ 00\ 00\ 00_x$. The method finds 30 bits of K8. 18 additional key bits can be found using similar manipulations on the pairs. The remaining eight key bits can be found using exhaustive search.

The following characteristic is used in this analysis:

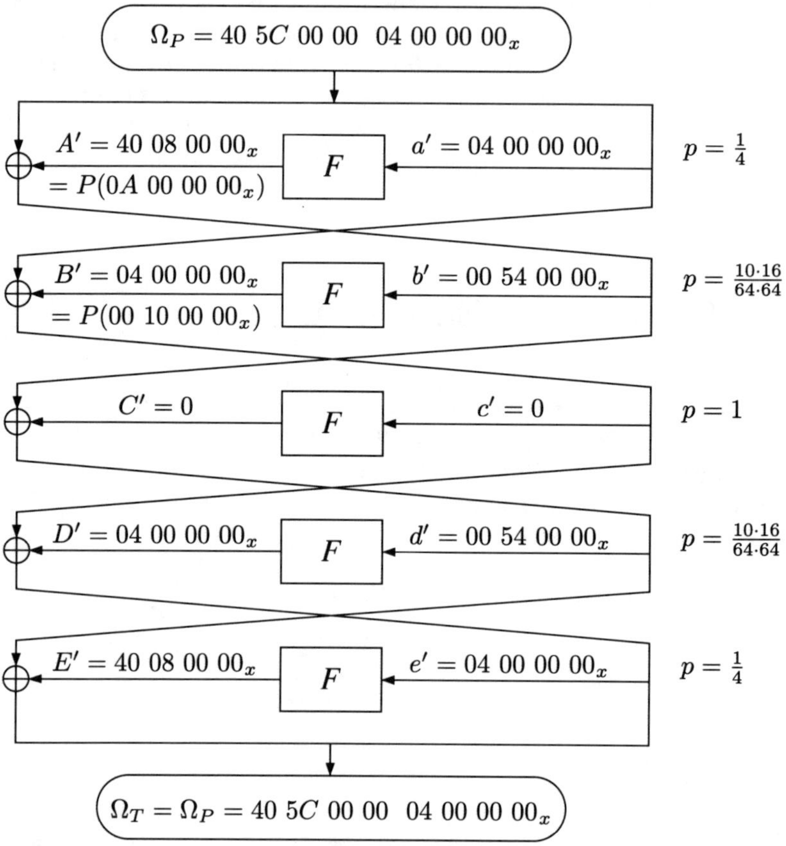

This characteristic has probability $\frac{1}{10485.76}$. The input XOR in the sixth round of a right pair is $f' = 40\ 5C\ 00\ 00_x$. Consequently, for five S boxes $S'_{Ef} = S'_{If} = 0$ and $S'_{Of} = 0$.

In right pairs, the five S boxes S2, S5, S6, S7 and S8 satisfy $S'_{Ef} = S'_{If} = 0$ and $S'_{Of} = 0$. By the formula $H' = T'_L \oplus g' = T'_L \oplus e' \oplus F'$ we can find the output XORs of the corresponding S boxes in the eighth round. The input data of the eighth round is known from the ciphertexts. Therefore, we can use the counting method to find the 30 subkey bits entering the five S boxes at the eighth round. The signal to noise ratio of this counting scheme is $S/N = \frac{2^{30}}{4^5 \cdot 10485.76} = 100$.

Counting on 30 subkey bits demands a huge memory of 2^{30} counters. In this case the clique method is not recommended since its computation time grows very fast (more than quadratically) with the number of pairs, while the computation time of the counting method is linear in the number of pairs. Nevertheless, we can reduce the amount of memory by counting on fewer subkey bits entering fewer S boxes. The remaining S boxes can be used for identification of some of the wrong pairs (in which $S'_{Eh} \not\rightarrow S'_{Oh}$). About 20% of the entries in the difference distribution tables are impossible and thus each remaining S box discards 20% of the wrong pairs. Counting on 24 key bits thus has $S/N = \frac{2^{24}}{4^4 \cdot 0.8 \cdot 10485.76} \approx 7.8$ and counting on 18 key bits has $S/N = \frac{2^{18}}{4^3 \cdot 0.8^2 \cdot 10485.76} \approx 0.6$.

In counting schemes that count on a reduced number of bits we can choose the reduced set of countable S boxes arbitrarily. In this particular case we can choose the reduced set in a way which maximizes the characteristic's probability and the signal to noise ratio by using a slightly modified characteristic which ignores output bits that are not counted anyway. The slightly modified characteristic is similar to the original one except that in the fifth round only one bit of $S2'_{Oe}$ is fixed and all the combinations of the other three are allowed:

$$e' = 04\ 00\ 00\ 00_x \rightarrow E' = P(0W\ 00\ 00\ 00_x) = X0\ 0Y\ Z0\ 00_x,$$

where $W \in \{0,1,2,3,8,9,A,B\}$, $X \in \{0,4\}$, $Y \in \{0,8\}$ and $Z \in \{0,4\}$. Therefore at the sixth round

$$f' = X0\ 5V\ Z0\ 00_x$$

where $V = Y \oplus 4$. The only possible combination in which $Z = 0$ is $04\ 00\ 00\ 00_x \rightarrow 40\ 08\ 00\ 00_x$ which has probability $\frac{16}{64}$. All the other combinations (in which $Z = 4$) have an overall probability $\frac{20}{64}$. We cannot count on the subkey bits $S5_{Kh}$ but it is still advisable to check the possibility of $S5'_{Eh} \rightarrow S5'_{Oh}$ which is satisfied by 80% of the pairs. Therefore, the probability of $e' \rightarrow E'$ is $\frac{16}{64} + 0.8\frac{20}{64} = \frac{32}{64} = \frac{1}{2}$. The probability of the five-round modified characteristic is $\frac{16 \cdot 10 \cdot 16}{64^3} \cdot \frac{16 \cdot 10 \cdot 32}{64^3} \approx \frac{1}{5243}$. The signal to noise ratio of a counting scheme which counts on the 24 subkey bits entering S2, S6, S7 and S8 is $S/N = \frac{2^{24}}{4^4 \cdot 0.8 \cdot 5243} \approx 15.6$. This signal to noise ratio makes it usually possible to identify the correct subkey bits with just five right pairs. Therefore, the attack uses a total amount of about 25000 pairs. The known plaintext variant of this attack needs about 2^{40} known plaintexts. The signal to noise ratio of a counting scheme which counts on 18 subkey bits entering three S boxes out of S2, S6, S7 and S8 is $S/N = \frac{2^{18}}{4^3 \cdot 0.8^2 \cdot 5243} \approx 1.2$. This 18-bit counting scheme needs 150000 pairs and has an average of about 24 counts for any wrong key value and about 53 counts for the right key value ($53 = 24 + \frac{150000}{5243} = 24 + 29$).

A summary of this cryptanalytic method, which can be easily implemented on a personal computer, is as follows:

1. Set up an array of $2^{18} = 256$K single-byte counters which is initialized

by zeroes. The array corresponds to the 2^{18} values of the 18 key bits of K8 entering S6, S7 and S8.

2. Preprocess the possible values of S_I that satisfy each $S'_I \rightarrow S'_O$ for the eight S boxes into a table. This table is used to speed up the program.

3. For each ciphertext pair do:

   (a) Assume $h' = T'_R$, $H' = T'_L$ and $h = T_R$. Calculate $S'_{Eh} = S'_{Ih}$ and S'_{Oh} for S2, S5, S6, S7 and S8 by h' and H'. Calculate S_{Eh} for S6, S7 and S8 by h.

   (b) For each one of the S boxes S2, S5, S6, S7 and S8 check if $S'_{Ih} \not\rightarrow S'_{Oh}$. If $S'_{Ih} \not\rightarrow S'_{Oh}$ for at least one of the S boxes then discard the pair as a wrong pair.

   (c) For each one of the S boxes S6, S7 and S8: fetch from the preprocessed table all the values of S_{Ih} which are possible for $S'_{Ih} \rightarrow S'_{Oh}$. For each possible value calculate $S_{Kh} = S_{Ih} \oplus S_{Eh}$. Increment by one the counters corresponding to all the possible 18-bit concatenations of one six-bit value suggested for $S6_{Kh}$, one six-bit value suggested for $S7_{Kh}$ and one six-bit value suggested for $S8_{Kh}$.

4. Find the entry in the array that contains the maximal count. The entry index is likely to be the real value of $S6_{Kh}$, $S7_{Kh}$ and $S8_{Kh}$ which is the value of the 18 bits (number $31, \ldots, 48$) of K8.

To find the other bits, we filter all the pairs and leave just the pairs with the expected S'_O value using the known values of h and the known bits of K8 entering S6, S7 and S8. The expected number of the remaining pairs is 53. This number is so small that we can afford to analyze each pair much more thoroughly than in the first phase, and thus recover more key bits.

The next bits we are looking for are the twelve bits of K8 that correspond to S2 and S5. We use a similar counting method (exploiting the enhanced signal to noise ratio created by the higher concentration of right pairs) and then filter more pairs. A wrong pair is not discarded by either this filter or its predecessor with probability 2^{-20} and thus almost all the remaining pairs are right pairs.

Using the known subkey bits of K8 we can calculate the values of 20 bits of each of H and H^* for each pair and thus 20 bits of each of g and g^* (by $g = T_L \oplus H$). Table 4.2 shows the dependence of the g bits and the subkey bits of K7 at the seventh round on the known and unknown subkey bits of K8 at the eighth round. The digits 1, 3 and 4 mean that they depend on the value of the unknown key bits entering the corresponding S box in the

Into S box number	g bits S_{Eg}	Key bits S_{Kg}
S1	+4++++	3+..4+
S2	++3++1	134333
S3	+14+++	+1+41+
S4	++++31	11..1+
S5	31++4+	+++.++
S6	4++13+	+.+.++
S7	3+4+++	+++.++
S8	++31+4	++++++

Table 4.2. Known bits at the seventh round.

eighth round. '+' means that it depends only on the known bits of K8. The eight key bits which are not used at all in K8 are marked by '.'.

The expected value of G' is known by the formula $G' = f' \oplus h'$. We can now look for the 18 missing bits of K8 by exhaustive search of 2^{18} possibilities for every pair. Thus we know H, H^* and g, g^* and 40 bits of K7. For each pair we check that the expected value of G' holds. For the right value of those 18 key bits the expected G' holds for almost all the filtered pairs. All the other possible values satisfy the expected G' value only for a few pairs (usually 2–3 pairs while the right value holds for 15 pairs). To save computer time we search primarily for the 12 key bits entering S1 and S4 in the eighth round. They suffice to compute $S3'_{Og}$ as seen in Table 4.2. After we find these 12 bits, we can find the other six bits. This completes the calculation of the 48 bits of K8. Only eight key bits are still missing and they can be found by exhaustive search of 256 cases, using one ciphertext pair, and verifying that the plaintext XOR is as expected.

To save disk space we can filter the pairs as soon as they are created and discard all the identifiable wrong pairs (leaving $0.8^5 \approx \frac{1}{3}$ of all the pairs). Therefore, in the case of counting on 24 bits, the 25000 pairs are reduced to about 7500 pairs. However, when the counting is carried out on 18 bits, the 150000 pairs are reduced to 50000 pairs. For this case, we devised another criterion which discards most of the wrong pairs while leaving almost all the right pairs. This criterion is based on a carefully chosen weighting function and discards any pair whose weight is lower than a particular threshold. This criterion is the extension of the filtering of the identifiable wrong pairs (where the threshold is actually zero) and is based on the idea that a right pair typically suggests more possible key values than a wrong pair. The weighting function is the product of the number of possible keys of each of the five countable S boxes (i.e., the number in the corresponding entry in the difference distribution tables). The threshold is

$S2_I$ 123456	$S2_I^*$ 123456	$S2_O$ 1234	$S2_O^*$ 1234
000010	001010	0001	1011
000110	001110	1110	0100
010001	011001	1100	0110
010101	011101	0001	1011
100000	101000	0000	1010
100010	101010	1110	0100
100100	101100	0111	1101
100110	101110	1011	0001

Table 4.3. The possible instances of $08_x \to A_x$ by S2 (in binary).

chosen to maximize the number of discarded pairs, while leaving as many right pairs as possible. The best threshold value was experimentally found to be 8192, which discards about 97% of the wrong pairs and leaves almost all the right pairs. This reduces the number of pairs we actually analyze from 150000 to about 7500, with a corresponding reduction in the running time of the attack.

The attacking program finds the key in less than two minutes on a personal computer using 150000 pairs with 95% success rate. Using 250000 pairs the success rate is increased to almost 100%. The program uses 460K bytes of memory, most of it for the counting array (one byte suffices for each counter since the maximum count is about 53, and thus the total array size is 2^{18} bytes), and the preprocessed speed up tables. The program which counts using 2^{24} memory cells finds the key using only 25000 pairs. A known plaintext attack needs about 2^{40} plaintexts.

4.3.1 Enhanced Characteristic's Probability

In addition to the statistical behavior of the characteristic we can use the possible values of individual input and output bits of the S boxes. Let us look at the first round of the characteristic. We have $08_x \to A_x$ by S2 with probability $\frac{16}{64}$. Table 4.3 describes the possible input and output values.

We can see that the input bits number 2 and 6 are always equal. In addition for $\frac{12}{16}$ of the input values they are both 0 and for $\frac{4}{16}$ of them they are both 1. If we know the XOR of the key bits entering these two bits of S2 in the first round (i.e., bits 57 and 42 of the key) we can use only plaintexts whose corresponding bits (i.e., bits 5 and 9) have the same XOR value (causing bits number 2 and 6 to be equal). Other pairs of plaintexts cannot satisfy the characteristic. The probability of the characteristic and the signal to noise ratio are then twice as good, and let us use less than half the number of pairs.

If we know the values of both bits in a key, we can choose the two bits in the plaintexts such that the bit values entering S2 are both zero. In this case the probability of S2 becomes $\frac{12}{16}$ instead of $\frac{16}{64}$. Thus, we get a factor of three in the probability and the signal to noise ratio. The higher signal to noise ratio lets us use less than $\frac{1}{3}$ of the pairs needed originally. A factor of four can be easily obtained by a characteristic that holds for all the inputs in which bit number 1 has value 1 and both bits number 2 and 6 have value 0.

4.3.2 Extension to Nine Rounds

The five-round characteristic can be extended to a six-round characteristic with probability of about $\frac{1}{1000000}$ by concatenating it to the following one-round characteristic:

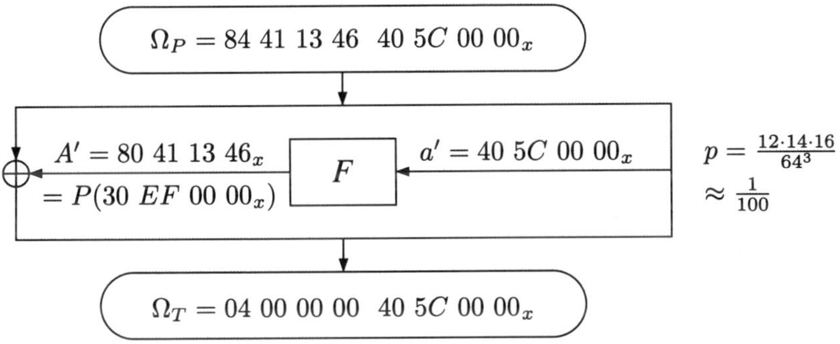

DES reduced to nine rounds can be broken using 30-million pairs by a method based on this six-round characteristic and using an array of size 2^{30} with $S/N = \frac{2^{30}}{4^5 \cdot 1000000} \approx 1$. The first part of the algorithm that finds the first 30 key bits is almost the same as in the eight-round algorithm except that it counts on all the 30 bits at once. The second part of the algorithm that uses Table 4.2 is slightly different since the key scheduling algorithm shifts only one bit at the ninth round rather than two bits at the eighth round. The input part stays the same. The known plaintext variant of this attack needs about 2^{45} plaintexts.

Number of rounds	Probability
3	$2^{-7.9} \approx 1/234$
5	$2^{-15.7} \approx 1/55000$
7	$2^{-23.6}$
9	$2^{-31.5}$
11	$2^{-39.4}$
13	$2^{-47.2}$
15	$2^{-55.1}$

Table 4.4. The probability of the iterative characteristic versus number of rounds.

4.4 DES with an Arbitrary Number of Rounds

The following two-round iterative characteristic with probability about $\frac{1}{234}$ can be used to cryptanalyze (at least in principle) variants of DES with an arbitrary number of rounds:

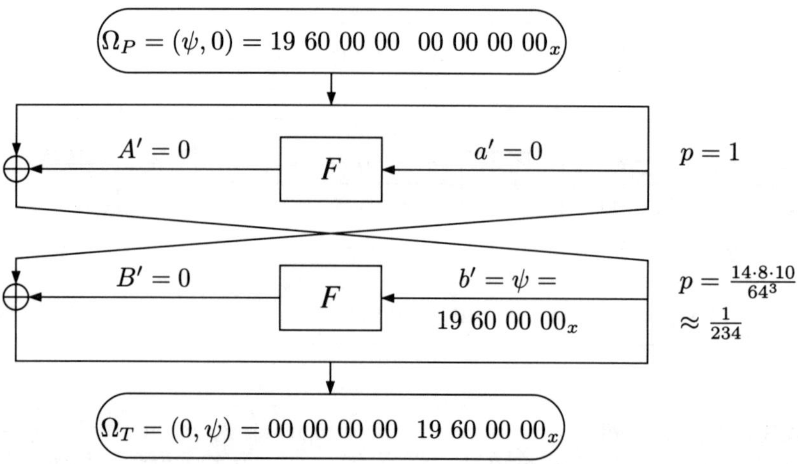

where $\psi = 19\ 60\ 00\ 00_x$. Due to the importance of this iterative characteristic, we call it *the iterative characteristic.*

By an iterative concatenation of the iterative characteristic with itself and with the one-round characteristic with probability 1 (described in Example 3.9) we get characteristics with odd numbers of rounds whose probabilities are summarized in Table 4.4. These characteristics have $\Omega_P = \Omega_T = 19\ 60\ 00\ 00\ \ 00\ 00\ 00\ 00_x = (\psi, 0)$. In the next round (if added to the characteristic) the input XOR of the F function is ψ and five of its S boxes satisfy $S'_E = 0$.

Note There is another value $\psi^\dagger = 1B\ 60\ 00\ 00_x$ for which the iterative characteristic has the same probability. There are several additional values for which the probabilities are smaller. The best of them is $\psi^\ddagger = 00\ 19\ 60\ 00_x$ for which the probability is exactly $\frac{1}{256}$. The extension of this iterative characteristic to 15 rounds has probability 2^{-56}.

There are several possible types of attacks, depending on the number of additional rounds in the cryptosystem that are not covered by the characteristic itself. The attack on DES reduced to eight rounds in Section 4.3 uses a five-round characteristic with three additional rounds which are not covered by the characteristic. This kind of attack is called a *3R-attack*. The other kinds of attacks are a *2R-attack* with two additional rounds and a *1R-attack* with one additional round. A *0R-attack* is also possible but it can be reduced to a 1R-attack with a better probability and the same signal to noise ratio. A 0R-attack has the advantage that the right pairs can be recognized almost without mistakes (the probability of a wrong pair to survive is 2^{-64}) and thus the memory requirements can become negligible using the clique method. For a fixed cryptosystem it is advisable to use the shortest possible characteristic due to its better probability. Thus, a 3R-attack is advisable over a 2R-attack and both are advisable over a 1R-attack.

In the following subsections, actual attacks on DES reduced to 8–15 rounds are described. All these attacks find some bits of the subkey of the last round. The other bits of the subkey of the last round can be calculated by using these known bits with similar techniques. Only eight bits do not appear in the subkey of the last round and they can be found by trying all the 256 possible keys.

4.4.1 3R-Attacks

In 3R-attacks, counting can be done on the bits of the subkey of the last round that enter S boxes whose corresponding S boxes in the round which follows the last round of the characteristic have zero input XORs. The four, six, eight and nine-round attacks described in the previous sections are of this type.

In DES reduced to eight rounds the first 30 subkey bits can be found using the iterative characteristic with five rounds (whose probability is about $\frac{1}{55000}$) by an attack which is similar to the one described in Section 4.3. Using an array of size 2^{24} we have $S/N = \frac{2^{24}}{4^4 \cdot 0.8 \cdot 55000} = 1.5$, and we need about 2^{20} pairs. Using an array of size 2^{30} we have $S/N = \frac{2^{30}}{4^5 \cdot 55000} = 19$.

About 67% ($1 - 0.8^5$) of the wrong pairs can be discarded a-priori.

For DES reduced to ten or more rounds, the signal to noise ratio of the 3R-attacks becomes too small, and thus 3R-attacks on these variants are not recommended.

4.4.2 2R-Attacks

In 2R-attacks counting can be done on all the bits of the subkey of the last round. Wrong pairs can be discarded if the input XORs of the S boxes in the previous round may not cause the expected output XORs. An S box whose input XOR is zero should also have an output XOR of zero, i.e., the success rate of this check is $\frac{1}{16}$. For the other S boxes the success rate is about 0.8.

In DES reduced to nine rounds the 48 bits of K9 can be found using 2^{26} pairs using the seven-round characteristic. We know that a right pair satisfies at its final rounds:

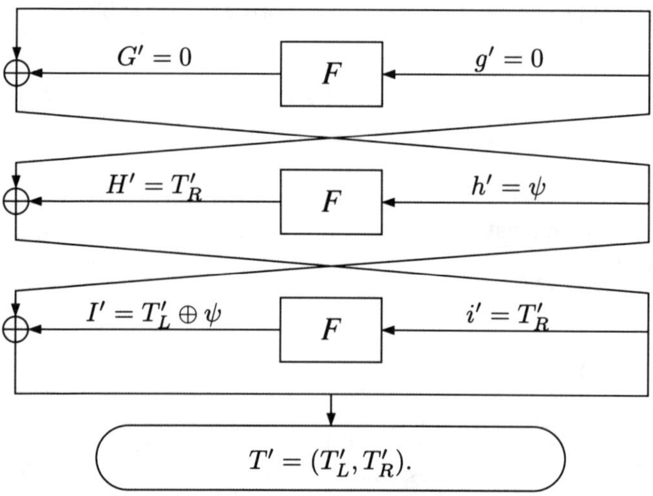

We can discard wrong pairs in which $\psi \not\rightarrow T'_R$ or $T'_R \not\rightarrow T'_L \oplus \psi$ and count the possible occurrences of the key bits in the remaining pairs. At $h' \rightarrow H'$ five S boxes satisfy $S'_{Eh} = S'_{Ih} = 0$ and thus S'_{Oh} must be zero (which happens for wrong pairs with probability $\frac{1}{16}$), while the other three S boxes satisfy $S'_{Ih} \rightarrow S'_{Oh}$ (which happens for wrong pairs with probability 0.8). Therefore the counting on all the 48 bits of K9 has $S/N = \frac{2^{48} \cdot 2^{-23.6}}{4^8 \cdot 0.8^3 \cdot (\frac{1}{16})^5} \approx 2^{29}$ and counting on 18 bits has $S/N = \frac{2^{18} \cdot 2^{-23.6}}{4^3 \cdot 0.8^5 \cdot 0.8^3 \cdot (\frac{1}{16})^5} \approx 2^{11}$. Even a separate counting on the six key bits entering each S box is possible with

$S/N = \frac{2^6 \cdot 2^{-23.6}}{4 \cdot 0.8^7 \cdot 0.8^3 \cdot (\frac{1}{16})^5} = 12$. The identification of the wrong pairs leaves only $0.8^3 \cdot \left(\frac{1}{16}\right)^5 \cdot 0.8^8 \approx 2^{-23.5}$ of the wrong pairs and thus only about one wrong pair remains per each right pair. The characteristic's probability is $2^{-23.6}$ and thus we need about 2^{26} pairs for the cryptanalysis. This attack needs more data than the previous 3R-attack on DES reduced to nine rounds but needs much less memory. Due to the very good identification of wrong pairs (only about eight pairs are not discarded, four right pairs and four wrong pairs) it is possible to use the clique method on all the 48 bits.

The eleven-round variant can be broken by using the nine-round characteristic with an array of size 2^{18} and $S/N = \frac{2^{18} \cdot 2^{-31.5}}{4^3 \cdot 0.8^5 \cdot 0.8^3 \cdot (\frac{1}{16})^5} \approx 8$ using 2^{35} pairs. The clique method can still be used when we count on 48 subkey bits with $S/N = \frac{2^{48} \cdot 2^{-31.5}}{4^8 \cdot 0.8^3 \cdot (\frac{1}{16})^5} \approx 2^{21}$ with an identification that leaves only about $2^{31.5} \cdot 2^{-23.5} = 2^8$ wrong pairs per each right pair.

The 13-round variant can be broken using the eleven-round characteristic with an array of size 2^{30} and $S/N = \frac{2^{30} \cdot 2^{-39.4}}{4^5 \cdot 0.8^3 \cdot 0.8^3 \cdot (\frac{1}{16})^5} \approx 6$ using 2^{43} pairs. The clique method is not applicable since $2^{39.4} \cdot 2^{-23.5} \approx 2^{16}$ wrong pairs are not discarded per each right pair. Counting schemes on 18 and 24 bits are not advisable due to the low signal to noise ratio.

The 15-round variant can be broken using the 13-round characteristic with an array of size 2^{42} and $S/N = \frac{2^{42} \cdot 2^{-47.2}}{4^7 \cdot 0.8 \cdot 0.8^3 \cdot (\frac{1}{16})^5} \approx 4$ using 2^{51} pairs. This is still faster than exhaustive search, but requires unrealistic amounts of space and ciphertexts.

4.4.3 1R-Attacks

In 1R-attacks counting can be done on all the bits of the subkey of the last round which enter S boxes with non-zero input XORs. Verification of the values of T'_R itself and checks on all the other S boxes in the last round to find whether the input XOR may cause the output XOR can be done. For those S boxes with a zero input XOR the output XOR should be zero too, i.e., the check's success rate is $\frac{1}{16}$. Since the input XOR of the last round is constant, we cannot distinguish between several subkey values. However, the number of such values is small (eight in all the 1R-attacks described here) and each can be checked later in parallel by the next part of the algorithm (either via exhaustive search or by a differential cryptanalytic method).

The ten-round variant can be broken using the nine-round characteristic. We know that a right pair satisfies at its final rounds:

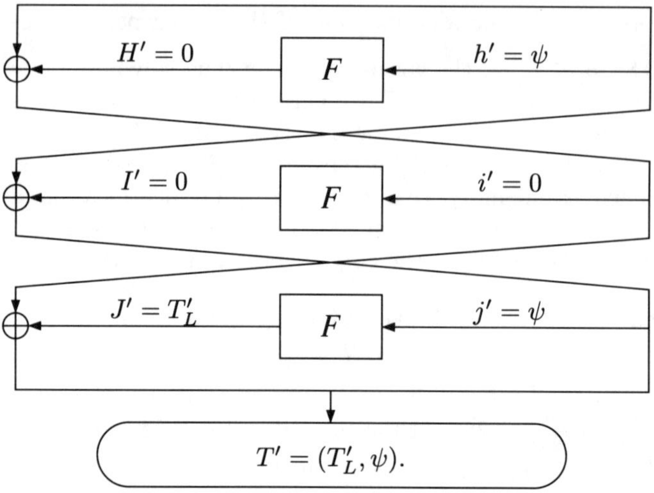

We can identify the right pairs easily. Those pairs satisfy $T'_R = \psi$, and the 20 bits in T'_L going out of S4, ..., S8 are zero. This also holds for 2^{-52} of the wrong pairs. For the other three S boxes we count the possible values of their 18 key bits with $S/N = \frac{2^{18} \cdot 2^{-31.5}}{4^3 \cdot 2^{-52}} \approx 2^{33}$. Thus we need about 2^{34} pairs.

The twelve-round variant can be broken using the eleven-round characteristic with $S/N = \frac{2^{18} \cdot 2^{-39.4}}{4^3 \cdot 2^{-52}} \approx 2^{25}$ and with 2^{42} pairs.

The 14-round variant can be broken using the 13-round characteristic with $S/N = \frac{2^{18} \cdot 2^{-47.2}}{4^3 \cdot 2^{-52}} \approx 2^{17}$ and with 2^{50} pairs.

For the 16-round DES, the signal to noise ratio is $S/N = \frac{2^{18} \cdot 2^{-55.1}}{4^3 \cdot 2^{-52}} \approx 2^9$ using the 15-round characteristic. This variant can be broken using 2^{57} pairs. However, the creation of 2^{57} pairs is more time-consuming than exhaustive search for the 2^{56} possible keys, and thus the successful cryptanalysis of the full 16-round DES requires the refined techniques introduced in Chapter 5.

4.4.4 Summary

For the sake of clarity, we summarize in Table 4.5 all the cryptanalytic results obtained so far, even though they are not the best attacks described in this book. The various columns in Table 4.5 are:

No. of Rounds: The number of rounds in the cryptosystem.

No. of Rounds	Needed Pairs	Analyzed Pairs	Found Bits	Characteristic		S/N		Chosen Plains	Known Plains
4	2^3	2^3	42	1	1	16	[6]	2^4	2^{33}
6	2^7	2^7	30	3	1/16	2^{16}	*	2^8	2^{36}
8	2^{15}	2^{13}	30	5	1/10486	15.6	[24]	2^{16}	2^{40}
9	2^{25}	2^{24}	30	6	1/1000000	1.0	[30]	2^{26}	2^{45}
10	2^{34}	4	18	9	$2^{-31.5}$	2^{33}	*	2^{35}	2^{49}
11	2^{35}	2^{11}	48	9	$2^{-31.5}$	2^{21}	*	2^{36}	2^{50}
12	2^{42}	4	18	11	$2^{-39.4}$	2^{25}	*	2^{43}	2^{53}
13	2^{43}	2^{19}	48	11	$2^{-39.4}$	6	[30]	2^{44}	2^{54}
14	2^{50}	4	18	13	$2^{-47.2}$	2^{17}	*	2^{51}	2^{57}
15	2^{51}	2^{27}	48	13	$2^{-47.2}$	4	[42]	2^{52}	2^{58}
16	2^{57}	2^5	18	15	$2^{-55.1}$	2^9	*	2^{58}	2^{61}

The known plaintext attack is faster than exhaustive search for variants with up to 13 rounds. The chosen plaintext attack is faster than exhaustive search for variants with up to 15 rounds. The best results described in this book are summarized in Table 5.2.

Table 4.5. Cryptanalysis of reduced variants of DES: intermediate summary.

Needed Pairs: The number of pairs encrypted during the data collection phase.

Analyzed Pairs: The number of pairs which are actually analyzed by the data analysis phase of the attack. This number excludes the identifiable wrong pairs which can be easily discarded during the data collection phase.

Found Bits: The number of key bits found in the first part of the attack by using a single characteristic. The other key bits are found later by a variety of other techniques.

Characteristic: The number of rounds and the probability of the characteristic used in the attack.

S/N: The signal to noise ratio of the attack. The number in brackets (if any) denotes the number of initial bits found with that signal to noise ratio. An asterisk denotes that the clique method is preferable over the counting method and then the S/N is based on the number of found bits.

Chosen Plains: The number of chosen plaintexts needed by the chosen plaintext attack.

Known Plains: The number of known plaintexts needed by the known plaintext variant of the attack.

$S2_I$ 123456	$S2_I^*$ 123456	$S2_O = S2_O^*$ 1234
000111	110101	0111
001111	111101	1110
010101	100111	0001
010111	100101	1010

Table 4.6. Possible inputs and outputs for $32_x \to 0$ by S2 (in binary).

$S3_I$ 123456	$S3_I^*$ 123456	$S3_O = S3_O^*$ 1234
000010	101110	0000
000011	101111	0111
000111	101011	1001
001111	100011	1010
010001	111101	0010

Table 4.7. Possible inputs and outputs for $2C_x \to 0$ by S3 (in binary).

4.4.5 Enhanced Characteristic's Probability

As described in Section 4.3.1, we can use the individual values of the input and output bits of the S boxes in order to marginally improve the probability of our characteristics. In this subsection we show how to apply this idea to the iterative characteristic.

When $32_x \to 0$ by S2 in the iterative characteristic the values of the input bits number 4 and 6 are both always 1 (see Table 4.6). Since in the first round the input XOR is zero, it cannot be used as in Section 4.3.1. In addition, when $2C_x \to 0$ by S3, in $\frac{8}{10}$ of the cases bit number 2 equals 0 and in $\frac{2}{10}$ of the cases bit number 2 equals 1 (see Table 4.7).

The XOR value of bit 6 of $S2_I$ and of bit 2 of $S3_I$ equals the XOR value of the corresponding key bits in $S2_K$ and $S3_K$ since the corresponding bits in $S2_E$ and $S3_E$ are the same bit due to the E expansion. If the XOR value of these key bits is known to be 1 then the probability of the two-round iterative characteristic becomes $\frac{14\cdot 8\cdot 8}{64^2\cdot 32} = \frac{7}{2^{10}} \approx \frac{1}{146}$. If their XOR value is known to be 0 then the probability becomes $\frac{14\cdot 8\cdot 2}{64^2\cdot 32} = \frac{7}{2^{12}} \approx \frac{1}{585}$.

The other characteristic described with the same probability has an opposite behavior. When $36_x \to 0$ by S2 the value of bit number 6 is always 0 and thus the probabilities are exchanged. If the XOR of the key bits is 0

No. of equals	keys ratio	probability of first characteristic	probability of other characteristic	sum of probabilities	No. chosen ciphertexts
0	$\frac{1}{128}$	$1.6 \cdot 2^{-51}$	$1.6 \cdot 2^{-65}$	$1.6 \cdot 2^{-51}$	$1.25 \cdot 2^{52}$
1	$\frac{7}{128}$	$1.6 \cdot 2^{-53}$	$1.6 \cdot 2^{-63}$	$1.6 \cdot 2^{-53}$	$1.25 \cdot 2^{54}$
2	$\frac{21}{128}$	$1.6 \cdot 2^{-55}$	$1.6 \cdot 2^{-61}$	$1.625 \cdot 2^{-55}$	$1.23 \cdot 2^{56}$
3	$\frac{35}{128}$	$1.6 \cdot 2^{-57}$	$1.6 \cdot 2^{-59}$	2^{-56}	2^{58}
4	$\frac{35}{128}$	$1.6 \cdot 2^{-59}$	$1.6 \cdot 2^{-57}$	2^{-56}	2^{58}
5	$\frac{21}{128}$	$1.6 \cdot 2^{-61}$	$1.6 \cdot 2^{-55}$	$1.625 \cdot 2^{-55}$	$1.23 \cdot 2^{56}$
6	$\frac{7}{128}$	$1.6 \cdot 2^{-63}$	$1.6 \cdot 2^{-53}$	$1.6 \cdot 2^{-53}$	$1.25 \cdot 2^{54}$
7	$\frac{1}{128}$	$1.6 \cdot 2^{-65}$	$1.6 \cdot 2^{-51}$	$1.6 \cdot 2^{-51}$	$1.25 \cdot 2^{52}$

Table 4.8. Probabilities by number of key bits equalities.

then the probability is $\frac{1}{146}$ and if it is 1 then the probability is $\frac{1}{585}$.

Consider for example, an attack on DES with 16 rounds. There are seven rounds in which the input XOR is assumed to be ψ. Suppose that, out of these seven rounds, we have n rounds ($0 \leq n \leq 7$) whose key bit number 6 of $S2_K$ equals key bit number 2 of $S3_K$. In this case, the probability of the 15-round characteristic is

$$\left(\frac{7}{2^{12}}\right)^n \left(\frac{7}{2^{10}}\right)^{7-n} \approx 1.6\frac{4^{7-n}}{2^{65}}.$$

For the other characteristic the probability is $1.6\frac{4^n}{2^{65}}$. Table 4.8 describes the probabilities for each number n of equalities among the key bits and the relative frequency of such keys.

To increase the probability (especially in the worse cases) we use quartets based on both characteristics. Since both characteristics allow counting on the same S boxes we can use them simultaneously. We can see from the table that we can use this method to break the full 16-round DES with less than 2^{56} encryptions, provided that the key bits satisfy certain relations. However, such keys can also be exhaustively searched in less than 2^{56} encryptions, and thus the small improvement in the complexity of the attack for such keys does not make it faster than exhaustive search.

4.5 Modified Variants of DES

In this section we study the intricate relationship between the structure and the security of DES by modifying DES in a variety of ways and applying differential cryptanalytic techniques to the modified variants. The modified operations are the P permutation, the S boxes and their order in the encryption process, the XOR operation, and the E expansion. The results shed considerable light on the (unpublished) design rules of the DES.

4.5.1 Modifying the P Permutation

The choice of the P permutation has a major influence on the existence of high probability characteristics. Many modifications of the P permutation would weaken the variants of DES. An extreme case is when the P permutation is replaced by the identity permutation (or eliminated). In this case the two middle output bits of each S box would enter as the two middle (private) bits of the same S box in the following round, and this would give rise to the following iterative characteristic:

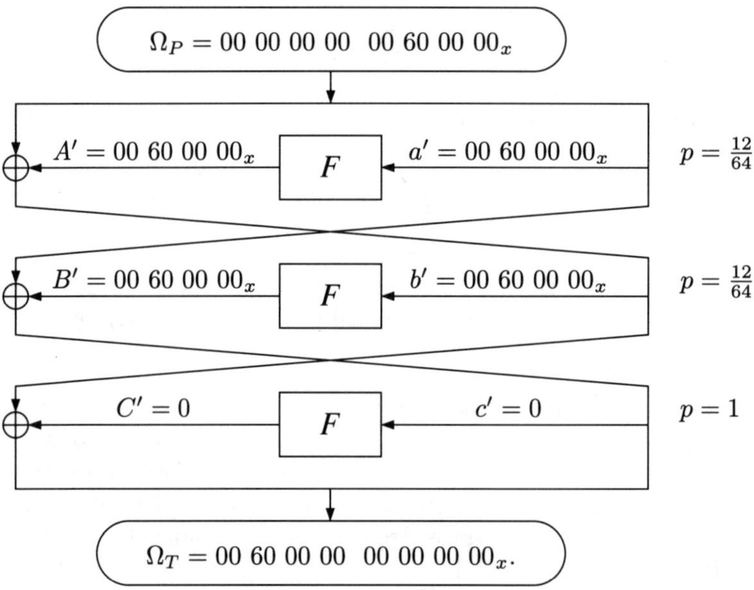

This characteristic can be iterated to a 10-round characteristic with probability about $2^{-14.5}$. Due to the small avalanche in this cryptosystem (the output of an S box affects only the inputs of itself and the two neighboring S boxes in the following round), we can extend this characteristic so that with probability about $2^{-16.5}$ the input XORs and the output XORs of five S boxes in round 14 are zero, and in this case 18 bits of the ciphertext XOR of right pairs are zero. Therefore, we can easily discard almost all the wrong pairs. This attack requires up to 2^{20} pairs. Attacks in which two output bits of an S box enter as the two private bits of the same S box in the following round may be mounted for about 9% of the replacements of P by random permutations, and their complexity is between 2^{20}–2^{42}. Many other random permutations may be attacked using other characteristics.

However, attacks based on characteristics in which the output XORs of all the F functions are zero, are not influenced by the choice of the P permutation. Therefore, all the attacks based on the iterative characteristic are independent of the choice of the P permutation and thus the replacement of the P permutation by any other permutation cannot make DES stronger.

4.5.2 Modifying the Order of the S Boxes

The DES cryptosystem specifies a certain order of the eight S boxes. Even a modification of the order of the S boxes can make the cryptosystem much weaker. Consider for example the case in which $S1$, $S7$ and $S4$ are brought together in this order (without loss of generality, in the first three S box entries) and the other S boxes are set in any order. Then there is a similar two-round iterative characteristic, denoted by $\psi^{\bullet} = 1D\ 40\ 00\ 00_x$ whose probability is about $\frac{1}{73}$:

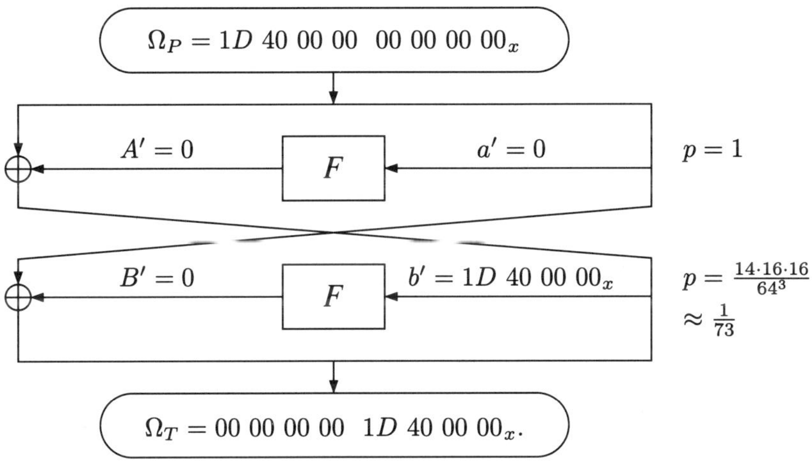

The 15-round characteristic has probability $\frac{1}{73^7} \approx 2^{-43}$ and thus the 16-round cryptosystem can be attacked using about 2^{46} chosen plaintexts with $S/N = \frac{2^{18} \cdot 2^{-43}}{4^3 \cdot 2^{-52}} = 2^{21}$ or using about 2^{55} known plaintexts.

The 17-round characteristic has probability $\frac{1}{73^8} \approx 2^{-50}$ and thus the 18-round cryptosystem can be attacked using about 2^{53} chosen plaintexts with $S/N = \frac{2^{18} \cdot 2^{-50}}{4^3 \cdot 2^{-52}} = 2^{14}$.

In these attacks the clique method can be used due to the excellent identification of wrong pairs (only 2^{-53} of them remain). As in the attack based on the iterative characteristic this attack is independent of the choice of the P permutation.

4.5.3 Replacing XORs by Additions

In DES there are two XOR operations in each round. The first XORs the expanded input with the subkey within the F function while the other XORs the output of the F function with the other half of the input data. The following subsections describe three possible modifications which replace some of the XOR operations by addition operations. The same analysis applies when the XORs are replaced by subtraction operations.

4.5.3.1 Replacing the XORs Within the F Function

If we replace the XOR operation within the F function by an addition operation we get a much weaker cryptosystem. The attack uses the following iterative characteristic:

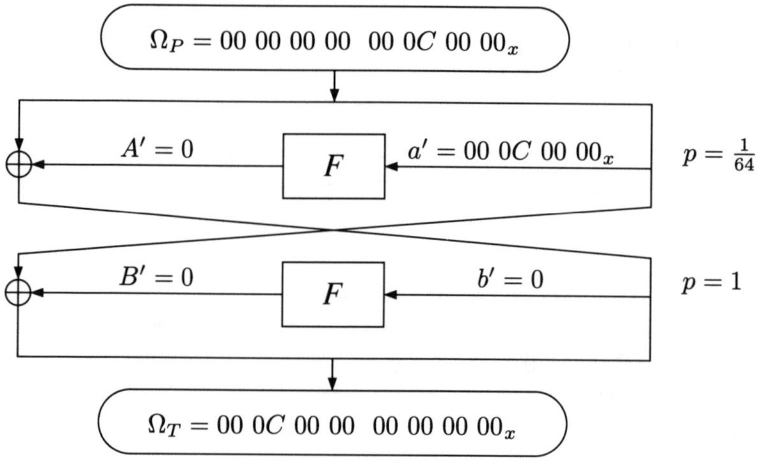

The $00\ 0C\ 00\ 00_x \rightarrow 0$ should be explained: $00\ 0C\ 00\ 00_x$ is the input XOR of the F function. The expansion to 48 bits is 000058000000_x. The addition of the key causes the input XOR to become 000028000000_x with probability $\frac{1}{16}$. Thus the input XORs of all the S boxes except S4 is zero, while $S4'_I = 28_x$. However, $28_x \rightarrow 0$ by S4 with probability $\frac{1}{4}$.

The 15-round characteristic has probability $(\frac{1}{64})^7 = 2^{-42}$. The 1R-attack counting scheme which finds the six subkey bits entering S4 in the sixteenth round has $S/N = \frac{2^6}{2^{42} \cdot 2^{-32} \cdot 2^{-24} \cdot 4} = 2^{18}$. Thus the attack on this modified 16-round DES requires about 2^{44} pairs of encryptions. The six key bits entering S3 can then be found using the same encryptions with even higher signal to noise ratio. Either exhaustive search of the 2^{44} possible keys (with 12 fixed bits) or similar analysis with other characteristics recover the right key. The total complexity of this attack is thus 2^{45}. The known plaintext variant of this attack needs about 2^{54} known plaintexts.

4.5.3.2 Replacing All the XORs

Modifying all the XORs by additions changes the probability of this characteristic from 2^{-6} to 2^{-8}. This happens because the additional addition operation (for example $c = a + B$) does not change the input XOR ($c' = a'$ for $B' = 0$) with probability $\frac{1}{4}$. Thus the 16-round characteristic has probability 2^{-64}, the 15-round characteristic has probability 2^{-58}, the 14-round characteristic has probability 2^{-56} and the 13-round characteristic has probability 2^{-50}.

The analysis of this attack shows that 2^{52} pairs are needed to cryptanalyze the 14-round cryptosystem. The attacks on the 15-round and 16-round cryptosystems are slower than exhaustive search.

4.5.3.3 Replacing All the XORs in an Equivalent DES Description

DES has an equivalent description in which the expansion is moved to the end of the F function and all the calculations are done using 48 bits instead of 32 bits. The cryptosystem which results from the replacement of all the XORs in this description by additions is not equivalent to the modified standard cryptosystem as described in the previous subsection. In this subsection we show that this cryptosystem is much weaker than the modified standard cryptosystem. We can save the repeated cancellation of non-zero input XORs entering S3 in the previous characteristic by doing it in the first addition, since during the various rounds the data bits entering each S box are kept expanded. We get a two-round iterative characteristic with probability $\frac{1}{16}$ which is concatenated to a single occurrence of a one-round characteristic with probability $\frac{1}{16}$ at the first round. Thus an n-round characteristic with an odd n has probability $\frac{1}{16} \cdot (\frac{1}{16})^{\frac{n-1}{2}} = 2^{-2-2n}$.

The 15-round characteristic has probability 2^{-32}. A 1R-attack on the 16-round cryptosystem which counts on the six key bits entering S4 in the last round has $S/N = \frac{2^6}{2^{32} \cdot 2^{-48} \cdot 2^{-42} \cdot 1} = 2^{64}$. Thus, only about 2^{34} pairs are needed. The other key bits entering the last round can be found using similar characteristics. The best three characteristics have probabilities between 2^{-32} and 2^{-35}, and the attacks based on them can find 18 key bits. Therefore, about 2^{37} pairs are needed to find the first 18 key bits. The value of the remaining 38 key bits can be found by exhaustive search. The total complexity of this attack is thus 2^{39}. The known plaintext variant of this attack needs about 2^{51} known plaintexts.

4.5.4 Random and Modified S Boxes

In a random S box there is a very high probability (about 0.998) that there are two different inputs that differ in the two middle input bits of an S box (which do not affect the neighboring S boxes) which have the same output. In this case there is an iterative characteristic which is (without loss of generality the S box is S1 and $S1'_I = C_x$):

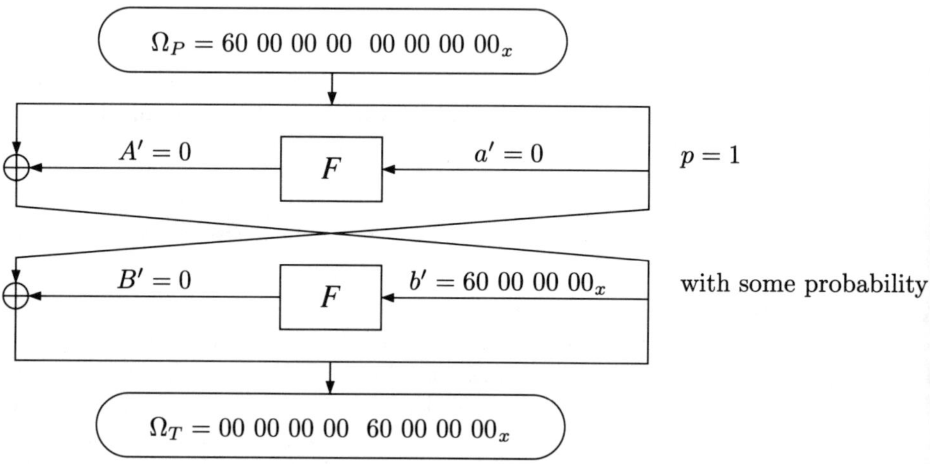

97% of the sets of eight S boxes have such iterative characteristic with probability $\frac{1}{8}$ or more. The corresponding 13-round characteristics have probability 2^{-18} and the 3R-attack on 42 subkey bits needs 2^{20} pairs with $S/N = 2^{10}$. Table 4.9 describes the relationship between the probability of the characteristic, the number of pairs needed, and the probability that a set of random S boxes has such a characteristic.

In S boxes chosen as four random permutations (as in the original DES S boxes) two different inputs that differ only in the private bits of one S box must have different outputs. But there is a high probability that there are two different inputs differing in the input bits of two S boxes which

Char. Prob.	Prob. 8 S boxes	13-round char. prob.	13-round S/N	Chosen Pairs
1/32	1.00000	2^{-30}	2^{-2}	
2/32	1.00000	2^{-24}	2^{4}	2^{27}
3/32	0.99991	$2^{-20.5}$	$2^{7.5}$	2^{23}
4/32	0.97079	2^{-18}	2^{10}	2^{20}
5/32	0.68375	$2^{-16.1}$	$2^{11.9}$	2^{18}
6/32	0.27330	$2^{-14.5}$	$2^{13.5}$	2^{17}
7/32	0.07240	$2^{-13.2}$	$2^{14.8}$	2^{15}
8/32	0.01499	2^{-12}	2^{16}	2^{14}
9/32	0.00260	$2^{-11.0}$	$2^{17.0}$	2^{13}
10/32	0.00039	$2^{-10.1}$	$2^{17.9}$	2^{12}

Table 4.9. Characteristic probabilities with random S boxes.

have the same output. In this case there is an iterative characteristic which is (without loss of generality the difference is in S1 and S2, and the input XOR is $7E\ 00\ 00\ 00_x$):

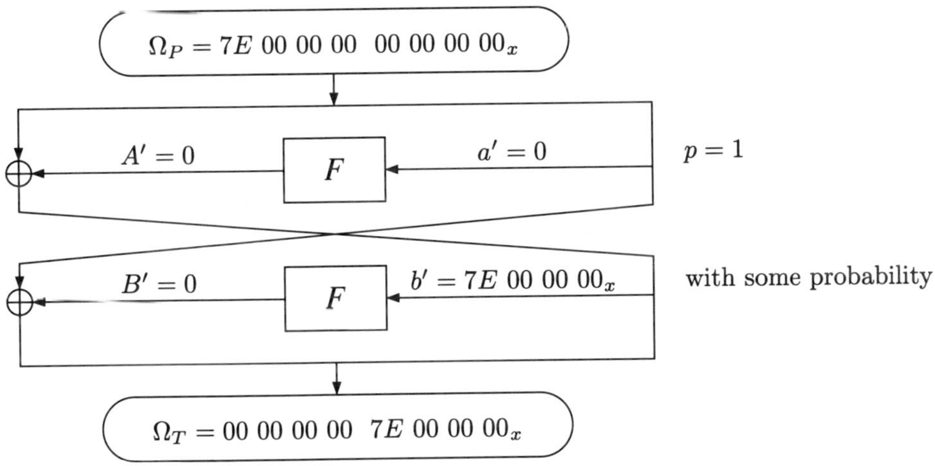

In random tests we found several attacks that use between 2^{43} to 2^{47} pairs. We estimate that attacks that use this number of pairs can be found for more than 90% of the 16-round cryptosystems which use S boxes chosen as four random permutations.

The security of DES can be devastated even by minor modifications of the S boxes. With a single modification in one entry of one of the original S boxes of DES[1] we can force this S box to have two inputs which differ

[1]This modification violates the permutation property in the S boxes of DES.

only in one private input bit of the S box and have the same output. For example, such a modification may set the value of $S(4)$ to be equal to $S(0)$ (i.e., the third value in the first line to be equal to the first value in the first line). Then, the two inputs 0 and 4 have the same output, and thus the probability of $4 \rightarrow 0$ by this S box is $\frac{1}{32}$. A two-round iterative characteristic based on this property has probability $\frac{1}{32}$ and is (without loss of generality the difference is in S1):

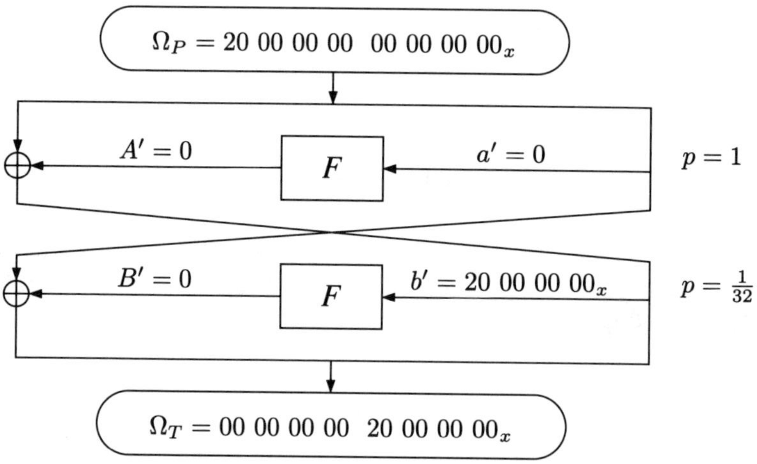

Therefore the probability of the 15-round characteristic is $\frac{1}{32^7} = 2^{-35}$. Using a 1R-attack, 2^{37} pairs are required to attack the 16-round modified DES with $S/N = \frac{2^6 \cdot 2^{-35}}{4 \cdot 2^{-60}} = 2^{29}$ in order to find two indistinguishable values of the first six key bits.

4.5.5 S Boxes with Uniform Difference Distribution Tables

After we published our initial results on differential cryptanalysis, several researchers [1,11,30] claimed that DES can be made immune to this attack by using S boxes whose difference distribution tables have the same value (e.g., 4) in all their entries, except the unavoidable irregularities at the first row. They suggested in particular using bent functions as S boxes, since these functions satisfy the uniformity condition[2].

[2] Note that any function with a uniform difference distribution table must have a non-uniform output distribution in which some output values result from more input values than others. This unavoidable property can be used by the cryptanalyst to design efficient non-differential attacks, in addition to the differential attacks described in this subsection.

Variants of DES with such S boxes turn out to be easier to attack. The regularity implies that the input XORs which modify only private input bits of the S boxes (which are not replicated to two S boxes) may cause zero output XOR with probability $\frac{4}{64} = \frac{1}{16}$. Therefore, the following two-round iterative characteristic has probability $\frac{1}{16}$:

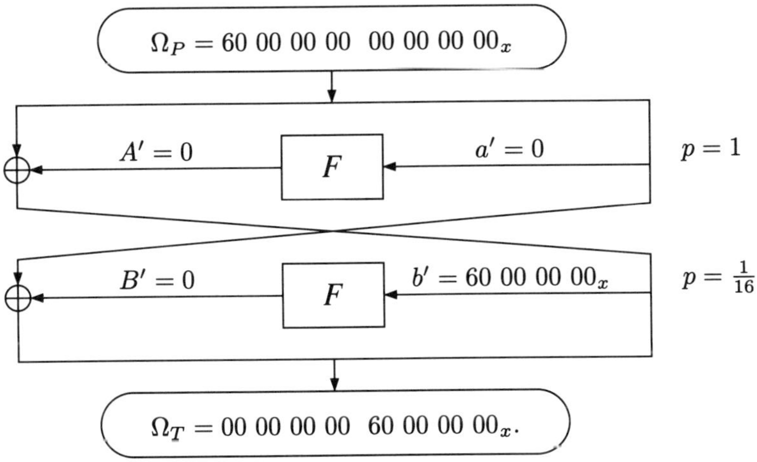

This probability is much higher than of the iterative characteristic of the original DES. There are two other such characteristics which modify the input bits of S1 and similar characteristics which modify the input bits of the other S boxes. The iteration of this characteristic to 15 rounds has probability $\left(\frac{1}{16}\right)^7 = 2^{-28}$ and a 1R-attack on the 16-round cryptosystem needs about 2^{30} pairs with $S/N = \frac{2^6 \cdot 2^{-28}}{4 \cdot 2^{-28} \cdot 2^{-32}} = 2^{36}$. Even 29-round variants of such a cryptosystem are still weaker than DES, and thus the cure is worse than the original problem.

4.5.6 Eliminating the E Expansion

A cryptosystem similar to DES in which the E expansion is eliminated and the S boxes map four bits to four bits is quite weak. Even the cryptosystems that use permutations derived from the original S boxes are easily attacked. For example, using the first lines of the original six-bit to four-bit S boxes as the new four-bit to four-bit S boxes, we can find the following four-round iterative characteristic with probability $\frac{1}{256}$:

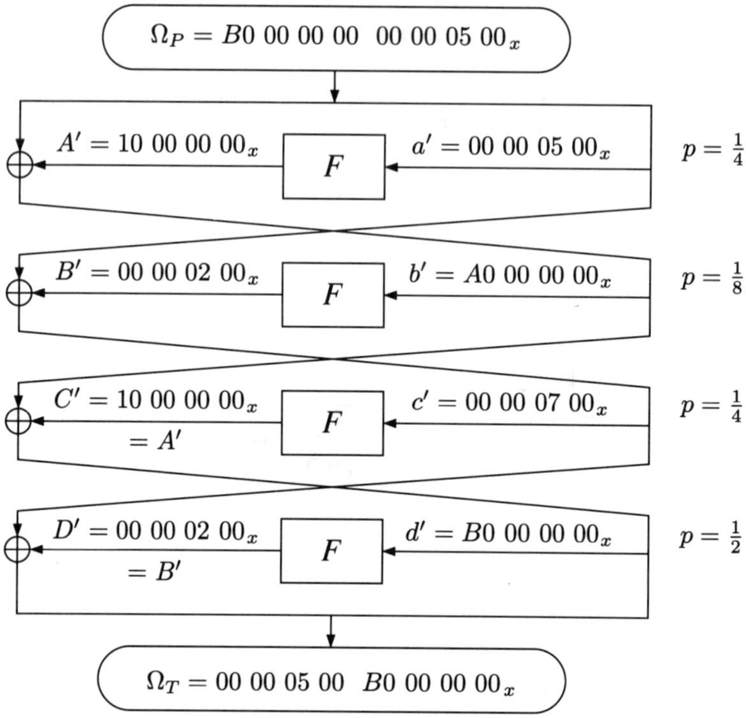

Only 2^{28} pairs are needed to break the 16-round cryptosystem using a 2R-attack. There are several additional characteristics that can be used to attack the cryptosystem with a similar number of pairs.

4.5.7 Replacing the Order of the E Expansion and the XOR with the Subkeys

A cryptosystem similar to DES in which the order of the E expansion and the XOR with the subkeys is reversed (and thus the length of the subkeys is reduced to 32 bits) is slightly weaker than DES. This variant has a two-round iterative characteristic with probability about $\frac{1}{146}$. This characteristic is just the second iterative characteristic described in Section 4.4 whose original probability is about $\frac{1}{234}$ and whose probability was shown (in Subsection 4.4.5) to depend on the value of the subkey. In our case, the subkey bits on which the probability depends are the same, and thus we receive the same probability for any valid key. Therefore, the 13-round characteristic has probability about $2^{-43.1}$ and the 15-round characteristic has probability $2^{-50.3}$ (rather than $2^{-55.1}$). Thus, an attack on the 16-round modified cryptosystem requires only about 2^{52} pairs (rather than 2^{57} pairs).

4.6 DES with Independent Keys

In this section we describe attacks on variants DES with independent keys (those whose subkeys are not derived from a 56-bit key by the key scheduling algorithm). We concentrate on the eight-round and the 16-round variants of DES, and conclude that DES with independent keys is not much stronger than DES with dependent keys, in spite of its longer keys.

4.6.1 Eight Rounds

The attack on DES reduced to eight rounds with independent keys is basically similar to the attack on DES reduced to eight rounds described in Section 4.3. We start by using the same algorithm to find the first 30 bits of K8 and then proceed to find the remaining bits of K8 and the bits of all the other subkeys by variants of this algorithm. The attack uses the same characteristic as in the attack described in Section 4.3 plus 100 pairs with two additional characteristics.

After finding the first 30 bits of K8, we filter the pairs, identify the right pairs and discard all the wrong pairs (with relatively few errors). The other 18 bits of K8 cannot be found yet since we cannot assume that the subkeys are related to each other by the key scheduling algorithm. To avoid this problem we first look for bits of K7. Table 4.2 shows the bits in g that can be calculated for any given ciphertext (the known key bits there are irrelevant to our case). For each of the eight S boxes of the seventh round and for each of its 64 possible key values we count the number of pairs for which this key value is possible. A key value is possible for an S box in a pair if there is an input pair to the S box whose computable bits have the calculated value, the other bits have any value and the output XOR is as expected by the characteristic and the ciphertexts (by $G' = f' \oplus h' = f' \oplus T'_R$). The most frequent key value is likely to be the right key value. Since there is not enough data to make this key value unique we look for the set of key values with maximal counts and choose the bits that have the same value in all the members of this set. Those bits are likely to have the right values. The other bits stay unknown. Experience has shown that the known bits of $S1_{Kg}$, $S3_{Kg}$ and $S4_{Kg}$ are at the locations denoted by '1' bits in $2F_x$, 27_x and $3C_x$ respectively. If some of these bits are unknown it is almost certainly due to a mistaken value of the known bits of K8.

By the knowledge of the subkey bits of the eighth round we can calculate several input bits of the seventh round for any ciphertext. The input to the seventh round g has missing bits that enter all the S boxes. There is one S box whose input depends just on one missing bit while the inputs of all the other S boxes depend on two missing bits at least. This S box is S1 whose input bit could be calculated if the output of S4 of the eighth round were known. To find the key bits of $S4_{Kh}$ we try all the 64 possibilities of its value for each pair, and find the key bits value by the counting method. Now each of the inputs of $S3_{Eg}$ and $S4_{Eg}$ have one missing bit: $S3_{Eg}$ could be calculated if $S1_{Oh}$ were known and $S4_{Eg}$ could be calculated if $S3_{Oh}$ were known. To find these subkey bits we try all the 128 possibilities of $S1_{Kh}$ and the missing bit of $S3_{Kg}$ and then the 128 possibilities of $S3_{Kh}$ and the missing bit of $S4_{Kg}$. Now K8 is completely known. To find K7 we repeat the algorithm of finding K7 described above with the difference that now we know K8 completely. Only one bit of K7 remains indistinguishable. This bit is bit number 2 of $S1_{Kg}$.

So far we have used the filtered pairs. These pairs are assumed to be right pairs whose f' is as expected. They cannot help finding K6 since the input XORs of five of the S boxes are zero, and thus 30 bits of K6 cannot be found at all. The other three S boxes have constant input XORs so there are two indistinguishable values for the subkey bits entering each S box. In order to find K6 we have to use wrong pairs for which the characteristic holds in the first three of the five rounds. From now on we use all the pairs and filter them by a different criterion in each phase of the cryptanalysis.

• K6: To find K6 we decrypt two rounds of the ciphertexts and get the values of f and f^*. We assume that the first three rounds of the characteristic hold in the chosen pairs so d' is as expected with zero input XORs entering six S boxes. Thus we can calculate the output XORs of these S boxes in the sixth round by $F' = c' \oplus D' \oplus g'$. Since $c' = 0$ and S'_{Ed} is zero in the six S boxes, we get that $F' = g'$ in the output bits of these S boxes. The filtering chooses all the pairs for which f' and F' satisfy $S'_{Ef} \rightarrow S'_{Of}$ for S1, S2, S5, ..., S8. Using the resultant pairs we count on the 12 subkey bits entering S1 and S2 and the missing bit of K7 (needed for the decryption of the seventh round).

To find the other bits of K6 we filter the pairs again by using the known bits of K6 to check the output XOR of S1 and S2, and count on $S5_{Kf}, \ldots, S8_{Kf}$, a separate counting for each S box (we have a very good filtering so the signal to noise ratio is high enough). In parallel we count on $S3_{Kf}$ and on $S4_{Kf}$, using the assumption that e' is as expected by the characteristic (four rounds hold) and using the filter that discards any pair for which $S'_{Oe} \neq 0$ for S1, S3, ..., S8 (since only $S2'_{Ee} \neq 0$). Several possibilities are found for some of the S boxes' key bits, and the following phases are applied on each one of them in parallel.

• K5: We assume $c' = 0$ and $d' = b'$. Then $D' = e'$ where e and e^* are calculated by partial decryption. S'_{Od} must be zero in the six S boxes in which $S'_{Ed} = 0$. We filter the pairs and leave only those that have $S'_{Od} = 0$. Then we count on each of the eight S boxes of the fifth round. Several possibilities can be found for some of the S_{Ke}'s. A list of all the possibilities of K5 is created and used to try each one of them in parallel in the following phases.

• K4: At the second round there must be $S2'_{Eb} = S6'_{Eb} = 0$ for any pair (these S box inputs do not depend on the differing bits of the plaintexts). d and d^* are found by partial decryption. In addition $D' = a' \oplus B' \oplus e'$ so $S2'_{Od}$ and $S6'_{Od}$ are known and there must be $S2'_{Ed} \rightarrow S2'_{Od}$ and $S6'_{Ed} \rightarrow S6'_{Od}$. If it does not hold for even one pair it is not a filtering problem: it can only result from a wrong value of the subkeys K5, ..., K8. A separate counting is done for each of the six S boxes S1, S2, S5, ..., S8. The counting on the other S boxes S3 and S4 is done only for pairs whose d' is as expected by the characteristic, since otherwise we cannot know the value of $S3'_{Od}$ and $S4'_{Od}$ because $S3'_{Ob}$ and $S4'_{Ob}$ are unknown. Since $S3'_{Ed}$ and $S4'_{Ed}$ are constants there are two indistinguishable values for each of their keys. As usual we create a list of the possible K4 values and try them in parallel.

• K3: c and c^* can be found by partial decryption of the last five rounds using K4, ..., K8. $S'_{Ea} = 0$ in all the S boxes except S2. Thus S'_{Oc} can be found for S1, S3, ..., S8 by $C' = P'_L \oplus A' \oplus d'$. For every pair there must be $S'_{Ec} \rightarrow S'_{Oc}$. Therefore, even if only one S box (S1 or S3, ..., S8) of one pair does not match $S'_{Ec} \rightarrow S'_{Oc}$ then the values of K4, ..., K8 are wrong. If this does not happen, the counting is done in parallel for all the S boxes except S2 using all the pairs. $S2'_{Ea} \neq 0$, thus the calculation of $S2'_{Oc}$ is impossible without further assumptions. Therefore we assume that the values of A' and b' are as expected by the characteristic. The filtering discards any pair that does not have $S'_{Ob} = 0$ for S1, S2 and S5, ..., S8 using $B' = a' \oplus c' = P'_R \oplus c'$ (since we assume $S'_{Eb} = 0$ in these S boxes). The counting of $S2_{Kc}$ is done using the filtered pairs.

• K2 and K1: The plaintext XOR used above is useless to find K2 and K1 since all the pairs have $S2'_{Eb} = S6'_{Eb} = 0$ and for all the S boxes of the first round except S2 there is $S'_{Ea} = 0$. The key bits cannot be found at all for these S boxes. Therefore, in order to find K1 and K2 we must use additional plaintext XORs. We need only 100 pairs with the additional plaintext XORs, which can be obtained without adding new ciphertexts by arranging some of the original ciphertexts in quartets. These plaintext XORs and the algorithm of finding K1 and K2 are very similar to the case of K1 and K2 in the four round version. See the end of Section 4.1 for more details.

This attack was implemented in C on a personal computer. It finds the key in less than two minutes with 95% success rate using 150000 pairs. Using 250000 pairs the success rate is almost 100%. The program uses 460K bytes of memory, most of it for the counting array (of size 2^{18} bytes) and the preprocessed optimization tables. The program which counts using 2^{24} memory cells finds the key using only 25000 pairs. The known plaintext variant of this attack needs about 2^{40} known plaintexts. As demonstrated by these figures, DES reduced to eight rounds with independent keys is almost as easy to solve as the corresponding variant with dependent keys, even though the number of key bits is increased from 56 to $8 \cdot 48 = 384$.

4.6.2 Sixteen Rounds

DES with independent keys with an arbitrary number of rounds is vulnerable to similar attacks. We showed in Section 4.4 that for 16-round DES we can find eight possibilities for 18 bits of K16 using 2^{57} pairs. Three characteristics can be used to cover K16 completely. The three characteristics are the iterative characteristic itself, a similar iterative characteristic which has non-zero input XORs to S3, S4 and S5 whose 15 round probability is 2^{-56}, and a similar characteristic with non-zero input XORs to S6, S7 and S8 whose 15 round probability is about 2^{-57}. Altogether, about 2^{59} pairs are needed to find two possibilities for the six bits entering each of the S boxes, except S2 whose bits are completely determined by two characteristics. Therefore 2^7 possibilities for K16 are found. We try in parallel all the 128 possibilities of the value of K16 and reduce the cryptanalytic problem to a DES reduced to 15 rounds. Since we know how to attack DES reduced to 15 rounds with 2^{52} chosen ciphertexts (that exist in the pool we already have), trying the 128 possibilities takes about 2^{59} steps. Most of the possibilities are discarded during this reduction, and all the subsequent reductions to fewer rounds have even smaller complexities. Therefore, the cryptanalysis of DES with 16 rounds with independent keys takes about 2^{60} steps and uses 2^{59} pairs which are formed by 2^{60} chosen plaintexts. The known plaintext variant of this attack needs about $2^{61.5}$ known plaintexts using several characteristics. Even though these are impractical complexity bounds, they are much faster than the 2^{768} complexity of exhaustive search.

4.7 The Generalized DES Scheme (GDES)

In this section, we analyze a structurally-modified variant of DES, called GDES, and show that it is much weaker than the original DES even though it is based on the same F function.

The Generalized DES Scheme (GDES) is a faster version of DES which was suggested by Schaumuller-Bichl[31,33]. The speed-up is obtained by increasing the ratio between the block size and the number of evaluations of the F function.

The GDES blocks are divided into q parts of 32 bits each. The F function is calculated once per round on the rightmost part, and the result is XORed into all the other parts, which are then cyclically rotated to the right. After the last round the order of the parts is exchanged to make the encryption and decryption differ only in the order of the subkeys. The scheme is shown in Figure 4.2, where n is the number of rounds of the GDES cryptosystem,

$$\begin{aligned} B_i^{(j)} &= B_{i-1}^{(j-1)} \oplus F(B_{i-1}^{(q)}, Ki) & j \in \{2,\ldots,q\}, i \in \{1,\ldots,n\} \\ B_i^{(1)} &= B_{i-1}^{(q)} & i \in \{1,\ldots,n\}, \end{aligned}$$

$B_0 = (B_0^{(1)},\ldots,B_0^{(q)})$ is the plaintext and $B_n^t = (B_n^{(q)},\ldots,B_n^{(1)})$ is the ciphertext.

4.7.1 GDES Properties

This subsection describes several properties of GDES.

1. In GDES with $n < q$,

$$B_0^{(i)} \oplus \varphi = B_n^{(n+i)} \qquad \forall i \in \{1,\ldots,q-n\}$$

where $\varphi = \bigoplus_{j=1}^{n} F(B_{j-1}^{(q)}, Kj)$.

Thus, the following formulae are satisfied for any $i, j \in \{1,\ldots,q-n\}$:

$$B_0^{(i)} \oplus B_0^{(j)} = B_n^{(n+i)} \oplus B_n^{(n+j)}$$

$$B_0^{(i)} = B_0^{(j)} \Longleftrightarrow B_n^{(n+i)} = B_n^{(n+j)}$$

and for pairs of plaintexts for which $B_0^{(q-n+1)}, \ldots, B_0^{(q)}$ are kept constant (i.e., $B_0'^{(q-n+1)} = \ldots = B_0'^{(q)} = 0$):

$$B_0'^{(i)} = B_m'^{(m+i)} = B_n'^{(n+i)} \qquad \forall i \in \{1,\ldots,q-n\}, \forall m \in \{0,\ldots,n\}.$$

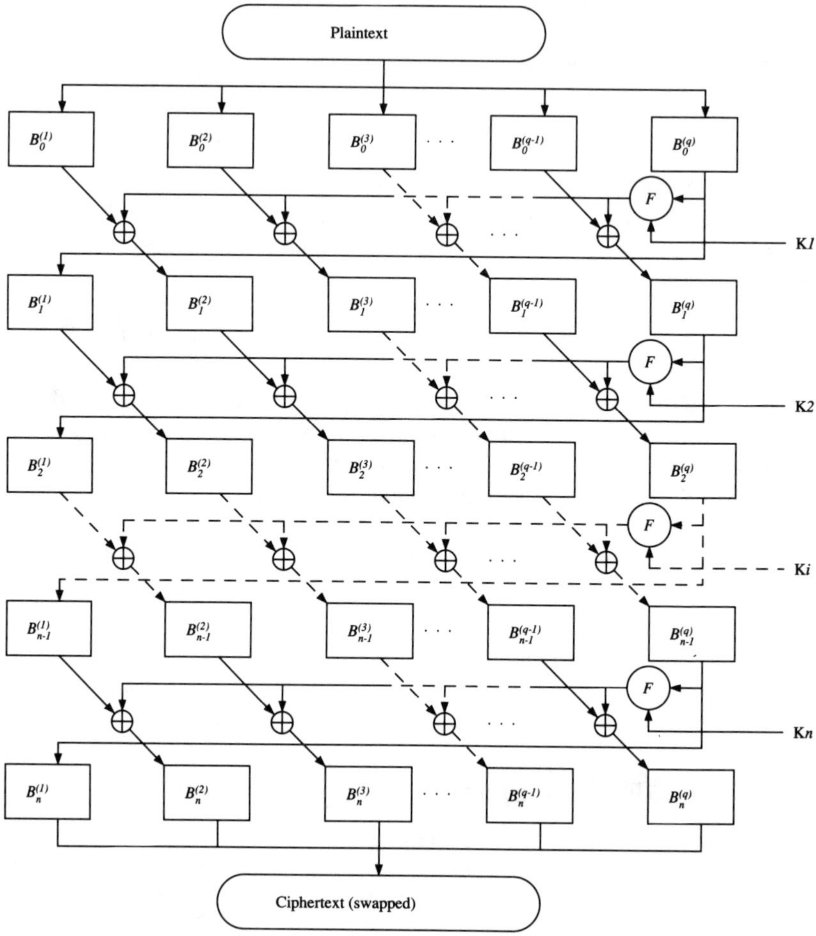

Figure 4.2. The Generalized DES Scheme.

2. In GDES with $n \leq q$, any pair of encryptions in which $B_0^{(q-n+2)}, \ldots, B_0^{(q)}$ are kept constant satisfies:

$$B_0'^{(q-n+1)} = B_{n-1}'^{(q)} = B_n'^{(1)}.$$

3. For any odd q and any n the following equation is satisfied:

$$\bigoplus_{j=1}^{q} B_0^{(j)} = \bigoplus_{j=1}^{q} B_m^{(j)} = \bigoplus_{j=1}^{q} B_n^{(j)} \qquad \forall m \in \{0, \ldots, n\}.$$

4. In GDES with $n = q - 1$,
$$B_0'^{(j)} = 0 \qquad \forall j \in \{2, \ldots, q\}$$
implies that
$$B_n'^{(j)} = 0 \qquad \forall j \in \{1, \ldots, q-1\}$$
and
$$B_n'^{(q)} = B_0'^{(1)}.$$

5. In GDES with $n = 2q - 2$,
$$\begin{aligned} B_0'^{(1)} &= \eta_1 \\ B_0'^{(2)} &= \eta_2 \\ B_0'^{(j)} &= 0 \qquad \forall j \in \{3, \ldots, q\} \end{aligned}$$
where $\eta_1 = 44\ 08\ 00\ 00_x$ and $\eta_2 = 04\ 00\ 00\ 00_x$ or $\eta_1 = 00\ 20\ 04\ 08_x$ and $\eta_2 = 00\ 00\ 04\ 00_x$ implies that
$$\begin{aligned} B_n'^{(j)} &= 0 \qquad \forall j \in \{1, \ldots, q-2\} \\ B_n'^{(q-1)} &= \eta_2 \\ B_n'^{(q)} &= \eta_1 \end{aligned}$$
with probability $\frac{1}{16}$ since $\eta_2 \to \eta_1 \oplus \eta_2$ with probability $\frac{1}{4}$. There are additional values for η_1 and η_2 with smaller probabilities.

6. In GDES with $n = 2q - 1$,
$$B_0'^{(1)} = \psi$$
and
$$B_0'^{(j)} = 0 \qquad \forall j \in \{2, \ldots, q\}$$
(where ψ is the value used in Section 4.4: $\psi = 19\ 60\ 00\ 00_x$) implies that
$$B_n'^{(j)} = 0 \qquad \forall j \in \{1, \ldots, q-1\}$$
and
$$B_n'^{(q)} = \psi$$
with probability about $\frac{1}{234}$. GDES with $n = lq - 1$ satisfies it for any $l \geq 2$ with probability about $\left(\frac{1}{234}\right)^{l-1}$.

4.7.2 Cryptanalysis of GDES

This subsection describes how to cryptanalyze GDES for various values of n and q. We assume that q is even (as suggested in [31,33]), but note that odd q can be attacked by variants of our technique. All the attacks can find the independent keys, and thus are not affected by the key scheduling algorithm. The special case of $q = 8$ and $n = 16$ which is suggested in [31,33] as a faster and more secure alternative to DES is breakable with just six ciphertexts in a fraction of a second on a personal computer.

4.7.2.1 A Known Plaintext Attack for $n = q$

Using a known plaintext attack we are given several plaintexts (each one of the form $B_0 = (B_0^{(1)},\ldots,B_0^{(q)})$) and the corresponding ciphertexts (each one of the form $B_n^t = (B_n^{(q)},\ldots,B_n^{(1)})$). Then

$$\bigoplus_{j=1}^{n} F(B_{j-1}^{(q)}, Kj) = \bigoplus_{j=1}^{q} \left(B_0^{(j)} \oplus B_n^{(j)}\right)$$

and for any $i \in \{1,\ldots,n\}$

$$\bigoplus_{\substack{j=1 \\ j\neq i}}^{n} F(B_{j-1}^{(q)}, Kj) = B_0^{(q+1-i)} \oplus B_n^{(q+1-i)}.$$

Thus, the output of the F function in round i is

$$F(B_{i-1}^{(q)}, Ki) = B_0^{(q+1-i)} \oplus B_n^{(q+1-i)} \oplus \bigoplus_{j=1}^{q} \left(B_0^{(j)} \oplus B_n^{(j)}\right)$$

and the input of the F function in round i is

$$B_{i-1}^{(q)} = B_0^{(q+1-i)} \oplus \bigoplus_{j=1}^{i-1} F(B_{j-1}^{(q)}, Kj).$$

Therefore, we can easily calculate S_E and S_O of each one of the $8n$ S boxes. As a result we get only four choices for the six subkey bits of each S box. Using two or three encryptions the choices can be filtered by leaving only the ones that appear in all the encryptions, and thus all the subkey bits can be found.

4.7.2.2 A Second Known Plaintext Attack for $n = q$

Using pairs whose plaintext XORs are known we can compute the input and output XORs of the F functions by the same method used in the known plaintext attack. We can thus find all the subkeys (starting with the subkey of the last round and working backwards towards the first round) using three pairs of ciphertexts with different plaintext XORs.

4.7.2.3 A Chosen Plaintext Attack for $n = 2q - 1$

Using a chosen plaintext attack with pairs satisfying

$$B'^{(j)}_0 = 0 \qquad \forall j \in \{2, \ldots, q\}$$

and any $B'^{(1)}_0 \neq 0$, we get

$$B'^{(j)}_{q-1} = 0 \qquad \forall j \in \{1, \ldots, q-1\}$$

and

$$B'^{(q)}_{q-1} = B'^{(1)}_0.$$

The rest of the encryption is based on q rounds and thus an attack similar to the second known plaintext attack for $n = q$ can be used to find q subkeys by analyzing three ciphertext pairs.

The other $q - 1$ subkeys can be found using a similar attack with two additional ciphertexts.

4.7.2.4 A Chosen Plaintext Attack for $n = 3q - 2$

This attack is similar to the previous one, and uses ciphertext pairs satisfying:

$$B'^{(1)}_0 = \eta_1$$
$$B'^{(2)}_0 = \eta_2$$
$$B'^{(j)}_0 = 0 \qquad \forall j \in \{3, \ldots, q\}.$$

where η_1 and η_2 are defined in Subsection 4.7.1. The right pairs with respect to the corresponding $(2q - 2)$-round characteristic are about $\frac{1}{16}$ of all the pairs. We can identify most of the wrong pairs by checking that the input XOR cannot cause the output XOR. This happens with probability about 0.8 for each S box. Thus only $0.8^{8q} = 0.16^q$ of the wrong pairs remain. When $q \geq 3$ this is less than $0.8^{8 \cdot 3} = \frac{1}{250}$ of the pairs. This excellent identification makes it possible to consider only 48 pairs, and identify the three expected occurrences of right pairs among them. We can further decrease this amount to 24 pairs by using quartets of two characteristics.

4.7.2.5 A Chosen Plaintext Attack for $n = lq - 1$

This attack works for $n = lq - 1$ rounds for $l \geq 3$. It is similar to the previous ones using

$$B'^{(1)}_0 = \psi = 19\ 60\ 00\ 00_x$$

$$B_0'^{(j)} = 0 \qquad \forall j \in \{2,\ldots,q\}.$$

The $((l-1)q-1)$-round characteristic holds with probability about $\left(\frac{1}{234}\right)^{l-2}$. The identification leaves about $0.8^{8q-5}\cdot\left(\frac{1}{16}\right)^5$ of the wrong pairs. Thus, if $0.8^{8q-5}\cdot 2^{-20} \ll \left(\frac{1}{234}\right)^{l-2}$ (i.e., for $q=8$: $l\leq 7$ and $n\leq 55$) then the identification is excellent and only three right pairs are needed (among the $3\cdot 234^{l-2}$ pairs considered) for counting the occurrences for each S box separately. Otherwise we can count on several S boxes simultaneously using more memory and a better signal to noise ratio. Counting on the 48 bits of the subkey of the last round has

$$S/N = \frac{2^{48}\cdot 2^{-8(l-2)}}{4^8\cdot 0.8^{8q-13}\cdot 2^{-20}} \approx 2^{64-8l+2.5q}.$$

This attack shows that any GDES which is faster than DES is also less secure than DES. GDES with $n=8q$ rounds is just as fast as DES. Consider GDES with $n=8q-1$ which is slightly faster than DES. The usable characteristic has $7q-1$ rounds and six repetitions of the iterative characteristic. Thus its probability is about $\left(\frac{1}{234}\right)^6 \approx 2^{-48}$. Counting on all the 48 bits of the subkey of the last round has

$$S/N = \frac{2^{48}\cdot 2^{-48}}{4^8\cdot 0.8^{8q-13}\cdot 2^{-20}} \approx 2^{2.5q}.$$

Therefore, about 4–8 right pairs are needed, giving a total of $8\cdot 2^{48} = 2^{51}$ pairs. This complexity decreases rapidly when we try to make GDES even faster by making n substantially smaller than $8q$.

4.7.2.6 The Actual Attack on the Recommended Variant

The recommended parameters for GDES are $q=8$ and $n=16$. In this subsection we show that even the independent-key version of any GDES with $n=2q$ can be broken with just 16 ciphertexts with particular differences in the plaintexts. The complexity can be reduced to six ciphertexts if the subkeys are derived from the standard key scheduling algorithm.

The ciphertexts corresponding to the following 16 plaintexts are required by the attack:

- A random plaintext P.
- The nine plaintexts obtained from P by XORing $66\ 00\ 00\ 00_x$, $60\ 60\ 00\ 00_x$, $60\ 00\ 60\ 00_x$, $60\ 00\ 00\ 60_x$, $60\ 00\ 00\ 06_x$, $9E\ 5F\ AC\ 7D_x$,

$F7\ A5\ 35\ C7_x$, $7A\ FA\ 78\ D5_x$ and $21\ 22\ E3\ 2C_x$ into $B_0^{(1)}$ (the first 32 bits of P).

- The six plaintexts obtained from P by XORing $A6\ BD\ EF\ B7_x$, $F4\ F3\ 82\ 3C_x$, $4F\ 5C\ 37\ 51_x$, $2B\ 76\ 7A\ DB_x$, $5A\ 19\ F9\ 68_x$ and $33\ EE\ DD\ FF_x$ into all the $B_0^{(i)}$ blocks.

These XOR values are chosen by the following criteria:

1. The first plaintext is the randomly chosen basis for the differential attack.
2. Five plaintexts have the maximal number of unchanged inputs to S boxes in the qth round compared with P and with each other. At least five of the inputs to each S box in the qth round are unchanged, which makes it possible to find the subkey of the last round.
3. Four other plaintexts have a maximal difference in the S boxes of the qth round. This is used to find the subkeys of the $q+1^{\text{th}}$ and all the subsequent rounds (There is not enough variability in the previous values to find all those subkeys).
4. Six plaintexts have a maximal difference in the S boxes of the first q rounds. This makes it possible to find the first q subkeys.

The cryptanalytic algorithm is as follows. At first the attacker tries to find the subkey of the last round. Each one of the 15 pairs formed by the first six encryptions has a different set of six S boxes whose input XORs in $B_0^{(1)}$ are zero. All the other $B_0^{(i)}, i \in \{2, \ldots, q\}$ have input XORs which are trivially zero. Thus, the F functions of the first $q-1$ rounds have zero input and output XORs in all the pairs. The F function of the qth round has zero input and output XORs in six of the eight S boxes. Therefore, we can calculate the output XOR of these six S boxes in the last ($2q^{\text{th}}$) round by the formula:

$$F'(B_{n-1}^{(q)}, Kn) = \bigoplus_{j=2}^{q} B_n'^{(j)}.$$

The input XOR is easily computed as $B_{n\ 1}'^{(q)} = B_n'^{(1)}$ and the input itself is $B_n^{(1)}$. Now we try all the possible key bits for each S box separately and check that for the given input XOR we get the given output XOR value. For each S box there are at least five pairs which can distinguish values of the key bits. The (almost certainly unique) value suggested by all the pairs is the key of the corresponding S box. Therefore, the complete subkey of the last round is found. Now partial decryption of the last round can be done, effectively reducing the cryptosystem to $2q-1$ rounds.

Note that if the subkeys are derived by the key scheduling algorithm of DES then 48 bits out of the 56 key bits are known at this point. The others can be easily found by trying all the 256 possibilities of the missing eight key bits. We thus proceed to analyze the case of independent keys, which requires 10 additional ciphertexts.

In the following $q-1$ rounds we get the input and the input XOR of the F function from the (partially decrypted) ciphertexts. The output XOR is calculated by the formula:

$$F'(B_{r-1}^{(q)}, Kr) = B_0'^{(1)} \oplus \bigoplus_{j=2}^{q} B_r'^{(j)}$$

where r is the round number ($r \in \{q+1, \ldots, 2q-1\}$). In this case the first ten ciphertexts are used. The additional four ciphertexts are needed primarily to find K($q+1$) since in the first six encryptions there are too many zero XOR bits and more variety is needed. These additional ciphertexts cannot help in the nth round because the output XORs of the S boxes in the qth round have to be zero.

In the remaining q rounds we use all the 16 ciphertexts. The additional ciphertexts have non-zero differences in all the S boxes in all the rounds, whereas the first ten had a constant value during the first $q-1$ rounds. The input XOR is calculated by the formula:

$$F'(B_{r-1}^{(q)}, Kr) = \varphi \oplus \bigoplus_{j=2}^{q} B_r'^{(j)}$$

where r is the round number ($r \in \{1, \ldots, q\}$) and φ is

$$\varphi = \begin{cases} B_0'^{(1)}, & \text{if } r < q; \\ B_0'^{(2)}, & \text{if } r = q. \end{cases}$$

4.7.2.7 Summary

GDES with $n = q = 8$ is breakable using a known plaintext attack with three ciphertexts. With a key scheduling similar to DES, GDES is vulnerable to a known plaintext attack when $n = q+1$ as well.

The recommended parameters for GDES are $q = 8$ and $n = 16$ [31,33]. The $n = 15$ variant is easily breakable using the $n = 2q-1$ attack with three ciphertexts. The recommended $n = 16$ variant is breakable with six ciphertexts in 0.2 seconds on a personal computer. If independent keys are used then it is breakable with 16 ciphertexts in three seconds on the same computer.

GDES with $q = 8$ and $n = 22$ is breakable using the $n = 3q - 2$ attack with 48 ciphertexts (24 pairs). GDES with $q = 8$ and $n = 31$ is breakable using the $n = 4q - 1$ attack with 250000 pairs and $S/N = \frac{2^{18}}{234^2 \cdot 0.8^{13}} \approx 2^7$ with memory of size 2^{18}. In general, any GDES which is faster than DES is also less secure than DES. The known plaintext variants of these attacks are not advisable since the block size is very large and therefore the conversion needs a huge number of known plaintexts.

5

Differential Cryptanalysis of the Full 16-Round DES

In this chapter we describe the first known attack which is capable of breaking the full 16-round DES in less than the complexity of exhaustive search of 2^{55} keys. The data analysis phase computes the key by analyzing about 2^{36} ciphertexts in 2^{37} time. The 2^{36} usable ciphertexts are obtained during the data collection phase from a larger pool of 2^{47} chosen plaintexts by a simple bit repetition criteria which discards more than 99.9% of the ciphertexts as soon as they are generated. This attack is not applicable to the independent-key variant of DES.

The attack on the 15-round variant of DES described in the previous chapter is based on the following two-round iterative characteristic:

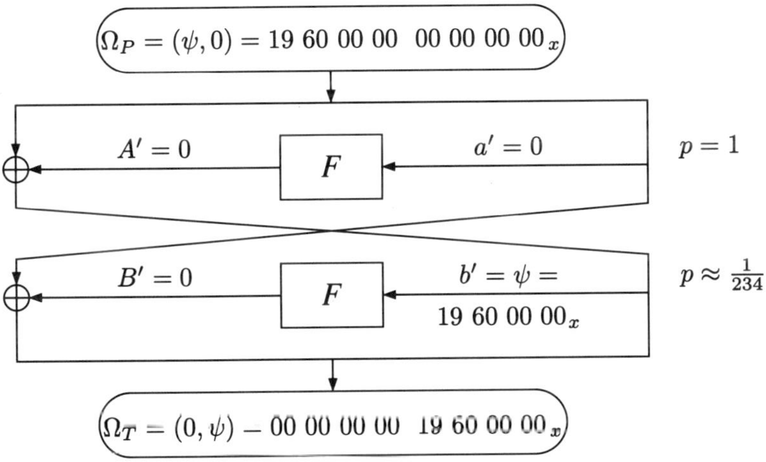

A 13-round characteristic can be obtained by iterating this characteristic six and a half times and its probability is about $2^{-47.2}$. The attack uses this characteristic in rounds 1 to 13, followed by a 2R-attack on the last two rounds 14 to 15. The attack tries many pairs of plaintexts, and eliminates any pair which is obviously a wrong pair due to its known input and output values. However, since the cryptanalyst cannot actually determine the intermediate values, the elimination process is imperfect and leaves behind a mixture of right and wrong pairs.

In the previous chapter, each surviving pair suggested several possible values for certain key bits. Right pairs always suggested the correct value for these key bits (along with several wrong values), while wrong pairs suggested random values. When sufficiently many right pairs were analyzed, the correct value (signal) overcame the random values (noise) by becoming the most frequently suggested value. The actual algorithm was to keep a separate counter for the number of times each value was suggested, and to output the index of the counter with the maximal final value. This approach required a huge memory (with up to 2^{42} counters in the attack on the 15-round variant of DES), and had a negligible probability of success when the number of analyzed pairs was reduced below the threshold implied by the signal to noise ratio.

In this chapter, we work somewhat harder on each pair, and suggest a list of complete 56-bit keys rather than possible values for a subset of key bits. As a result, we can immediately test each suggested key via trial encryption, without using any counters. By eliminating the counters, we can carry out the attack with very small memory, and the algorithm is guaranteed to discover the correct key as soon as the first right pair is encountered.

The key to success in such an attack is to use a high probability characteristic, which makes it possible to consider fewer wrong pairs before the first occurrence of a right pair. The probability of the characteristic used in the attack on the 15-round variant of DES is about $\left(\frac{1}{234}\right)^6 = 2^{-47.2}$. The obvious way to extend the attack to 16 rounds is to use the above iterative characteristic one more time, but this reduces the probability of the characteristic from $2^{-47.2}$ to $2^{-55.1}$, which makes the attack slower than exhaustive search. In this chapter we add the extra round without reducing the probability at all.

The assumed evolution of the differences during the encryption of a right pair in this 16-round attack is summarized in Figure 5.1, which consists of the old 15-round attack on rounds 2 to 16, preceded by a new round 1. For convenience, we employ the notation of an eight-round cryptosystem to the 16-round DES.

Our goal is to generate without loss of probability pairs of plaintexts whose XORed outputs after the first round are the required XORed inputs $(\psi, 0)$ into the 13-round characteristic of rounds 2 to 14. Let P be an arbitrary 64-bit plaintext, and let $v_0, \ldots, v_{4095}$ be the 2^{12} 32-bit constants which consist of all the possible values at the 12 bit positions which are

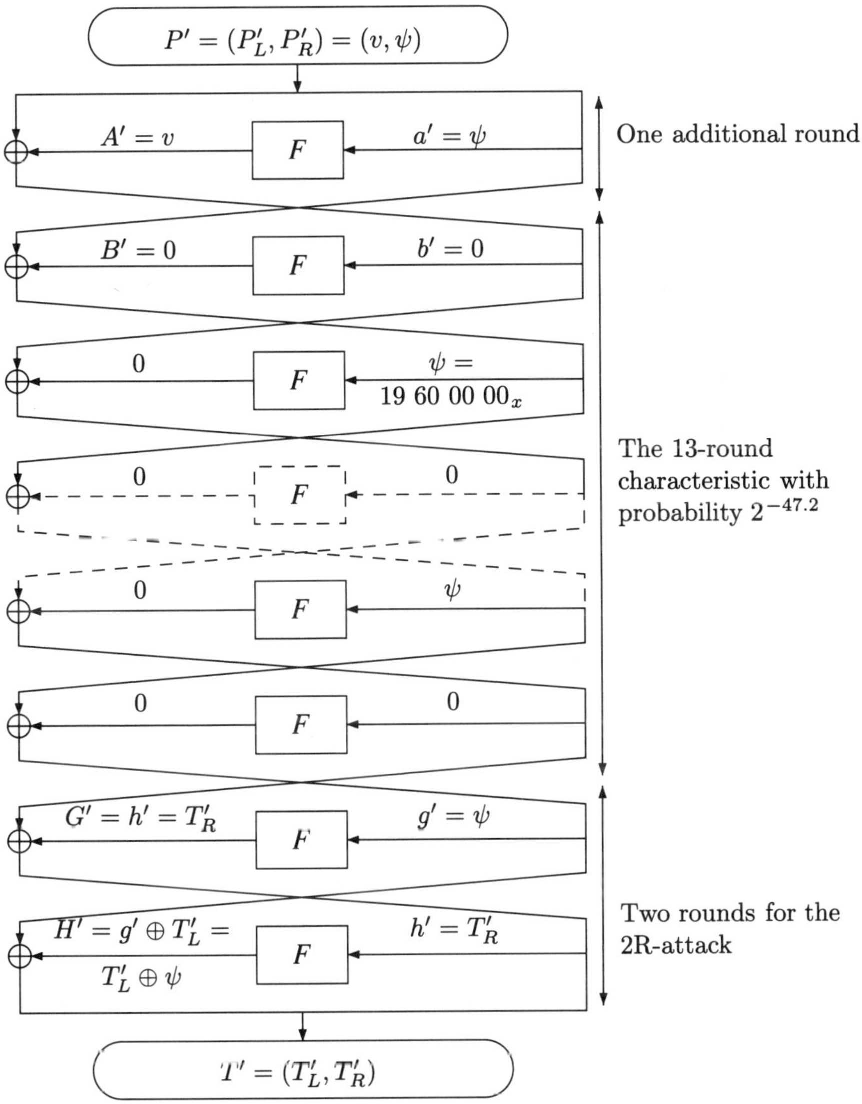

Figure 5.1. The attack on the full 16-round DES.

XORed with the 12 output bits of S1, S2 and S3 after the first round, and 0 elsewhere. We now define a structure which consists of 2^{13} plaintexts:

$$P_i = P \oplus (v_i, 0) \qquad \bar{P}_i = (P \oplus (v_i, 0)) \oplus (0, \psi) \qquad \text{for } 0 \le i < 2^{12}$$
$$T_i = \text{DES}(P_i, K) \qquad \bar{T}_i = \text{DES}(\bar{P}_i, K)$$

The plaintext pairs we are interested in are all the 2^{24} pairs $(P_i, \bar{P}_j)$ with $0 \le i, j < 2^{12}$. Their plaintext XOR is always of the form (v_k, ψ), and each v_k occurs exactly in 2^{12} pairs. Since the processing of the F function on the inputs P_R and $P_R \oplus \psi$ in the first round causes an output XOR which can be non-zero only at the outputs of S1, S2 and S3, this output XOR is one of the v_k. As a result, for exactly 2^{12} of the pairs, the output XOR of the first F function is exactly cancelled by XORing it with the left half of the plaintext XOR, and thus the output XOR of the first round (after swapping the left and right halves) is the desired input XOR $(\psi, 0)$ into the iterative characteristic. Therefore, each structure has a probability of about $2^{12} \cdot 2^{-47.2} = 2^{-35.2}$ to contain a right pair.

The problem in this approach is that we do not know the actual value of v_k, which cancels the output XOR of the first F function, and thus we do not know on which 2^{12} plaintext pairs to concentrate. Trying all the 2^{24} possible pairs takes too long, but we can use their cross-product structure to isolate the right pairs among them in just 2^{12} time. In any right pair, the ciphertext XOR should have 20 zero bits at its right half at the positions corresponding to the outputs of the five S boxes S4, ..., S8 in the 15th round. We can thus sort (or hash) the two groups of 2^{12} ciphertexts T_i, $\bar{T}_j$ by these 20 bit positions, and detect all the repeated occurrences of values among the 2^{24} ciphertext pairs in about 2^{12} time. Any pair of plaintexts which fails this test has a non-zero ciphertext XOR at those 20 bit positions, and thus cannot be a right pair by definition. Since each one of the 2^{24} possible pairs passes this test with probability 2^{-20}, we expect about $2^4 = 16$ pairs to survive. By testing additional S boxes in the first, fifteenth, and sixteenth rounds and eliminating all the pairs whose XOR values are indicated as impossible in the difference distribution tables of the various S boxes, we can discard about 92.55% of these surviving pairs[1] leaving only $16 \cdot 0.0745 = 1.19$ pairs per structure as the expected output of the data collection phase. All these additional tests can be implemented by a few table lookup operations into small precomputed tables, and their

[1] A fraction of about $\left(\frac{14}{16} \cdot \frac{13}{16} \cdot \frac{15}{16}\right)^2 \cdot 0.8^8 = 0.0745$ of these pairs remain and thus a fraction of about 0.9255 of them are discarded. The input XOR values of the S boxes in the first and the fifteenth rounds of right pairs are known and fixed, and thus we use the fraction of non-zero entries of the corresponding lines in the difference distribution tables whose values are $\frac{14}{16}$, $\frac{13}{16}$ and $\frac{15}{16}$, rather than the fraction of the non-zero entries in the whole tables, which is approximated by 0.8.

time complexity is much smaller than the time required to perform one trial encryption during an exhaustive search. Note that this filtering process removes only wrong pairs but not all of them and thus the input of the data analysis phase is still a mixture of right and wrong pairs.

The data analysis phase of the attacks described in the previous chapter uses huge arrays of up to 2^{42} counters to find the most popular values of certain key bits. The new attack described in this chapter uses only negligible space. We want to count on all the key bits simultaneously but cannot afford an array of 2^{56} counters. Instead, we immediately try each suggested value of the key. A key value is suggested when it can create the output XOR values of the last round as well as the expected output XOR of the first round and the fifteenth round for the particular plaintexts and ciphertexts. In the first round and in the fifteenth round the input XORs of S4 and S5, ..., S8 are always zero. Due to the key scheduling algorithm, all the 28 bits of the left key register are used as inputs to the S boxes S1, S2 and S3 in the first and the fifteenth rounds and S1, ..., S4 in the sixteenth round. Only 24 bits of the right key register are used in the sixteenth round. Thus, $28 + 24 = 52$ key bits enter these S boxes. The fraction of 52-bit values that remain after comparing the output XOR of the last round to its expected value and discarding the ones whose values are not possible is $\frac{2^{-32}}{0.8^8}$. Only a fraction of $\frac{2^{-12}}{\frac{14}{16}\cdot\frac{13}{16}\cdot\frac{15}{16}}$ of the remaining ones exist after comparing the output XOR of the three S boxes in the first round to its expected value. A similar fraction of the remaining 52-bit values remain by analyzing the three S boxes in the fifteenth round. Each analyzed pair suggests about $2^{52} \cdot \frac{2^{-32}}{0.8^8} \cdot \frac{2^{-12}}{\frac{14}{16}\cdot\frac{13}{16}\cdot\frac{15}{16}} \cdot \frac{2^{-12}}{\frac{14}{16}\cdot\frac{13}{16}\cdot\frac{15}{16}} = 0.84$ values for these 52 bits of the key, each value corresponding to 16 possible values of the full 56-bit key. Therefore, each structure suggests about $1.19 \cdot 0.84 \cdot 16 = 16$ choices for the whole key. By peeling off two additional rounds we can verify each such key by performing about one quarter of a DES encryption (i.e., executing two rounds for each one of the two members of the pair), leaving only about 2^{-12} of the choices of the key. This filtering costs about $16 \cdot \frac{1}{4} = 4$ equivalent DES operations per structure. Each remaining choice of the 56-bit key is verified via trial encryption of one of the plaintexts and comparing the result to the corresponding ciphertext. If the test succeeds, there is a very high probability that this key is the right key. Note that the signal to noise ratio of this counting scheme is $S/N = \frac{2^{52}\cdot 2^{-47.2}}{1.19/2^{12}\cdot 0.84} = 2^{16.8}$.

This data analysis can be carried out efficiently by carefully choosing the order in which we test the various key bits. We first enumerate all the possible values of the six key bits of $S4_{Kh}$, and eliminate any value which does not give rise to the expected output XOR of this S box. This leaves four out of the 64 possibilities of $S4_{Kh}$ in average. Table 5.1 shows the number of common bits entering the S boxes in the first round and in the

		K16									
		Left Key Register (C)					Right Key Register (D)				
		S1	S2	S3	S4	X	S5	S6	S7	S8	X
K1	S1		2	1	1	2					
	S2	2		1	2	1					
	S3	2			3	1					
	S4	2	3	1							
	X		1	3							
	S5							1	2	2	1
	S6						3		2	1	
	S7							2		2	2
	S8						2	3			1
	X						1		2	1	

X denotes the key bits which are not used in the subkey.

Table 5.1. The number of common bits entering the S boxes in the first round (K1) and in the sixteenth round (K16).

sixteenth round. We see that three of the bits of $S4_{Kh}$ are shared with $S3_{Ka}$. We complete the three missing bits of $S3_{Ka}$ in all possible ways, and reduce the average number of possibilities to two. Two bits of $S1_{Kh}$ are shared with $S3_{Ka}$. By completing the four missing bits of $S1_{Kh}$ and then the two missing bits of $S2_{Ka}$ we can reduce the average number of possibilities to about half. After completing the 13 remaining bits of the left key register in a similar way, the average number of values suggested for this half of the key is one.

To compute bits from the right key register, we first extract actual S box input bits from their assumed XORed values. In the fifteenth round we know the input XORs and the output XORs of S1, S2 and S3. We can thus generate about 4–5 candidate inputs for each one of these S boxes, and deduce the corresponding bits in g by XORing with the known bits of the left key register. In a similar way, we can calculate the outputs of the S boxes S1, S2, S3 and S4 in the sixteenth round, XOR these bits of H with the known bits of the left half of the ciphertext T_L and get 16 bits of g, from which two bits enter S1, two bits enter S2 and three bits enter S3 in the fifteenth round. By comparing these bit values to the candidate inputs of the S boxes we end up with about one candidate input for S1, one for S2, and only about half of the trials would result with a candidate input for S3. We can now deduce all the bits of g which enter these three S boxes and deduce the corresponding bits of H by $H = g \oplus T_L$. Two of these bits are outputs of S5, two bits are outputs of S6, three are outputs of S7 and one is an output of S8. For each of these four S boxes we know the input XOR and the output XOR, and can deduce about 4–5 possible inputs. Since we also know actual output bits, the number of possible inputs is reduced to about one for S5 and S6, two for S8, but only half of the trials would result with a candidate for S7. We can deduce 24 out of the 28 bits of the right key register by XORing the 24 computed bits at the inputs of these four S boxes with the expanded value of the known right half of the ciphertext.

We can now summarize the performance of this attack in the following way. Each structure contains a right pair with probability $2^{-35.2}$. The data collection phase encrypts a pool of about 2^{35} structures, which contain about $2^{35} \cdot 2^{13} = 2^{48}$ chosen plaintexts, from which about $2^{35} \cdot 1.19 = 2^{35.25}$ pairs ($2^{36.25}$ ciphertexts) remain as candidate inputs to the data analysis phase. The probability that at least one of them is a right pair is about 58%, and the analysis of any right pair is guaranteed to lead to the correct key. The time complexity of this data analysis phase is about $2^{35} \cdot 4 = 2^{37}$ equivalent DES operations.

In order to further reduce the number of chosen plaintexts and in order to avoid the dependence of the probability on the unknown key (described in Subsection 4.4.5), we can use an extended notion of quartets. Since the basic collection of plaintexts in this attack is a structure rather than a pair, we create metastructures which contain 2^{14} chosen plaintexts, built from two structures which correspond to the standard iterative characteristic and from two structures which correspond to the following iterative characteristic:

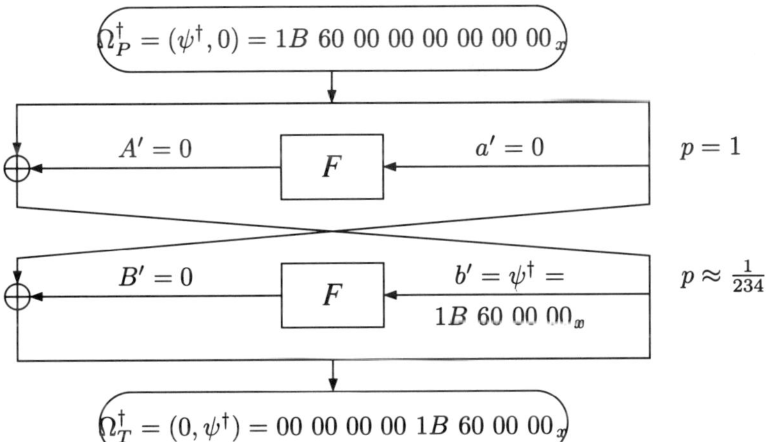

This characteristic has the same probability as the previous one. With these metastructures, we can obtain four times as many pairs from twice as many plaintexts, and thus reduce the number of chosen plaintexts encrypted in the data collection phase from 2^{48} to 2^{47}.

Since the instances of processing different structures are unrelated, this attack can be carried out on a parallel machine with up to 2^{33} disconnected processors with very small local memories with linear speedup. In addition, this attack can be carried out even if the analyzed ciphertexts are derived from up to 2^{33} different keys due to frequent key changes during the data collection phase. The attack can be carried out incrementally with any number of available ciphertexts, and its probability of success grows linearly with this number (e.g., when 2^{29} usable ciphertexts are generated from a smaller pool of 2^{40} plaintexts, the analysis time decreases to 2^{30} and the probability of success is about 1%).

This specific attack is not directly applicable to plaintexts consisting solely of ASCII characters since such plaintexts cannot give rise to the desired XOR differences. By using several other iterative characteristics we can attack the full 16-round DES with a pool of about 2^{49} chosen ASCII plaintexts (out of the 2^{56} possible ASCII plaintexts).

5.1 Variants of the Attack

The general form of this attack can be summarized in the following way: Given a characteristic with probability p and signal to noise ratio S/N for a cryptosystem with k key bits, we can apply an attack which encrypts $\frac{2}{p}$ chosen plaintexts in the data collection phase and whose complexity is $\frac{2^k}{S/N}$ trial encryptions in the data analysis phase. The number of chosen plaintexts can be reduced to $\frac{1}{p}$ by using appropriate metastructures, and the effective time complexity can be reduced by a factor of $f \leq 1$ if a tested key can be discarded by carrying out only a fraction f of the rounds. Therefore, this attack can be mounted whenever $p > 2^{1-k}$ and $S/N > 1$. This attack requires fewer chosen plaintexts compared to the corresponding counting schemes, but if the signal to noise ratio is too low or if the number of the key bits on which we count is small, the time complexity of the data analysis phase may be higher than the corresponding complexity of the counting scheme.

In the attack described in this chapter, $p = 2^{-47.2}$, $k = 56$, $f = \frac{1}{4}$ and $S/N = 2^{16.8}$. Therefore, the number of chosen plaintexts is $\frac{2}{p} = 2^{48.2}$ which can be reduced to $\frac{1}{p} = 2^{47.2}$ by using metastructures, and the complexity of the data analysis phase is $2^{37.2}$ equivalent DES operations.

This is currently our best attack on DES, and its performance for various variants with reduced number of rounds is summarized in Table 5.2.

No. of Rounds	Chosen Plaintexts	Known Plaintexts	Analyzed Plaintexts	Complexity of Analysis
8	2^{14}	2^{38}	4	2^{9}
9	2^{24}	2^{44}	2	2^{32} †
10	2^{24}	2^{43}	2^{14}	2^{15}
11	2^{31}	2^{47}	2	2^{32} †
12	2^{31}	2^{47}	2^{21}	2^{21}
13	2^{39}	2^{52}	2	2^{32} †
14	2^{39}	2^{51}	2^{29}	2^{29}
15	2^{47}	2^{56}	2^{7}	2^{37}
16	2^{47}	2^{55}	2^{36}	2^{37}

† The complexity of the analysis can be greatly reduced for these variants by using about four times as many plaintexts with the clique method.

Table 5.2. Cryptanalysis of variants of DES: our best results.

Variants with an even number of rounds n have a characteristic with probability $p = \left(\frac{1}{234}\right)^{(n-4)/2}$, require p^{-1} chosen plaintexts, and analyze $p^{-1} \cdot 2^{-10.75}$ plaintexts in time complexity $p^{-1} \cdot 2^{-10}$. The known plaintext variant of this attack needs about $2^{31.5} \cdot p^{-0.5}$ known plaintexts (using the symmetry of the cryptosystem which makes it possible to double the number of known encryptions by reversing the roles of the plaintexts and the ciphertexts). Variants with an odd number of rounds n have a characteristic with probability $p = \left(\frac{1}{234}\right)^{(n-3)/2}$, require p^{-1} chosen plaintexts, and analyze $p^{-1} \cdot 2^{-40.2}$ plaintexts in time complexity $p^{-1} \cdot 2^{-10}$. For such odd values of n, if $p > 2^{-40.2}$ then the number of analyzed plaintexts is two and the complexity of the data analysis phase is 2^{32}. However, using about four times as many chosen plaintexts, we can use the clique method (described in Section 4.2) and reduce the time complexity of the data analysis phase to less than a second on a personal computer. The known plaintext attacks need about $2^{32} \cdot p^{-0.5}$ known plaintexts (in this case the symmetry does not help).

In the previous chapter we analyzed several modified variants of DES. The results of the application of the technique introduced in this chapter to these 16-round variants are summarized in Table 5.3.

Modified Operation	Chosen Plaintexts
Full DES (no modification)	2^{47} (dependent key)
P permutation	Cannot strengthen
Identity permutation	2^{19}
Order of S boxes	2^{38}
XORs by additions	2^{39}, 2^{31}
S boxes:	
Random	2^{21}
Random permutations	2^{44}–2^{48}
One entry	2^{33}
Uniform tables	2^{26}
Elimination of the E expansion	2^{26}
Order of E and subkey XOR	2^{44}
GDES (width $q = 8$):	
16 rounds	6, 16
64 rounds	2^{49} (independent key)

Table 5.3. Cryptanalysis of modified variants of DES: our best results.

6

Differential Cryptanalysis of FEAL

FEAL was suggested as a software-oriented cryptosystem which can be easily and efficiently implemented on microprocessors. The structure of FEAL is similar to DES with a modified F function, initial and final permutations and key scheduling algorithm. In the F function, the P permutation and the S boxes of DES are replaced by byte rotations and addition operations. The S boxes S_0 and S_1 of FEAL get two input bytes and calculate one output byte as $S_i(x, y) = \mathrm{ROL2}(x + y + i \pmod{256})$, where ROL2 rotates its input byte two bits to the left. The F function gets a 32-bit input and a 16-bit subkey and calculates a 32-bit output by applying the S boxes four times sequentially. The initial and the final permutations are replaced by initial and final transformations, in which the whole 64-bit data is XORed with 64-bit subkeys and the right half of the data is XORed with the left half. Figure 6.1 describes the structure of an eight-round FEAL and its F function. The key scheduling algorithm is replaced by a key processing algorithm, which makes the subkeys depend on the key in a more complex way. The key processing algorithm and its F_k function are described in Figure 6.2.

Originally, FEAL was suggested as a four-round cryptosystem[36], called FEAL-4. After the cryptanalysis of FEAL-4 by Den-Boer[12], the eight-round variant FEAL-8 was suggested[35,26]. Later, FEAL-N with an arbitrary number of rounds[23] and FEAL-NX with increased size 128-bit key[24] were also introduced. In this chapter we show that differential cryptanalytic techniques can be used to break FEAL with up to 31 rounds, and that the eight-round variant FEAL-8 is easily breakable.

The following FEAL-specific notations are used in this chapter:

The plaintext and the ciphertext: The plaintext and the ciphertext are denoted by P and T respectively. Unlike the case of DES, they denote the real plaintext and ciphertext without ignoring the initial and final transformations of FEAL. Thus, the characteristic's input XOR Ω_P is different from the corresponding plaintext XOR P'.

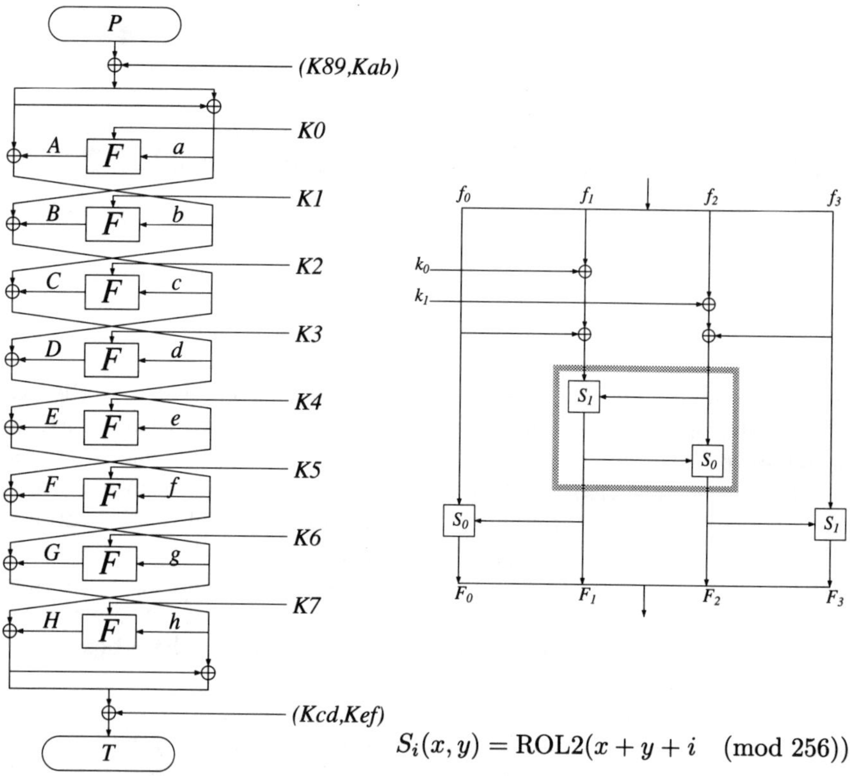

Figure 6.1. The outline of FEAL-8 and of the F function.

Rotation operations: The operations of cyclically rotating the byte X by n bits to the left and to the right are denoted by ROL$n(X)$ and ROR$n(X)$ respectively.

The S boxes: The S boxes of FEAL S_0 and S_1 are denoted by $S_i(X, Y)$ for the inputs X and Y and for $i \in \{0, 1\}$. Their definition is: $S_i(x, y) = \mathrm{ROL2}(x + y + i \pmod{256})$.

Selecting one byte or one bit: The ith byte of a multi-byte value X or the ith bit of the byte X are denoted by X_i. The jth bit of the ith byte of a multi-byte value X is denoted by $X_{i,j}$. The index 0 denotes the least significant byte and bit as appropriate.

Useful operations: The 32-bit value $(0, K_0, K_1, 0)$ where K is 16-bit long is denoted by am(K). The 16-bit value $(X_0 \oplus X_1, X_2 \oplus X_3)$ where X is 32-bit long is denoted by mx(X).

Since each S box has 16 input bits and only eight output bits it is not

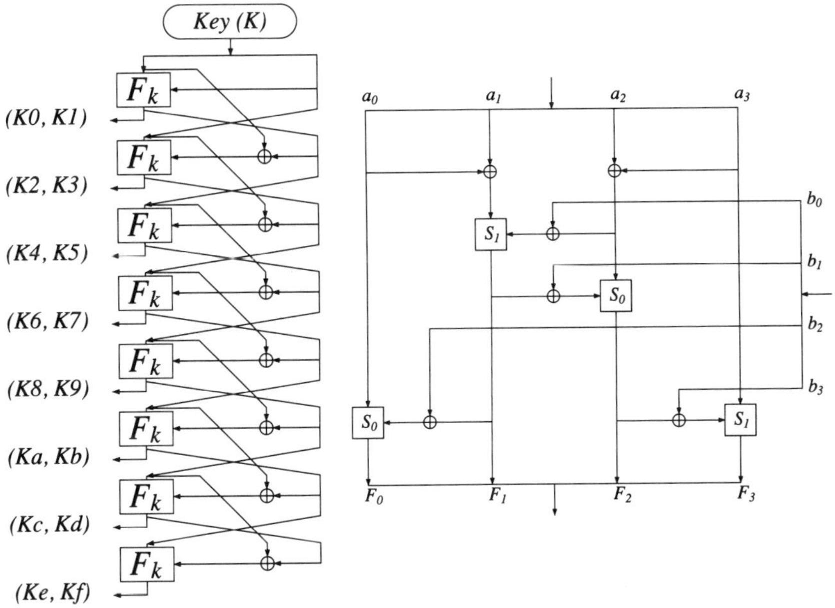

Figure 6.2. The key processing algorithm of FEAL-8 and its F_k function.

recommended to use the difference distribution tables directly. Instead, in the first stage of the analysis we use the joint distribution table of the two middle S boxes in the F function (inside the gray rectangle in Figure 6.1). This combination has 16 input bits and 16 output bits, and the table has many interesting entries. For example, there are two entries with probability 1 which are $00\ 00_x \rightarrow 00\ 00_x$ and $80\ 80_x \rightarrow 00\ 02_x$. About 98% of the entries are impossible (contain value 0). The average value of all the entries is 1, but the average value of the non-zero entries is about 50. In Section 6.3 we describe how we can easily decide whether $X \rightarrow Y$ for any particular X and Y without consulting the table.

The S boxes also have the following properties with respect to pairs: Let $Z = S_i(X, Y)$. If $X' = 80_x$ and $Y' = 80_x$ then $Z' = 00_x$. If $X' = 80_x$ and $Y' = 00_x$ then $Z' = 02_x$. For any input XORs X' and Y' of the S boxes the most probable output XOR is $Z' = \mathrm{ROL2}(X' \oplus Y')$. This output XOR is obtained with probability about $\frac{1}{2^{\#(X'|Y')}}$ (where $\#X$ is the number of bits set to 1 in the lower seven bits of the byte X and $|$ is the or operator) since each bit which is different in the pairs (in X and X^*, or in Y and Y^*) gives rise to a different carry with probability $\frac{1}{2}$.

The input of the F function in the last round is a function of the ciphertext XORed with an additional subkey of the final transformation rather than just a function of the ciphertext (as in DES). There is an equivalent description of FEAL in which the XOR with the subkeys in the final transformation is eliminated and the 16-bit subkeys XORed to the two middle bytes of the inputs of the F function in the various rounds are replaced by 32-bit values.

Definition 6.1 The 32-bit subkeys of the equivalent description in which the XOR with the subkeys in the final transformation is eliminated are called *actual subkeys.* The actual subkey which replaces the subkey Ki is denoted by AKi. The 16-bit XOR combinations $\mathrm{mx}(AKi) = (AKi_0 \oplus AKi_1, AKi_2 \oplus AKi_3)$ are called *16-bit actual subkeys.* The actual subkey of the last round of a cryptosystem is called the *last actual subkey.*

The actual subkeys in the even rounds $i+1$ are

$$AKi = Kcd \oplus Kef \oplus \mathrm{am}(Ki).$$

The actual subkeys in the odd rounds $i+1$ are

$$AKi = Kcd \oplus \mathrm{am}(Ki).$$

The actual subkeys of the initial transformation are

$$\begin{aligned} AK89 &= K89 \oplus Kcd \oplus Kef \\ AKab &= Kab \oplus Kef. \end{aligned}$$

The actual subkeys of the final transformation are eliminated and thus their equivalent values are zero. Our attack finds the actual subkeys rather than the subkeys themselves since it finds XORs of the ciphertexts and internal values in the F function.

The simplest example of a one-round characteristic with probability 1 is (for any L'):

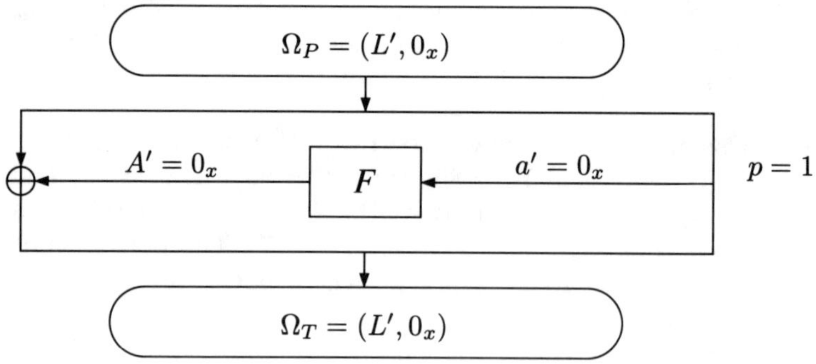

This characteristic is similar to the one-round characteristic with probability 1 of DES. Unlike the case of DES, FEAL has three other one-round characteristics with probability 1. A typical one is:

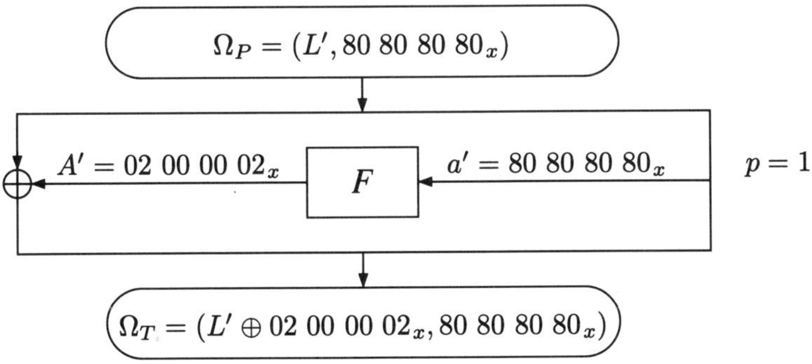

Three non-trivial three-round characteristics with probability 1 also exist. The one derived from the above one-round characteristic is:

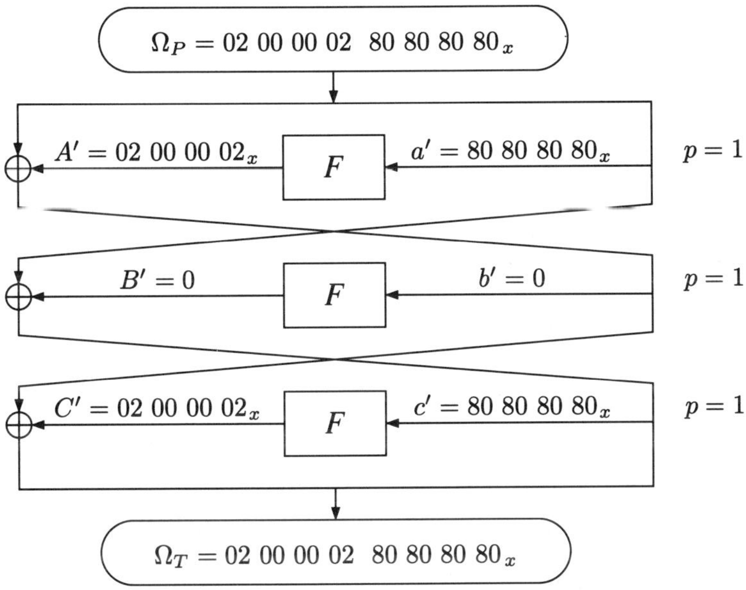

The following is a five-round characteristic with probability $\frac{1}{16}$:

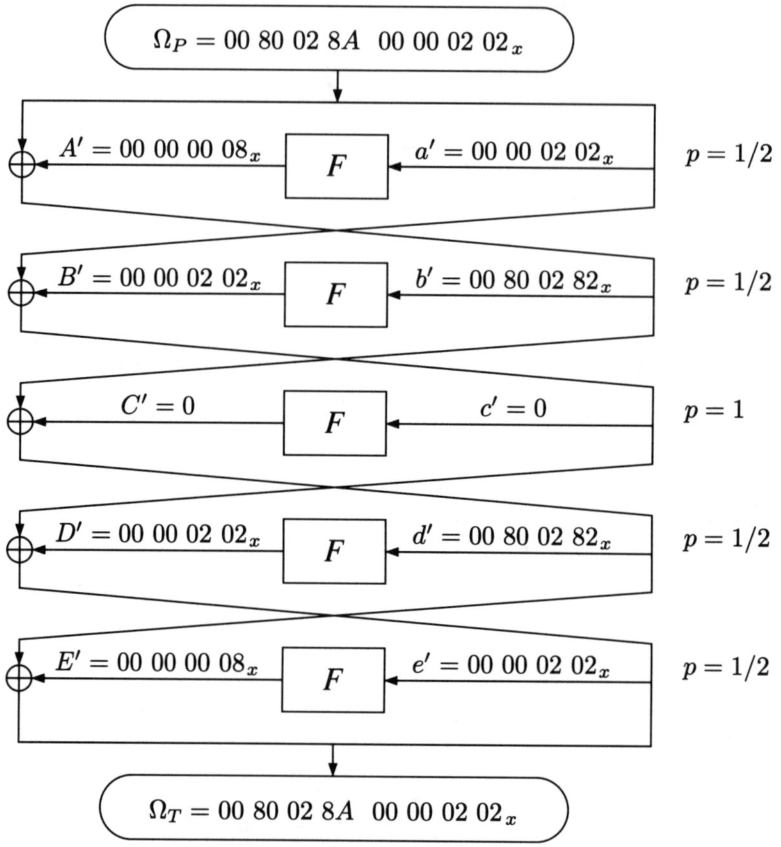

A second five-round characteristic with probability $\frac{1}{16}$ is described later.

The iterative characteristics of FEAL do not include one in which a non-zero input XOR of the F function may cause a zero output XOR (since the F function is reversible), but there are other kinds of iterative characteristics. For example, the following iterative characteristic has probability $\frac{1}{4}$ for each round:

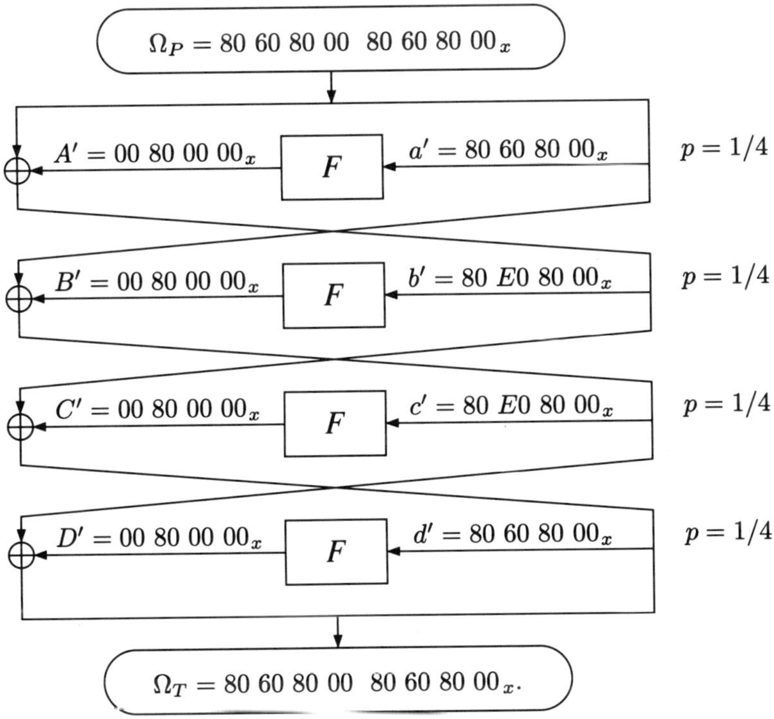

6.1 Cryptanalysis of FEAL-8

This differential cryptanalytic chosen plaintext attack on FEAL-8 requires about 128 pairs of ciphertexts whose corresponding plaintext XORs are $P' = A2\ 00\ 80\ 00\ 22\ 80\ 80\ 00_x$. It can be converted into a known plaintext attack which uses about 2^{36} known plaintexts and their corresponding ciphertexts. This plaintext XOR is motivated by the following five-round characteristic whose probability is 1/16:

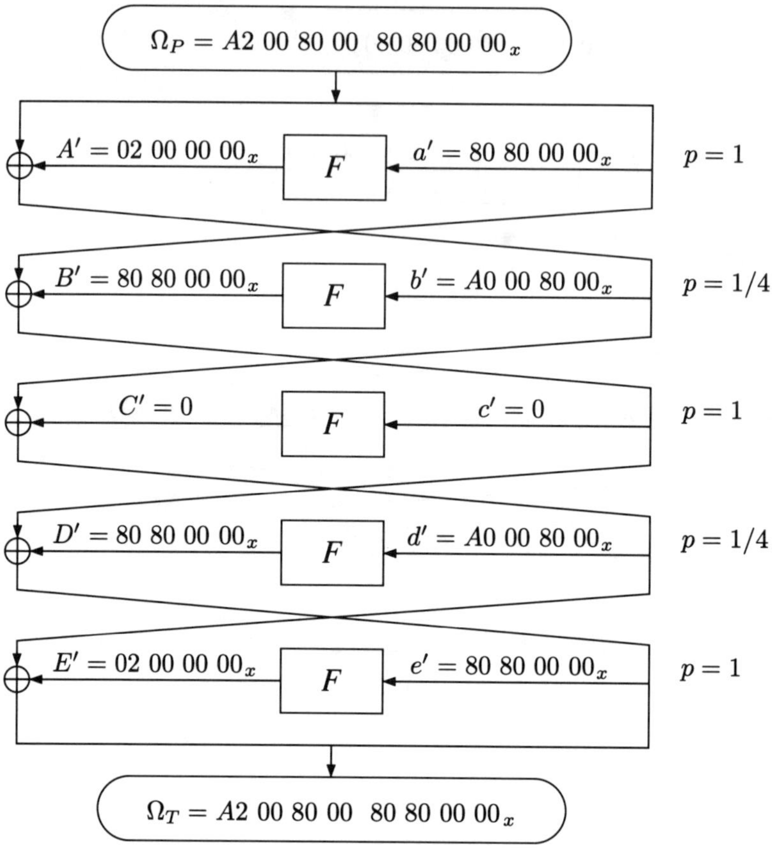

Four shorter characteristics are derived from the first rounds of this five-round characteristic. Each characteristic has a different number of rounds but all of them have the same value of Ω_P. The one-round characteristic which is derived from the first round of the five-round characteristic has probability 1. The two-round and the three-round characteristics which are derived from the first two and three rounds have probability 1/4. The four-round characteristic has probability 1/16.

6.1.1 Reducing FEAL-8 to Seven Rounds

Given the ciphertexts T and T^* of a right pair, we can deduce:

$$
\begin{aligned}
h &= T_L \oplus T_R \\
h' &= T'_L \oplus T'_R
\end{aligned}
$$

$$\begin{aligned} G' &= d' \oplus E' \oplus h' = A2\ 00\ 80\ 00_x \oplus T'_L \oplus T'_R \\ F' \oplus H' &= T'_L \oplus e' = T'_L \oplus 80\ 80\ 00\ 00_x. \end{aligned}$$

Before the counting method is used to find the 16-bit last actual subkey, filtering can be done to discard about $\frac{15}{16}$ of the wrong pairs. Since the addition operation is linear in its least significant bit and since $h' \rightarrow H'$, the following equations hold:

$$\begin{aligned} h'_{0,0} &= H'_{0,2} \oplus H'_{1,0} \\ h'_{3,0} &= H'_{3,2} \oplus H'_{2,0} \\ h'_{2,0} &= H'_{2,2} \oplus H'_{1,0} \oplus h'_{3,0} \\ h'_{1,0} &= H'_{1,2} \oplus h'_{0,0} \oplus h'_{2,0} \oplus h'_{3,0}. \end{aligned}$$

Similar equations hold for $f' \rightarrow F'$. Since these equations are linear and the value of $F' \oplus H'$ is known, we can deduce the XOR of these four bits in f' and in h': $f'_{i,0} \oplus h'_{i,0}$, $i \in \{0, \ldots, 3\}$. Both f' and h' are known for a right pair, and therefore by comparing these four bits to their expected values we can discard about $\frac{15}{16}$ of the wrong pairs. All the right pairs must be verified correctly. Since the right pairs occur with the characteristic's probability of $\frac{1}{16}$, about half of the remaining pairs are right pairs.

Then, a special form of a 3R-attack is applied. Instead of finding zero bits in F', deriving the corresponding bits in H' and trying all possible subkeys for success, we work here in the other direction. The counting scheme counts the number of pairs for which each value of the 16-bit last actual subkey mx($AK7$) is possible. For each such value we calculate $\hat{H}$ and $\hat{H}^*$ (where for any 32-bit X, $\hat{X}$ is the 16-bit value of its two middle bytes (X_1, X_2)), and receive $\hat{F}'$ (since $F' \oplus H'$ is known). Then we verify if f' may cause the calculated value of $\hat{F}^*$. The expected signal to noise ratio is

$$S/N = \frac{2^{16} \cdot 2^{-4}}{0.02 \cdot \frac{1}{4}} \approx 2^{20}$$

(the value $\frac{1}{4}$ replaces $\frac{1}{16}$ since part of it is also included within 0.02). This ratio is so high that only eight right pairs are typically needed for the attack, and thus the total number of pairs we have to examine is about $8 \cdot 16 = 128$. Note that we cannot distinguish between the right value of the 16-bit actual subkey and the same value XORed with $80\ 80_x$. Therefore, we find two possibilities for the 16-bit last actual subkey.

The following counting scheme is used to complete the last actual subkey. For each pair (out of all the pairs) we calculate $\hat{H}$ and $\hat{H}^*$ and get $\hat{H}'$. Then we calculate $\hat{g}' = \hat{T}'_L \oplus \hat{H}'$, $\hat{F}' = \hat{e}' \oplus \hat{g}'$ and a few other bits of g' and discard any pair for which we can conclude that $g' \not\rightarrow G'$ by the F function using the bits we have found.

We try the 128 possibilities for the lowest seven bits of $AK7_0$. For each value we calculate H_0, H_0^*, $H_0' = H_0 \oplus H_0^*$ and $F_0' = e_0' \oplus H_0' \oplus T_{L0}'$ and verify that f_0' (from the characteristic) and F_1' (from $\hat{F}'$) may cause this F_0'. We count the number of the pairs satisfying this condition. The value of $AK7_0$ which is counted most often is likely to be the right value. We cannot distinguish the upper bit of the value, so we try just 128 possibilities (instead of 256 as was expected) and then try the two possible values in the following steps, till the wrong one fails. In a similar way we find seven bits of $AK7_3$. As a result, we find eight possibilities for the last actual subkey $AK7$. Unlike the case of DES, we cannot easily deduce key bits from a single actual subkey. However, we can reduce the cryptosystem to a seven-round cryptosystem by "peeling off" the last round using the known last actual subkey, and can analyze the resultant cryptosystem by similar methods.

6.1.2 Reducing the Seven-Round Cryptosystem to Six Rounds

We assume that the last actual subkey is already known, and that the cryptosystem can be reduced to a seven-round cryptosystem. A right pair with respect to the five-round characteristic satisfies

$$\begin{aligned} f' &= \text{A2 00 80 00}_x \\ g' &= T_L' \oplus H' \\ G' &= h' \oplus f' = h' \oplus \text{A2 00 80 00}_x \\ F' &= e' \oplus g' = T_L' \oplus H' \oplus \text{80 80 00 00}_x. \end{aligned}$$

We verify that $f' \rightarrow F'$ and $g' \rightarrow G'$ and count in two steps: the first step counts on the 16-bit actual subkey and the second step counts on each one of the other two bytes of the actual subkey. The signal to noise ratio of the first step which finds the 16-bit actual subkey mx($AK6$) is

$$S/N = \frac{2^{16}}{16 \cdot \left(\frac{1}{7}\right)^4 \cdot \left(\frac{1}{7}\right)^2 \cdot 1} \approx 2^{29}.$$

The signal to noise ratio of the second step which finds $AK6_0$ and $AK6_3$ is

$$S/N = \frac{2^{8}}{16 \cdot \left(\frac{1}{7}\right)^4 \cdot 2^{-16} \cdot 1} \approx 2^{31}.$$

In the first step one bit is indistinguishable and in the second step two bits are indistinguishable. Therefore, we try all the eight resulting possibilities of $AK6$ in parallel in the following steps. In total we find at most

64 possibilities for the last two actual subkeys and can thus reduce the cryptosystem to six rounds.

6.1.3 Reducing the Cryptosystem to 5, 4, 3, 2 and 1 Rounds

Using the last two actual subkeys we can calculate H and G for any ciphertext T and reduce the cryptosystem to six rounds. All the right pairs with respect to the five-round characteristic satisfy $f' = h' \oplus G' = A2\ 00\ 80\ 00_x$ and $f' \rightarrow g' \oplus 80\ 80\ 00\ 00_x$ (g' can be calculated using the known $AK7$). Two bytes of $AK5$ equal their counterparts in $AK7$. We try all the 2^{16} possibilities of the 16-bit actual subkey mx($AK5$). For each possibility and each pair we calculate F, F^* and $F' = F \oplus F^*$. A right pair satisfies $F' = g' \oplus 80\ 80\ 00\ 00_x$. We count the number of pairs which satisfy $f' = A2\ 00\ 80\ 00_x$ (as is enforced by the five-round characteristic) and whose above values of F' are equal, and $f' \rightarrow F'$. The value of mx($AK5$) which is counted most often is likely to be the real value. The signal to noise ratio of this step is

$$S/N = \frac{2^{16}}{16 \cdot 2^{-32} \cdot 2^{-16}} = 2^{60}.$$

In this step we can always distinguish all the bits of the actual subkey.

Given $AK5$ we reduce the cryptosystem to five rounds and find $AK4$ using the three-round characteristic. Two bytes of AK4 have the same value as their counterparts in AK6. For each possible value of mx($AK4$) we count the number of pairs which satisfy $e' = g' \oplus F' \neq 80\ 80\ 00\ 00_x$ (the pairs whose $e' = 80\ 80\ 00\ 00_x$ are useless because they enforce a fixed output XOR), $e' \rightarrow E'$ and $d' \rightarrow D' = g' \oplus F'$. $AK3$ is calculated similarly by counting the pairs which satisfy $d' = A0\ 00\ 80\ 00_x$ and $d' \rightarrow D'$. $AK2$ is also calculated similarly using the one-round characteristic and counting the pairs which satisfy $c' \neq 0$, $c' \rightarrow C'$ and $b' \rightarrow B'$. $AK1$ is similarly calculated by counting the pairs which satisfy $b' \rightarrow B'$.

$AK0$ cannot be calculated using these pairs since their plaintext XOR always cause $A' = 02\ 00\ 00\ 00_x$ and thus all the possibilities succeed under the A' condition with equal probability. However, it can be found using other characteristics. The actual subkeys of the initial transformation $AK89$ and $AKab$ cannot be found without the value of a plaintext even if all the other actual subkeys are known. In our case $AK0$, $AK89$ and $AKab$ are not needed since the key itself can be obtained from the actual subkeys which we have already found.

Although we find the actual subkeys with the (correct) assumption that many actual subkeys have common values in two of their bytes, it is possible to extend this attack to the general case in which all the actual subkeys are independent (i.e., $8 \cdot 32 + 2 \cdot 32 = 320$ independent bits).

6.1.4 Calculating the Key Itself

Using the values of the actual subkeys $AK1$–$AK7$ the following XORs of the original subkeys can be obtained:

$$\begin{gathered} K5 \oplus K7 \\ K4 \oplus K6 \\ K3 \oplus K5 \\ K2 \oplus K4 \\ K1 \oplus K3. \end{gathered} \tag{6.1}$$

The key itself can be derived from these values by analyzing the structure of the key processing algorithm.

We start by trying all the 256 possible values of $K5_1$. For each value we calculate [the values in brackets are known from (6.1)]:

$$\begin{aligned} K7_1 &= K5_1 \oplus [K5_1 \oplus K7_1] \\ K3_1 &= K5_1 \oplus [K3_1 \oplus K5_1] \\ K1_1 &= K3_1 \oplus [K1_1 \oplus K3_1]. \end{aligned}$$

By the fourth round of the key processing algorithm:

$$\begin{aligned} K7_0 &= K1_1 \oplus K5_1 \oplus S_1^{-1}(K7_1, K3_1) \\ K5_0 &= K7_0 \oplus [K5_0 \oplus K7_0] \\ K3_0 &= K5_0 \oplus [K3_0 \oplus K5_0] \\ K1_0 &= K3_0 \oplus [K1_0 \oplus K3_0]. \end{aligned}$$

Now, we find two bytes of the key itself, one by the third round of the key processing algorithm and the other by the second round:

$$\begin{aligned} K_7 &= K3_1 \oplus K5_0 \oplus S_1^{-1}(K5_1, K1_1) \\ K_3 &= K1_1 \oplus K3_0 \oplus S_1^{-1}(K3_1, K_7) \end{aligned}$$

and verify by the first round of the key processing algorithm that

$$S_1(K1_0 \oplus K_7, K_3) = K1_1.$$

For each remaining value we try all the 256 possibilities of $K4_0$. Then

$$\begin{aligned} K6_0 &= K4_0 \oplus [K4_0 \oplus K6_0] \\ K2_0 &= K4_0 \oplus [K2_0 \oplus K4_0]. \end{aligned}$$

By the fourth round of the key processing algorithm:

$$\begin{aligned}
K6_1 &= K1_0 \oplus K5_0 \oplus S_0^{-1}(K6_0, K2_0) \\
K4_1 &= K6_1 \oplus [K4_1 \oplus K6_1] \\
K2_1 &= K4_1 \oplus [K2_1 \oplus K4_1] \\
K0_0 &= K4_0 \oplus K3_0 \oplus K3_1 \oplus S_1^{-1}(K6_1, K2_0 \oplus K2_1) \\
K0_1 &= K4_1 \oplus K6_1 \oplus S_0^{-1}(K7_0, K3_0 \oplus K3_1).
\end{aligned}$$

The rest of the key can be found by the third round of the key processing algorithm:

$$\begin{aligned}
K_4 &= K2_0 \oplus K1_0 \oplus K1_1 \oplus S_1^{-1}(K4_1, K0_0 \oplus K0_1) \\
K_5 &= K2_1 \oplus K4_1 \oplus S_0^{-1}(K5_0, K1_0 \oplus K1_1) \\
K_6 &= K3_0 \oplus K4_1 \oplus S_0^{-1}(K4_0, K0_0)
\end{aligned}$$

and by the second round:

$$\begin{aligned}
K_0 &= K0_0 \oplus K_6 \oplus K_7 \oplus S_1^{-1}(K2_1, K_4 \oplus K_5) \\
K_1 &= K0_1 \oplus K2_1 \oplus S_0^{-1}(K3_0, K_6 \oplus K_7) \\
K_2 &= K1_0 \oplus K2_1 \oplus S_0^{-1}(K2_0, K_4).
\end{aligned}$$

Given the key, we verify that it is really processed to the known actual subkeys and that the XOR of a decrypted pair of ciphertexts equals the chosen plaintext XOR value. If this verification succeeds, then the calculated key is very likely to be the real key.

6.1.5 Summary

This attack was implemented on a personal computer. It finds the actual subkeys and then the key in less than two minutes using 128 pairs. Using quartets with the two characteristics with probability $\frac{1}{16}$ we need only 128 ciphertexts for this attack. The program uses 280K bytes of memory. The known plaintext variant of this attack needs about 2^{36} known plaintexts.

6.2 Cryptanalysis of FEAL-N and FEAL-NX with $N \leq 31$ Rounds

FEAL-N[23] was suggested as an N-round extension of FEAL-8 after our attack on FEAL-8 was announced. FEAL-NX[24] is similar to FEAL-N but uses a longer 128-bit key and a different key processing algorithm. Since our attack ignores the key processing algorithm and finds the actual subkeys, we can apply it to both FEAL-N and FEAL-NX with identical complexity and performance.

The attack on FEAL with an arbitrary number of rounds is based on the following iterative characteristic (whose corresponding plaintext XOR is $P' = 80\ 60\ 80\ 00\ \ 00\ 00\ 00\ 00_x$):

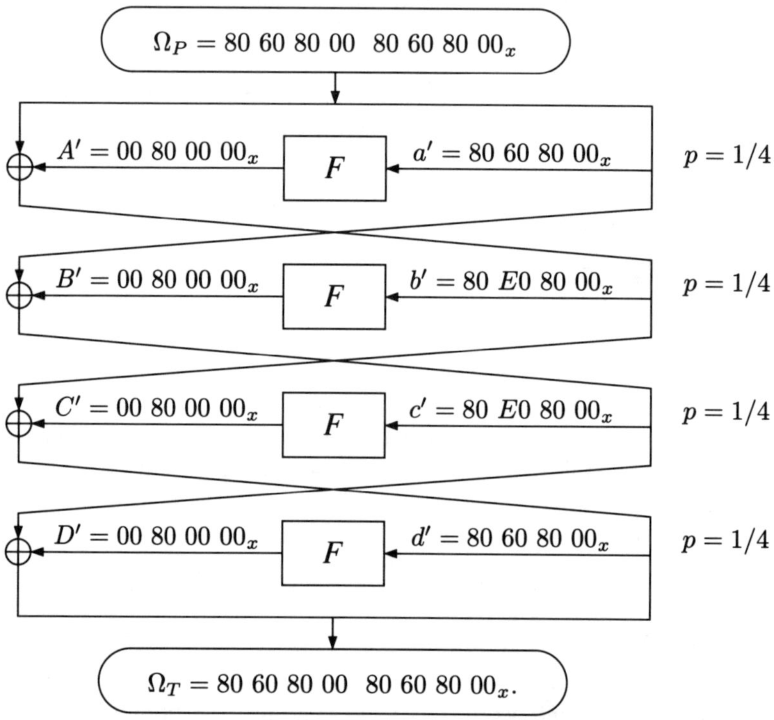

The probability of each round of this characteristic is 1/4, and it can be concatenated to itself any number of times since the swapped value of the two halves of Ω_P equals Ω_T. Thus, for any N, an N-round characteristic with probability $\frac{1}{4^N} = 2^{-2N}$ can be obtained.

A 2R-attack is based on a characteristic which is shorter by two rounds than the cryptosystem. In this case, we know the ciphertext XOR T' and the input XOR of the F function of the last round (without loss of generality we employ the notation of an eight-round cryptosystem) h' from the ciphertexts, and we know f' and g' from the characteristic. Thus, $G' = f' \oplus h'$ and $H' = g' \oplus T'_L$. Each pair is verified to have $g' \rightarrow G'$ and $h' \rightarrow H'$ and the resultant pairs are used in the process of counting the possibilities in order to find the last actual subkey. Two bits of the last actual subkey are indistinguishable. Therefore, we must try the following steps in parallel for the four possibilities of these two bits. The verification of $g' \rightarrow G'$ leaves only 2^{-19} of the pairs (since for either $g' = 80\ 60\ 80\ 00_x$ or $g' = 80\ E0\ 80\ 00_x$ there are only about 2^{13} possible output XORs G' and $2^{13} \cdot 2^{-32} = 2^{-19}$). The verification of $h' \rightarrow H'$ leaves 2^{-11} of the pairs (the fraction of the non-zero entries in the difference distribution table of the F function). The signal to noise ratio of this process is thus

$$S/N = \frac{2^{32}}{2^{2(N-2)} \cdot 2^{-19} \cdot 1} = 2^{55-2N}.$$

The identification leaves

$$I = 2^{2(N-2)} \cdot 2^{-19} \cdot 2^{-11} = 2^{2N-34}$$

wrong pairs for each right pair. Therefore, the right value of the last actual subkey is counted with a detectably higher probability than a random value up to $N \leq 28$ rounds, and thus we can break FEAL-N with 2R-attacks for any $N \leq 28$ rounds, faster than via exhaustive search. The results of these attacks and their known plaintext variants are shown in Table 6.1.

A 1R-attack is based on a characteristic which is shorter by one round than the cryptosystem. Using 1R-attacks (without loss of generality we employ the notation of an eight-round cryptosystem), we know T' and h' from the ciphertexts and g' and h' from the characteristic. Also, $H' = g' \oplus T'_L$. We can verify that the value of h' calculated from the ciphertexts equals the value of h' derived from the characteristic, and that $h' \rightarrow H'$. The successfully filtered pairs are used in the process of counting the number of times each possible value of the last actual subkey is suggested, and finding the most popular value. Complicating factors are the small number of bits set in h' (which is a constant defined by the characteristic), and the fact that many values of H' suggest many common values of the last actual subkey. The signal to noise ratio of this process is

$$S/N = \frac{2^{32}}{2^{2(N-1)} \cdot 2^{-32} \cdot 1} = 2^{66-2N}.$$

The identification leaves

$$I = 2^{2(N-1)} \cdot 2^{-32} \cdot 2^{-19} = 2^{2N-53}$$

wrong pairs for each right pair. Therefore, the right value of the last subkey is counted with detectably higher probability than a random value up to $N \leq 31$ rounds. A summary of the 1R-attacks on FEAL-N appears in Table 6.1, and shows that the differential cryptanalysis is faster than exhaustive search up to $N \leq 31$.

Note that in both the 1R-attacks and the 2R-attacks we use octets with four characteristics (this is a special case in which an octet can have four

No. of Rounds	2R-attack Char Prob	S/N	Pairs Needed	Chosen Plain	Known Plain	1R-attack Char Prob	S/N	Pairs Needed	Chosen Plain	Known Plain
8	2^{-12}	2^{39}	2^{14}	2^{13}	$2^{38.5}$	2^{-14}	2^{50}	2^{17}	2^{16}	2^{40}
9	2^{-14}	2^{37}	2^{16}	2^{15}	$2^{39.5}$	2^{-16}	2^{48}	2^{19}	2^{18}	2^{41}
10	2^{-16}	2^{35}	2^{18}	2^{17}	$2^{40.5}$	2^{-18}	2^{46}	2^{21}	2^{20}	2^{42}
11	2^{-18}	2^{33}	2^{20}	2^{19}	$2^{41.5}$	2^{-20}	2^{44}	2^{23}	2^{22}	2^{43}
12	2^{-20}	2^{31}	2^{22}	2^{21}	$2^{42.5}$	2^{-22}	2^{42}	2^{25}	2^{24}	2^{44}
13	2^{-22}	2^{29}	2^{24}	2^{23}	$2^{43.5}$	2^{-24}	2^{40}	2^{27}	2^{26}	2^{45}
14	2^{-24}	2^{27}	2^{26}	2^{25}	$2^{44.5}$	2^{-26}	2^{38}	2^{29}	2^{28}	2^{46}
15	2^{-26}	2^{25}	2^{28}	2^{27}	$2^{45.5}$	2^{-28}	2^{36}	2^{31}	2^{30}	2^{47}
16	2^{-28}	2^{23}	2^{30}	2^{29}	$2^{46.5}$	2^{-30}	2^{34}	2^{33}	2^{32}	2^{48}
17	2^{-30}	2^{21}	2^{32}	2^{31}	$2^{47.5}$	2^{-32}	2^{32}	2^{35}	2^{34}	2^{49}
18	2^{-32}	2^{19}	2^{34}	2^{33}	$2^{48.5}$	2^{-34}	2^{30}	2^{37}	2^{36}	2^{50}
19	2^{-34}	2^{17}	2^{36}	2^{35}	$2^{49.5}$	2^{-36}	2^{28}	2^{39}	2^{38}	2^{51}
20	2^{-36}	2^{15}	2^{38}	2^{37}	$2^{50.5}$	2^{-38}	2^{26}	2^{41}	2^{40}	2^{52}
21	2^{-38}	2^{13}	2^{40}	2^{39}	$2^{51.5}$	2^{-40}	2^{24}	2^{43}	2^{42}	2^{53}
22	2^{-40}	2^{11}	2^{42}	2^{41}	$2^{52.5}$	2^{-42}	2^{22}	2^{45}	2^{44}	2^{54}
23	2^{-42}	2^{9}	2^{44}	2^{43}	$2^{53.5}$	2^{-44}	2^{20}	2^{47}	2^{46}	2^{55}
24	2^{-44}	2^{7}	2^{46}	2^{45}	$2^{54.5}$	2^{-46}	2^{18}	2^{49}	2^{48}	2^{56}
25	2^{-46}	2^{5}	2^{49}	2^{48}	2^{56}	2^{-48}	2^{16}	2^{51}	2^{50}	2^{57}
26	2^{-48}	2^{3}	2^{52}	2^{51}	$2^{57.5}$	2^{-50}	2^{14}	2^{53}	2^{52}	2^{58}
27	2^{-50}	2	2^{55}	2^{54}	2^{59}	2^{-52}	2^{12}	2^{55}	2^{54}	2^{59}
28	2^{-52}	2^{-1}	2^{58}	2^{57}	$2^{60.5}$	2^{-54}	2^{10}	2^{57}	2^{56}	2^{60}
29	2^{-54}	2^{-3}				2^{-56}	2^{8}	2^{59}	2^{58}	2^{61}
30	2^{-56}					2^{-58}	2^{6}	2^{61}	2^{60}	2^{62}
31	2^{-58}					2^{-60}	2^{4}	2^{64}	2^{63}	$2^{63.5}$
32	2^{-60}					2^{-62}	2^{2}	2^{67}	2^{66}	

Table 6.1. Summary of the attacks on FEAL-N.

characteristics since $\Omega_P^4 = \Omega_P^1 \oplus \Omega_P^2 \oplus \Omega_P^3$). These four characteristics are the four possible rotations of the given characteristic. Thus, each octet gives rise to 16 pairs which greatly reduces the required number of chosen plaintexts. In both kinds of attacks there are two indistinguishable bits at each of the last two actual subkeys. The attacking program should try all the 16 possible values of these bits when analyzing the earlier subkeys.

6.3 Other Properties of FEAL

In this section we describe several properties of FEAL which can accelerate the implementation of the FEAL-breaking algorithms described in this chapter.

1. The F function is partially invertible even if the subkey is not known: Given the value $Y = F(X, K)$ we can find all the internal values inside the F function and half of the actual input bytes by:

$$\begin{aligned} X_0 &= S_0^{-1}(Y_0, Y_1) \\ X_3 &= S_1^{-1}(Y_3, Y_2) \\ X_2 \oplus K_1 &= X_2 \oplus X_3 \oplus K_1 = S_0^{-1}(Y_2, Y_1) \\ X_1 \oplus K_0 &= X_0 \oplus X_1 \oplus K_0 = S_1^{-1}(Y_1, [X_2 \oplus K_1]). \end{aligned}$$

2. The F_k function of the key processing algorithm is partially invertible: Let $Z = F_k(X, Y)$. Then, given any three values out of Z_2, Z_3, X_3, Y_3, the fourth value is easily calculated using the formula:

$$Z_3 = S_1(X_3, Z_2 \oplus Y_3).$$

   In particular,
$$Z_{3,2} = X_{3,0} \oplus Z_{2,0} \oplus Y_{3,0} \oplus 1$$
   since the S box is linear in the least significant bit of the addition operation.

3. The following equation of the subkeys is satisfied by FEAL-8:

$$Kef_{3,2} \oplus Kcd_{3,2} = Kcd_{3,0} \oplus Kef_{2,0} \oplus Kcd_{2,0} \oplus K7_{1,0}$$

   or using the actual subkeys notation:

$$AK7_{3,2} = AK6_{3,0} \oplus AK7_{2,0}.$$

   Therefore, given the value of $AK7$, it is easy to calculate the value of the bit $AK6_{3,0}$. This property is used to discard wrong values of AK6 during the search for the actual subkeys.

4. The key processing algorithm of FEAL-8 yields 256 subkey bits, of which 32 bits are redundant. Only 224 bits are needed during the encryption/decryption processes. They are:

$$\begin{aligned} K0^{\dagger} &= K0 \oplus \widehat{Kcd} \\ K1^{\dagger} &= K1 \oplus \widehat{Kcd} \oplus \widehat{Kef} \end{aligned}$$

$$
\begin{aligned}
K2^\dagger &= K2 \oplus \widehat{Kcd} \\
K3^\dagger &= K3 \oplus \widehat{Kcd} \oplus \widehat{Kef} \\
K4^\dagger &= K4 \oplus \widehat{Kcd} \\
K5^\dagger &= K5 \oplus \widehat{Kcd} \oplus \widehat{Kef} \\
K6^\dagger &= K6 \oplus \widehat{Kcd} \\
K7^\dagger &= K7 \oplus \widehat{Kcd} \oplus \widehat{Kef} \\
K89^\dagger &= K89 \oplus \mathrm{am}(\widehat{Kcd} \oplus \widehat{Kef}) \\
Kab^\dagger &= Kab \oplus \mathrm{am}(\widehat{Kef}) \\
Kcd^\dagger &= (Kcd_0, 0, 0, Kcd_3) \\
Kef^\dagger &= (Kef_0, 0, 0, Kef_3)
\end{aligned}
$$

where for any 32-bit X, $\hat{X}$ is the 16-bit value of its two middle bytes (i.e., (X_1, X_2)). The encryption and decryption using the new values of the subkeys give the same results as with the original values. Another equivalent description of the subkeys is denoted by the actual subkeys in which the subkeys of the rounds are extended to 32 bits and the subkey of the final transformation is eliminated.

5. The following property can be most useful in deciding whether some input XOR may cause some output XOR by the F function and to find actual values of input bits from the input XOR and the output XOR. The decision is done in parallel for each S box in the F function.

   Let $Z = S_i(X,Y)$ and $Z^* = S_i(X^*,Y^*)$. The least significant bit of the addition operation satisfies $Z'_2 = X'_0 \oplus Y'_0$. Let C be the byte of carries in the addition operation $(X+Y+i) \pmod{256}$ in S_i, defined as $C = (X+Y+i \pmod{256}) \oplus X \oplus Y$ (i is interpreted as the 0/1 carry into the least significant bit). C_j is the carry bit passed from the $(j-1)^{\text{th}}$ bit of the addition operation in S_i to the jth bit. Thus,

$$
\forall j \in \{1,\ldots,7\}: \; C_j = \begin{cases} 1, & \text{if } X_{j-1}+Y_{j-1}+C_{j-1} \geq 2; \\ 0, & \text{if } X_{j-1}+Y_{j-1}+C_{j-1} \leq 1 \end{cases}
$$

   and C'_j is the value of $C_j \oplus C^*_j$. $C_0 = i$ and thus the value of C'_0 is always zero. Since $C = \mathrm{ROR2}(Z) \oplus X \oplus Y$, C' can be easily calculated from the input XORs and the output XOR by

$$
C' = \mathrm{ROR2}(Z') \oplus X' \oplus Y'.
$$

   From the combination of the values of X'_j, Y'_j, C'_j and C'_{j+1} (for $j \in \{0,\ldots,6\}$) we can derive some new information. For example, assume that $X'_j = Y'_j = 0$ and $C'_j = 1$ and consider the two possibilities of C'_{j+1}. If $C'_{j+1} = 0$ then either (a) $X_j+Y_j+C_j \leq 1$ and $X^*_j+Y^*_j+C^*_j \leq 1$ and thus $X_j = Y_j = 0$, or (b) $X_j+Y_j+C_j \geq 2$ and $X^*_j+Y^*_j+C^*_j \geq 2$

X'_j	Y'_j	$C'_j = 1$	$C'_j = 0$
0	0	$X_j \oplus Y_j = C'_{j+1}$ ‡	$C'_{j+1} = 0$*
0	1	$Y_j \oplus C_j = C'_{j+1} \oplus 1$	$X_j \oplus C_j = C'_{j+1}$ †
1	0	$X_j \oplus C_j = C'_{j+1} \oplus 1$	$Y_j \oplus C_j = C'_{j+1}$ †
1	1	$C'_{j+1} = 1$*	$Z_{j+2} \oplus C_j = X_j \oplus Y_j = C'_{j+1} \oplus 1$ ‡

In Z_{j+2}, the index $(j+2)$ is modulo eight.

Table 6.2. Difference properties of the S boxes of FEAL.

and thus $X_j = Y_j = 1$. In both cases $X_j = Y_j$. If $C'_{j+1} = 1$ then similarly $X_j \neq Y_j$ and therefore in general $X_j \oplus Y_j = C'_{j+1}$. Table 6.2 generalizes this observation for all the combinations of X'_j, Y'_j and C'_j. The entries marked by * are particularly useful because they can be used to identify wrong pairs. The entries marked by † can be used to derive the values of the bits X_0 and Y_0. The entries marked by ‡ can be used to derive the value of $X_j \oplus Y_j$ and the value of Z_2).

7

Differential Cryptanalysis of Other Cryptosystems

7.1 Cryptanalysis of Khafre

Khafre[22] is a software-oriented cryptosystem with 64-bit blocks whose number of rounds (which should be a multiple of eight) is not specified. Each block is divided into two halves, called the right half and the left half. In each round the lowest byte of the right half is used as an eight-bit input to an S box with 32-bit output. The left half is XORed with the output of the S box. The right half is rotated and the two halves are exchanged. The rotation is such that every byte is used once every eight rounds as an input to an S box. Before the first round and after every eighth round the data is XORed with 64-bit subkeys. These subkeys are the only way the key is involved in the cryptosystem.

The differential cryptanalysis of Khafre is based upon the observation that the number of output bits of an S box is more than twice the number of input bits. Therefore, given an output XOR of an S box in a pair, the input pair is (usually) unique and it is easy to find the two inputs. Moreover, there are about $\frac{(2^8)^2}{2} = 2^{15}$ possible input pairs for each S box, and thus only about 2^{-17} of the 32-bit values are output XORs of some pair.

A second observation is that there are characteristics in which only one even round (or only one odd round) has non-zero input XOR to the S box. The output XOR of this round in a right pair is easily derivable from the plaintext XOR and the ciphertext XOR. Given this output XOR we can discard most of the wrong pairs by the first observation, leaving only a small fraction of about 2^{-17} of them.

The characteristics of Khafre are described by templates which choose between zero XORs and non-zero XORs. Each right pair may have a different value of the non-zero XORs. The following characteristic is used as an example of the cryptanalysis of Khafre with 16 rounds. This characteristic is described as the first characteristic of Khafre due to its simplicity. Better characteristics are described later in this section.

Rnd	Left Half				Right Half					Output XOR			
Ω_P	0	0	A	0	0	0	B	0					
1	0	0	A	0	0	0	B	0	$\rightarrow$	0	0	0	0
2	B	0	0	0	0	0	A	0	$\rightarrow$	0	0	0	0
3	A	0	0	0	B	0	0	0	$\rightarrow$	0	0	0	0
4	0	B	0	0	A	0	0	0	$\rightarrow$	0	0	0	0
5	0	A	0	0	0	B	0	0	$\rightarrow$	0	0	0	0
6	0	0	0	B	0	A	0	0	$\rightarrow$	0	0	0	0
7	0	0	0	A	0	0	0	B	$\rightarrow$	C	D	E	$A^\dagger$
8	0	0	B	0	C	D	E	0	$\rightarrow$	0	0	0	0
9	D	E	0	C	0	0	B	0	$\rightarrow$	0	0	0	0
10	B	0	0	0	D	E	0	C	$\rightarrow$	$F \oplus B^\ddagger$	G	H	I
11	0	C	D	E	F	G	H	I	$\rightarrow$	J	K	$D \oplus L^\ddagger$	$E^\dagger$
12	I	F	G	H	J	M^0	L	0	$\rightarrow$	0	0	0	0
13	0	J	M^0	L	I	F	G	H	$\rightarrow$	N	$P \oplus J^\ddagger$	Q	$L^\dagger$
14	G	H	I	F	N	P	R^0	0	$\rightarrow$	0	0	0	0
15	R^0	0	N	P	G	H	I	F	$\rightarrow$	S	T	U	$P^\dagger$
16	H	I	F	G	V	T	W^0	0	$\rightarrow$	0	0	0	0
Ω_T	T	W^0	0	V	H	I	F	G					

Each value 0 describes a byte which has equal values in both executions of the encryption of the pair (zero XOR). Each letter denotes a XOR value which is not zero. A letter with a superscript ^{0} denotes a XOR value which can be either zero or non-zero. The exact values of the non-zero XOR values may vary for different right pairs. The superscript † means that the byte of the output XOR must be equal to the corresponding byte of the left half in order to cause the input XOR byte of the S box in the next round to be zero. Each occurrence of † causes a reduction of the probability of the characteristic by $\frac{1}{255}$. The superscript ‡ means that the byte of the output XOR must not be equal to the corresponding byte of the left half in order to prevent a zero value in the corresponding byte in the next round, so that it can become zero in one of the following rounds, after XORing with another non-zero value. Each occurrence of ‡ causes a reduction of the probability of the characteristic by $\frac{254}{255}$. Therefore, the probability of this characteristic is $\left(\frac{1}{255}\right)^4 \cdot \left(\frac{254}{255}\right)^3 \approx 2^{-32}$. The input XOR Ω_P of the characteristic has two degrees of freedom: A and B, each one can have 255 possible values. Therefore, the characteristic has $255^2 \approx 2^{16}$ possible plaintext XORs.

Given a sufficient number of pairs, we can discard most of the wrong pairs using the byte in the ciphertext XOR with value zero. Only about 2^{-8} of the wrong pairs remain.

Looking at the characteristic we can see that the output XOR of the tenth round is easily extracted by XORing the right half of the plaintext

XOR with the right half of the ciphertext XOR and rotating the result by 16 bits (ROT16($P'_R \oplus T'_R$)). This happens since the tenth round is the only even round whose output XOR is not zero. There are 2^{32} possibilities for the value of ROT16($P'_R \oplus T'_R$). However, there are only about 2^{15} possible input pairs of the S box itself. Therefore, there are at most about 2^{15} possible output XORs in the tenth round. As a consequence, most of the remaining wrong pairs can be easily discarded, leaving only about 2^{-17} of the 2^{-8} of the wrong pairs that remained in the previous test. In addition, the two input values of the S box and the two output values can be identified uniquely.

The input XOR value C of the S box in the tenth round equals the upper byte of the output XOR in the seventh round. The input XOR B and the lower byte of the output XOR A of the S box in the seventh round are known from the plaintext XOR. There are only 128 possible pairs of inputs (with that input XOR) to the S box in the seventh round. 16 bits of the output XOR of this S box are known. Therefore, we can discard each pair whose corresponding 16 bit value is not as expected. The probability of a wrong pair to pass this test is about $2^7 \cdot 2^{-16} = 2^{-9}$.

For each of the remaining pairs, we can find the actual values of the inputs to the S box in the fifteenth round since we know its eight-bit input XOR and eight bits of its output XOR. There are only 2^7 pairs with this input XOR and therefore about half of the wrong pairs can be discarded. Then, we can calculate the input values to the S box in the thirteenth round by a similar calculation and discard about half of the remaining wrong pairs. The input values to the S box in the eleventh round can be found with much better identification, since all the 32 bits of the output XOR are known at this stage. We can discard most of the remaining wrong pairs and leave only about $2^7 \cdot 2^{-32} = 2^{-25}$ of them.

Up to now, we discarded almost all the wrong pairs, leaving only a negligible fraction of about $2^{-8} \cdot 2^{-17} \cdot 2^{-9} \cdot 2^{-1} \cdot 2^{-1} \cdot 2^{-25} = 2^{-61}$ of them. For the right pairs, we found the actual input values of the S boxes in all the five rounds with non-zero input XORs. However, we do not know which value belongs to which encryption in the pair, and thus we have two possible relations for each of these five values. We can find 16 possibilities for the lower byte of the left half of the last subkey by XORing through a trail from the tenth round forward to the ciphertext (two possible values of the input XOR of the tenth round and two possible values of the output XOR of each one of the eleventh, the thirteenth and the fifteenth rounds). Using the counting method with three right pairs among $3 \cdot 2^{32}$ pairs, we can uniquely identify the value of this byte of the subkey, identify the right pairs themselves, and identify the exact choice of inputs to the S boxes in the five rounds for each encryption in the right pairs. Identification of the values of the input to the S box of the last round is possible using the counting method which identifies two more bytes of the last subkey. A similar identification may be done for the fourteenth round and then to the twelfth round, each finding two more bytes of the subkey. In total we find seven bytes of the last subkey. We can complete the value of the last subkey using another characteristic in which the first non-zero input XOR to an S box is in the eighth round, and reduce the cryptosystem to eight rounds (since in Khafre the subkeys are XORed into the data only once every eight rounds). The eight-round cryptosystem is already known to be breakable even if the S boxes themselves are unknown (see [22]).

This attack on Khafre with 16 rounds needs about three right pairs obtained from a pool of about $3 \cdot 2^{32}$ pairs ($3 \cdot 2^{33}$ ciphertexts). This number of ciphertexts can be drastically reduced by using a compact structure of 2^{16} encryptions which contains about 2^{31} pairs. Therefore, the structure has probability about half to contain a right pair. The structure is simple: choose a constant random value for six of the bytes of the plaintexts, excluding the second and the sixth bytes. Choose all the 2^{16} possible values for the second and sixth bytes of the plaintexts and encrypt all the plaintexts. This structure also contains pairs with the additional characteristic needed to complete the last subkey. In order to have about three right pairs, we have to choose about six such structures, with a total of about $6 \cdot 2^{16} \approx 400000$ plaintexts.

The attacking program finds the last subkey in less than 45 minutes on a personal computer using 400000 encryptions with 90% success rate. Using about 590000 encryptions the success rate is increased to more than 99% and the execution time is increased to about an hour. The program uses about 500K bytes of memory, most of which is used to store the plaintexts and the ciphertexts.

This attack can be converted to a known plaintext attack using about $2^{41.5}$ plaintext/ciphertext pairs. In such an attack, the $2^{41.5}$ plaintexts can form $(2^{41.5})^2/2 = 2^{82}$ pairs. Since there are only 2^{64} possible plaintext XORs, about $2^{82}/2^{64} = 2^{18}$ pairs occur with each plaintext XOR. There are about 2^{16} usable input XORs of the characteristic and thus we get about $2^{16} \cdot 2^{18} = 2^{34}$ candidate pairs which can be used to break Khafre with 16 rounds.

Characteristics with improved probability of about 2^{-24} also exist. One such characteristic is:

Rnd	Left Half				Right Half					Output XOR			
Ω_P	0	0	A	0	0	0	0	0					
1	0	0	A	0	0	0	0	0	$\rightarrow$	0	0	0	0
2	0	0	0	0	0	0	A	0	$\rightarrow$	0	0	0	0
3	A	0	0	0	0	0	0	0	$\rightarrow$	0	0	0	0
4	0	0	0	0	A	0	0	0	$\rightarrow$	0	0	0	0
5	0	A	0	0	0	0	0	0	$\rightarrow$	0	0	0	0
6	0	0	0	0	0	A	0	0	$\rightarrow$	0	0	0	0
7	0	0	0	A	0	0	0	0	$\rightarrow$	0	0	0	0
8	0	0	0	0	0	0	0	A	$\rightarrow$	B	C	D	E
9	0	0	A	0	B	C	D	E	$\rightarrow$	F	G	$H^0 \oplus A$	I
10	D	E	B	C	F	G	H^0	I	$\rightarrow$	$J^0 \oplus D$	$K^0 \oplus E$	$L \oplus B^{\ddagger}$	$C^{\dagger}$
11	H^0	I	F	G	J^0	K^0	L	0	$\rightarrow$	0	0	0	0
12	0	J^0	K^0	L	H^0	I	F	G	$\rightarrow$	M	$N \oplus J^{0\ddagger}$	$P^0 \oplus K^0$	$L^{\dagger}$
13	G	H^0	I	F	M	N	P^0	0	$\rightarrow$	0	0	0	0
14	P^0	0	M	N	G	H^0	I	F	$\rightarrow$	$Q^0 \oplus P^0$	R	$S^0 \oplus M$	$N^{\dagger}$
15	I	F	G	H^0	Q^0	R	S^0	0	$\rightarrow$	0	0	0	0
16	R	S^0	0	Q^0	I	F	G	H^0	$\rightarrow$	$T^0 \oplus R$	$U^0 \oplus S^0$	V^0	$W^0 \oplus Q^0$
Ω_T	F	G	H^0	I	T^0	U^0	V^0	W^0					

Using characteristics with probability about 2^{-24} we need about $3 \cdot 2^{24}$ pairs which are formed by $3 \cdot 2^{25}$ encryptions. Using structures of 2^8 encryptions which contain 2^{15} pairs the attack needs about $3 \cdot 2^{17}$ encryptions (the same as with the characteristic with probability about 2^{-32}). Known plaintext differential cryptanalytic attacks based on this characteristic need about $2^{41.5}$ encryptions (since $\frac{(2^{41.5})^2}{2 \cdot 2^{64}} \cdot 2^8 = 2^{26} > 3 \cdot 2^{24}$). The above characteristic can be extended to a 24-round characteristic with probability about 2^{-56}. Attacks on 24-round Khafre based on this characteristic need about 2^{60} pairs. Using structures of 2^8 encryptions with 2^{15} pairs they need about 2^{53} encryptions. The differential cryptanalytic known plaintext attack on 24-round Khafre based on this characteristic needs about $2^{58.5}$ encryptions (since $\frac{(2^{58.5})^2}{2 \cdot 2^{64}} \cdot 2^8 = 2^{60}$).

The best usable characteristic of Khafre that we have found is the fol-

No. of rounds	Char. prob.	Pairs needed	Chosen plaintexts	Known plaintexts
16	2^{-16}	$3 \cdot 2^{16}$	1536	$2^{37.5}$
24	2^{-56}	2^{60}	2^{53}	$2^{58.5}$

Table 7.1. Summary of the attacks on Khafre.

lowing 16-round characteristic whose probability is about 2^{-16}:

Rnd	Left Half				Right Half					Output XOR			
Ω_P	0	0	A	0	0	0	0	0					
1	0	0	A	0	0	0	0	0	$\rightarrow$	0	0	0	0
2	0	0	0	0	0	0	A	0	$\rightarrow$	0	0	0	0
3	A	0	0	0	0	0	0	0	$\rightarrow$	0	0	0	0
4	0	0	0	0	A	0	0	0	$\rightarrow$	0	0	0	0
5	0	A	0	0	0	0	0	0	$\rightarrow$	0	0	0	0
6	0	0	0	0	0	A	0	0	$\rightarrow$	0	0	0	0
7	0	0	0	A	0	0	0	0	$\rightarrow$	0	0	0	0
8	0	0	0	0	0	0	0	A	$\rightarrow$	B	C	D	E
9	0	0	A	0	B	C	D	E	$\rightarrow$	F	G	$H^0 \oplus A$	I
10	D	E	B	C	F	G	H^0	I	$\rightarrow$	$J^0 \oplus D$	$K^0 \oplus E$	$L \oplus B^\ddagger$	$M \oplus C^\ddagger$
11	H^0	I	F	G	J^0	K^0	L	M	$\rightarrow$	$N^0 \oplus H$	$P^0 \oplus I$	$Q \oplus F^\ddagger$	$R \oplus G^\ddagger$
12	M	J^0	K^0	L	N^0	P^0	Q	R	$\rightarrow$	$S^0 \oplus M$	$T \oplus J^{0\ddagger}$	$U^0 \oplus K^0$	$L^\dagger$
13	R	N^0	P^0	Q	S^0	T	U^0	0	$\rightarrow$	0	0	0	0
14	U^0	0	S^0	T	R	N^0	P^0	Q	$\rightarrow$	$V^0 \oplus U^0$	W	$X^0 \oplus S^0$	$T^\dagger$
15	P^0	Q	R	N^0	V^0	W	X^0	0	$\rightarrow$	0	0	0	0
16	W	X^0	0	V^0	P^0	Q	R	N^0	$\rightarrow$	$Y^0 \oplus W$	$Z^0 \oplus X^0$	α^0	$\beta^0 \oplus V^0$
Ω_T	Q	R	N^0	P^0	Y^0	Z^0	α^0	β^0					

Two of the odd rounds (the ninth and the eleventh rounds) have non-zero output XORs. The XOR of these two output XORs (with a rotation of one of them) can be easily extracted for right pairs. Since this XOR is a combination of four outputs (rather than two as in the previous characteristics), the identification of the right pairs is much more complex, but is still possible. The differential cryptanalytic chosen plaintext attack based on this characteristic needs three right pairs which are likely to be found in a pool of $3 \cdot 2^{16}$ pairs. Using structures of 2^8 encryptions which contain 2^{15} pairs about $\frac{2^8}{2^{15}} \cdot 3 \cdot 2^{16} = 1536$ encryptions are needed. The implementation of this chosen plaintext attack takes about an hour on a personal computer. The known plaintext differential cryptanalytic attack based on this characteristic needs about $2^{37.5}$ encryptions (since $\frac{(2^{37.5})^2}{2 \cdot 2^{64}} \cdot 2^8 = 2^{18} > 3 \cdot 2^{16}$).

A summary of our best results for 16-round Khafre and 24-round Khafre is given in Table 7.1 which describes the number of pairs needed for the attack, the number of chosen plaintexts needed, and the number of known plaintexts needed. Note that these complexities are independent of the actual choice of the S boxes as long as the S boxes themselves are known to the attacker, and remain valid even if different S boxes are used in different rounds.

7.2 Cryptanalysis of REDOC-II

REDOC-II[38,8] is a ten-round cryptosystem with 70-bit blocks (arranged as ten bytes of seven bits). Each round contains six phases: (1) First variable substitution, (2) Second variable substitution, (3) First variable key XOR, (4) Variable enclave, (5) Second variable key XOR and (6) Variable permutation. Each phase modifies the data using tables. There are 16 predefined substitution tables which are used by the variable substitutions. There are 128 predefined permutation tables used by the variable permutation. There are 128 predefined enclave tables used by the variable enclave. All these tables are fixed and are given as part of the definition of REDOC-II. In addition, 128 ten-byte key tables and nine mask tables are calculated for each key by a key processing algorithm. In each variable key XOR phase one table is chosen by XORing the value of a specific byte in the data with a specific byte in the mask tables. The resulting value is the table number. All the bytes of the data except the choosing byte are XORed with the corresponding bytes in the chosen key table. In each variable substitution phase one table is chosen by XORing the value of a specific byte in the data with a specific byte in the mask tables. The table number is the resulting value modulo 16. All the bytes of the data except the choosing byte are substituted by the chosen substitution table. In each variable permutation phase one table is chosen by adding (modulo 128) all the ten bytes of the data and XORing the result with a specific byte in the mask tables. The resulting value is the table number. The data bytes are permuted by the chosen permutation.

The variable enclave phase is more complicated. The predefined enclave tables have five rows and three columns. Each entry contains a number between one and five. There are two properties which an enclave table should satisfy: each column should be a permutation of the numbers 1–5 and each row should contain three different numbers. Processing an enclave table on a half-block is as follows:

1. Each entry in the table contains an index of a byte in the half-block.
2. Add the values of the three bytes pointed to by the numbers in the first row of the table and store the result in the byte pointed to by the first column in this row.

3. Add the resultant values of the three bytes pointed to by the numbers in the second row of the table and store the result in the byte pointed to by the first column in the row.
4. Similarly add according to the third, fourth and fifth rows.

Each variable enclave phase uses four enclave tables as follows:

1. Divide the block into two half-blocks of five bytes each. The half-blocks are called the left half and the right half.
2. XOR the values of two particular bytes in the right half (in the first round: the first two bytes) with two particular mask bytes. The resultant two bytes are indexes of two enclave tables.
3. Process the left half by the first enclave table indexed by the above two bytes.
4. Process the resultant left half by the second enclave table indexed by the above two bytes.
5. XOR the values of two particular bytes in the resultant left half (in the first round: the first two bytes) with two particular mask bytes. The resultant two bytes are indexes of two enclave tables.
6. XOR the left half to the right half.
7. Process the resultant right half by the first enclave table indexed by the above two bytes.
8. Process the resultant right half by the second enclave table indexed by the above two bytes.
9. XOR the right half to the left half.

An important property of the enclave tables is that they are linear operations in terms of addition which can be simulated by a matrix-vector product. By modifying only most significant bits in the input, only most significant bits in the output are modified. Moreover, the linear modification table of the most significant output bits by the most significant input bits uniquely identifies the enclave table used. This property can even be used in the variable enclave phase. The left half of the input with two of the bytes of the right half affect the choice of the enclave tables used in this phase. However, three of the bytes of the right half do not affect the choice of the enclave tables (in the first round they are the eighth, ninth and tenth bytes) and thus the modifications of the most significant bits of the output are linear functions of the modifications of the most significant bits of these input bytes. Note that since we XOR the right half to the left half as the last step in the variable enclave phase we get a symmetric modification in both halves and therefore, an even number of modified most significant bits.

In this attack we use the following one-round characteristic:

After Phase	Data XOR										
Ω_P	0	0	0	0	0	0	0	A	0	0	
First Subst	0	0	0	0	0	0	0	B	0	0	For some B
Second Subst	0	0	0	0	0	0	0	64	0	0	$p \approx 1/128$
Key XOR	0	0	0	0	0	0	0	64	0	0	
Enclave	C	0	D	E	F	C	0	D	E	F	$p \approx 1/2$
Key XOR	C	0	D	E	F	C	0	D	E	F	
Permutation	Some permutation of C,0,D,E,F,C,0,D,E,F										
Ω_T	Some permutation of C,0,D,E,F,C,0,D,E,F										

where $A, B \in \{1, \ldots, 127\}$ and $C, D, E, F \in \{0, 64\}$ (not all of them zero). In total, this characteristic has probability about $\frac{1}{256}$. The ciphertext XOR has 60 zero bits (six in each byte) and the XORed value of the most significant bits of the ciphertext XOR is zero as well. Similar characteristics exist in which the difference is at the ninth and tenth bytes rather than at the eighth byte. Differences in more than one of these three bytes is also possible with smaller probabilities, but if the difference is the same in all the differing bytes and the values of all the differing bytes in the plaintexts are equal then the probability remains about $\frac{1}{256}$.

Given sufficiently many pairs encrypted by one-round REDOC-II with the plaintext differences specified in the characteristics, we can discard (almost) all the wrong pairs by verifying that the 61 bits of the ciphertext XORs $(60 + 1)$ are really zero. Only a negligible fraction of 2^{-61} of the wrong pairs may remain. In practice, only right pairs remain.

For each of the $16 \cdot 16 = 256$ possible values of the masks of the substitution phases we count the number of pairs whose differing byte after the two substitutions resulting from the masks differ only by the most significant bit. For each one of the 128 possible values of the mask of the permutation phase we count the number of pairs whose ciphertext XOR permuted by the resulting inverse permutation is symmetric and has zeroes in the second and the seventh bytes. The right values of these mask bytes are likely to be the ones counted most frequently and thus can be identified. This attack needs about 1000 pairs and finds three masks of the processed key.

The attack can be enhanced by using structures of 32 encryptions with identical nine bytes and whose tenth byte has 32 different values. In such a structure there are 496 pairs. There are only 128 possible differences after the second substitution and thus there are about four pairs which differ only by one most significant bit after the substitution phases. These four pairs use the same enclave tables and thus with probability about half the structure contains four right pairs, and with probability about half does not contain any right pair. Using three such structures with identical eight bytes, where 32 plaintexts differ by the ninth byte, 32 differ by the tenth byte and 32 differ by both the ninth and the tenth bytes with equal values in both bytes in each plaintext, we are guaranteed to have at least one structure whose choosing byte of the second key XOR has no difference and thus to have about four right pairs. This enhanced attack needs only 96 chosen plaintexts.

REDOC-II with more than one round is also vulnerable to this attack. The following characteristic is a two-round extension of the above characteristic (for simplicity we use in the second round the same choosing bytes as in the first round, rather than the new choosing bytes of the second round).

After Phase	Data XOR										
Ω_P	0	0	0	0	0	0	0	A	0	0	
First Subst	0	0	0	0	0	0	0	B	0	0	For some B
Second Subst	0	0	0	0	0	0	0	64	0	0	$p \approx 1/128$
Key XOR	0	0	0	0	0	0	0	64	0	0	
Enclave	C	0	D	E	F	C	0	D	E	F	$p \approx 4/31$ (see †)
Key XOR	C	0	D	E	F	C	0	D	E	F	
Permutation	0	0	0	0	0	0	0	G	H	I	$p \approx 1/15$ (see ‡)
First Subst	0	0	0	0	0	0	0	J	K	0	Some J and K
Second Subst	0	0	0	0	0	0	0	64	64	0	$p \approx (1/128)^2$
Key XOR	0	0	0	0	0	0	0	64	64	0	
Enclave	L	0	M	N	P	L	0	M	N	P	$p \approx 1/2$
Key XOR	L	0	M	N	P	L	0	M	N	P	(see •)
Permutation	Some permutation of $L,0,M,N,P,L,0,M,N,P$										
Ω_T	Some permutation of $L,0,M,N,P,L,0,M,N,P$										

† One of C, D, E and F is 64 and the others are zero.

‡ Two of G, H and I are 64 and the third is zero. The probability that the permutation takes the two 64's into G, H and I is $\binom{3}{2}/\binom{10}{2} = 3/45 = 1/15$. We assume without loss of generality that $I = 0$.

• L, M, N and P are either zero or 64.

This characteristic has probability about $\frac{1}{128} \cdot \frac{4}{31} \cdot \frac{3}{45} \cdot \left(\frac{1}{128}\right)^2 \cdot \frac{1}{2} \approx 2^{-29}$ and the attack needs about 2^{31} pairs. Using structures of 128 encryptions whose differences are restricted to a single byte (either the eighth, ninth or the tenth byte) we are guaranteed to have 64 pairs whose difference after the first two substitution phases is only in one most significant bit, and each of them has a probability of about 2^{-22} to be a right pair. Therefore, there is a right pair in such a structure with probability about 2^{-16} and the attack needs about $4 \cdot 2^{16} \cdot 128 = 2^{25}$ encryptions to find four right pairs and to deduce three masks. The extended three-round characteristic has probability about 2^{-50} and thus the attack needs about 2^{52} pairs. Using structures of 128 encryptions the attack needs about 2^{46} encryptions. The extended four-round characteristic has probability about 2^{-71} and thus the attack needs about 2^{73} pairs. Using structures of 128 encryptions the attack needs about 2^{67} encryptions. About $2^{73} \cdot 2^{-61} = 2^{12}$ wrong pairs may not be discarded, but the right values of the three masks can still be identified using the counting scheme which counts all the 15 bits simultaneously.

The conversion of the chosen plaintext attacks on REDOC-II into known plaintext attacks has the following results. Given $2^{35} \cdot \sqrt{2m}$ encryptions, there are about $\frac{(2^{35} \cdot \sqrt{2m})^2}{2 \cdot 2^{70}} = m$ pairs with each plaintext XOR value. There are $3 \cdot 2^7$ possible plaintext XORs of pairs differing by one of the three bytes and therefore about $3 \cdot 2^7 \cdot m$ pairs with the plaintext XORs required by the attack are likely to exist among them. Using the plaintext XORs which differ by more than one byte, this complexity changes to about $7 \cdot 2^7 \cdot m$. Since the attack on one-round REDOC-II needs about 1000 pairs, $7 \cdot 2^7 \cdot m = 1000$ and therefore $m \approx 1$. The number of encryptions needed for the known plaintext attack on one-round REDOC-II is about $2^{35} \cdot \sqrt{2m} \approx 2^{35.5}$. The attacks on REDOC-II with two, three and four rounds need about 2^{46}, $2^{56.5}$ and 2^{67} known plaintexts, respectively.

In addition to the chosen plaintext attacks, we can also mount chosen ciphertext attacks which use characteristics based on the differences in the ciphertexts and show their evolution towards the plaintexts (i.e., in the reverse direction). One such characteristic of the one-round variant is:

Before Phase	Data XOR										
Ω_T	Some permutation of two 64's and eight 0's										
Permutation	Same values in both half blocks where one 64 is at bytes $i \in \{1,3,4,5\}$ and the other at byte $i+5$										$p \approx 4/45$
Key XOR	The same										
Enclave	0	0	0	0	0	0	0	A	B	C	$p \approx 1/4$
Key XOR	0	0	0	0	0	0	0	A	B	C	
Second Subst	0	0	0	0	0	0	0	D	E	F	for some D, E, F
First Subst	0	0	0	0	0	0	0	G	H	I	$(G,H,I) \neq (0,0,0)$
Ω_P	0	0	0	0	0	0	0	G	H	I	

This characteristic has probability about $\frac{1}{45}$. Similar characteristics with four differing bytes in the ciphertexts, six differing bytes and eight differing bytes have probabilities about $\frac{1}{140}$, $\frac{1}{210}$ and $\frac{1}{180}$ respectively. Using special structures, we can attack one-round REDOC-II using 40 chosen ciphertexts in order to find the three mask bytes. The variants with two, three and four rounds can be attacked using 2^{24}, 2^{45} and 2^{66} chosen ciphertexts respectively. The conversion of these attacks to known plaintext attacks gives approximately the same complexities as the attacks based on the chosen plaintext attacks.

An extension of the chosen plaintext attack on the one-round variant of REDOC-II can find all the mask tables and the key tables. We assume here that the three masks were already found and that the cryptosystem is reduced to three phases. In order to find all the key tables we use several structures of 128 encryptions which differ by one of the three bytes as above, plus several encryptions which differ also by the first two bytes.

This extension starts by calculating the matrix which describes the double enclave of the right half of the enclave phase. In the first step we look for the value of the entry which corresponds to the influence of the eighth input byte on the second output byte by trying the triplets of the value XORed with the input byte before it is multiplied, the multiplication factor and the value added after the multiplication from the other four input bytes. For each such triplet we check whether all the pairs in the structure suggest the same value to be XORed with the sum to make the output byte. The right value of the triplet should be suggested by all the pairs in the structure. Usually several triplets remain undiscarded, and all of them have the same factor. This factor should be the value of the corresponding entry in the matrix. The two entries which correspond to the ninth and to the tenth input bytes can be found similarly. Using the values of these three entries we can find more bits of the twelve entries of the matrix which correspond to the same three input bytes and to the four other output bytes. These values usually suffice to identify uniquely the pair of enclave tables used in the double enclave and to complete the matrix.

The attacker should follow the following steps. First, find the values which are XORed with the inputs of the right half of the data (by the first key XOR phase and by the left half of the data after its double enclave). Then find the values which are XORed with the output of the right double enclave to make the outputs. Derive the relationship between the values XORed with the inputs and the values XORed with the outputs, derive some entries of the key tables and calculate the masks of the right double enclave and the XOR of the masks of the two key XOR phases. Find additional entries of the key tables by reversing the left double enclave and finding its masks. Complete the missing entries of the key tables using the additional encryptions (especially the second bytes of the key tables which cannot be found otherwise). Finally, derive the actual indexes of the key tables and calculate the actual values of the missing masks from the key tables.

The three masks of the substitution and the permutation phases of the one-round variant can be found within less than a second on a personal

No. of rounds	Char. prob.	Pairs needed	Chosen plains	Chosen ciphers	Known plains	Comments
1	2^{-8}	–	2300	–	–	All masks + key tables
1	2^{-8}	1000	96	40	$2^{35.5}$	Three masks
2	2^{-29}	2^{31}	2^{25}	2^{24}	2^{46}	Three masks
3	2^{-50}	2^{52}	2^{46}	2^{45}	$2^{56.5}$	Three masks
4	2^{-71}	2^{73}	2^{67}	2^{66}	2^{67}	Three masks

Table 7.2. Summary of the attacks on REDOC-II.

computer by a chosen plaintext attack. The program which attacks the one-round variant of REDOC-II finds all the masks and the key tables in about a minute using about 2300 encryptions with more than 90% success rate. Using about 3900 encryptions the success rate becomes better than 99%. The program uses about 150K bytes of memory. A summary of our best results on REDOC-II is given in Table 7.2.

7.3 Cryptanalysis of LOKI

LOKI[6] is a 64-bit key/64-bit block cryptosystem similar to DES which uses one twelve-bit to eight-bit S box (based on irreducible polynomials) replicated four times in each round. The E expansion and the P permutation are replaced by new choices and the initial and final permutations are replaced by XORs with the key. The permutations in the key scheduling algorithm are replaced by rotations and the subkeys become 32-bit long. The XOR of the input of the F function with the key is done before the expansion and therefore neighboring S boxes receive common bits. Two new modes of operation which convert LOKI into a hash function are defined.

The difference distribution table of the larger S box of LOKI has much smaller probabilities than the ones of DES (average $\frac{1}{256}$ and maximum $\frac{1}{64}$). However, it is possible to have non-zero input XORs in two S boxes resulting with the same output, whereas in DES this requires at least three S boxes. We have found the following two-round iterative characteristic with probability $\frac{118}{2^{20}} \approx 2^{-13.12}$ (this probability is calculated using the observation that two neighboring S boxes have four common input bits, otherwise we get a slightly smaller probability):

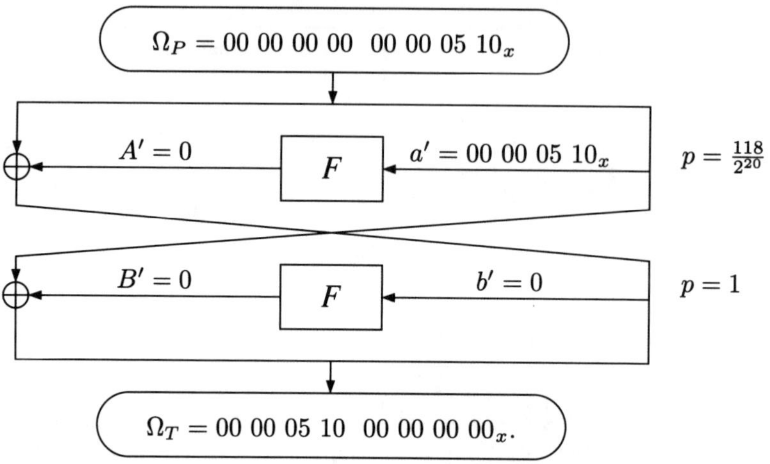

This characteristic can be iterated to nine rounds with probability about $2^{-52.5}$ and to eleven rounds with probability about $2^{-65.5}$. Since all the four S boxes of LOKI are the same and all the output XORs in this characteristic are zero, there are three similar characteristics in which the XOR pattern is rotated by multiples of eight bits. There is another eight-round iterative characteristic in which only non-replicated bits of some S box are different and the outputs differ only by one bit. This characteristic is:

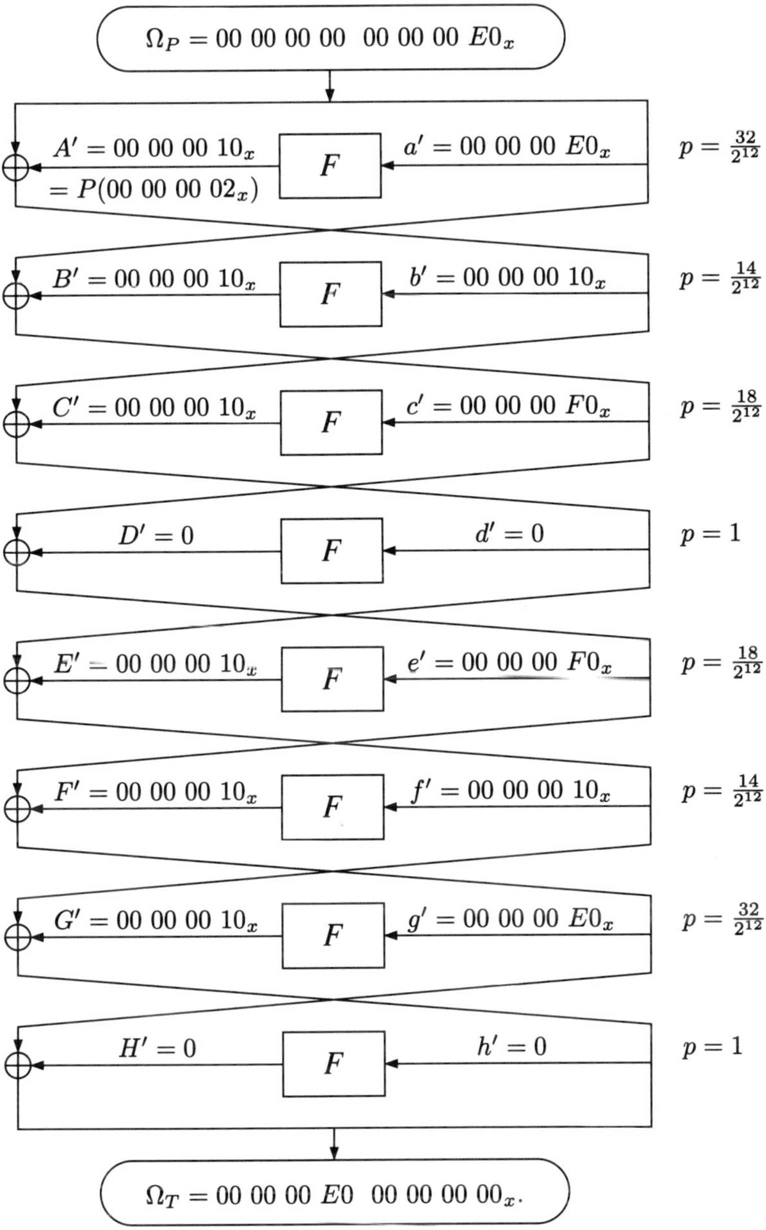

This iterative characteristic has probability about 2^{-46} and its extension to nine rounds has the same probability. Using this characteristic it is possible to break LOKI with up to eleven rounds with less than 2^{64} chosen or known plaintexts.

Careful analysis of the structure of LOKI has revealed that any key has 15 equivalent keys which encrypt any plaintext to the same ciphertext due to a key complementation property. These 15 keys are the original key XORed with the 15 possible 64-bit hexadecimal numbers whose digits are identical (i.e., $hhhhhhhhhhhhhhhh_x$ where $h \in \{1_x, \ldots, F_x\}$). Encryption with these keys results with the same inputs to the F functions in all the 16 executions. Therefore, most of the keys are redundant and a known plaintext attack can be carried out with a complexity of 2^{60} rather than 2^{64}.

Another complementation property is due to the observation that XORing the key with an hexadecimal value $gggggggghhhhhhhh_x$ and XORing the plaintext by $iiiiiiiiiiiiiiii_x$ where $g \in \{0_x, \ldots, F_x\}$, $h \in \{0_x, \ldots, F_x\}$ and $i = g \oplus h$ results in XORing the ciphertext by $iiiiiiiiiiiiiiii_x$. This property can be used to reduce the complexity of a chosen plaintext attack by a further factor of 16 to 2^{56}.

These observations result in major weaknesses when LOKI is used as a hash function. For any message it is easy to find 15 additional messages which hash to the same value by the Single Block Hash (SBH) mode of LOKI: the other messages are the given message XORed with each of the 15 hexadecimal values $hhhhhhhhhhhhhhhh_x$. Since the messages are used as the key of the LOKI primitive (XORed with the previous hash value which can be viewed as a fixed value) and the plaintext of LOKI is fixed, the outputs of all the executions are the same.

If we are allowed to choose the initial value, then for any message it is easy to find 255 other messages which hash to the same value by the Double Block Hash (DBH) mode of LOKI. This is done by XORing both H_{-1} and M_2 with $gggggggghhhhhhhh_x$ and XORing M_1 with $hhhhhhhhgggggggg_x$ without changing H_0 (where $g \in \{0_x, \ldots, F_x\}$ and $h \in \{0_x, \ldots, F_x\}$).

LOKI has 256 simple fixpoints of the form $\text{LOKI}(X, K) = X$ whose plaintexts and the ciphertexts are equal using keys of the form $K = gggggggghhhhhhhh_x$ and plaintexts of the form $X = iiiiiiiiiiiiiiii_x$, where $g, h \in \{0_x, \ldots, F_x\}$ and $i = g \oplus h$. In particular, LOKI encrypts the plaintext zero by the key zero to the ciphertext zero: $\text{LOKI}(0,0) = 0$. Therefore, the two hash function modes hash the zero messages with the zero initial value to zero. This observation shows that the zero initial value should be avoided since any number of zero-blocks (or any even number in the DBH mode) can be prepended to the message without modifying the hash value. Moreover, in the SBH mode all the 16 initial values $H_0 = hhhhhhhhhhhhhhhh_x$ should be avoided since the message $00000000hhhhhhhh_x$ and 15 others hash to the initial value $H_1 = hhhhhhhhhhhhhhhh_x$. In the DBH mode all the 256 initial values $H_{-1} = 0$ and $H_0 = gggggggghhhhhhhh_x$

should be avoided since the messages $M_1 = hhhhhhhhgggggggg_x$ and $M_2 = iiiiiiiiiiiiiiii_x$ where $i = g \oplus h$ hash to the initial value and can be prepended any number of times without affecting the hash value.

After this research was completed, Matthew Kwan[19,5] found the following three-round iterative characteristic of LOKI with probability $2^{-14.4}$:

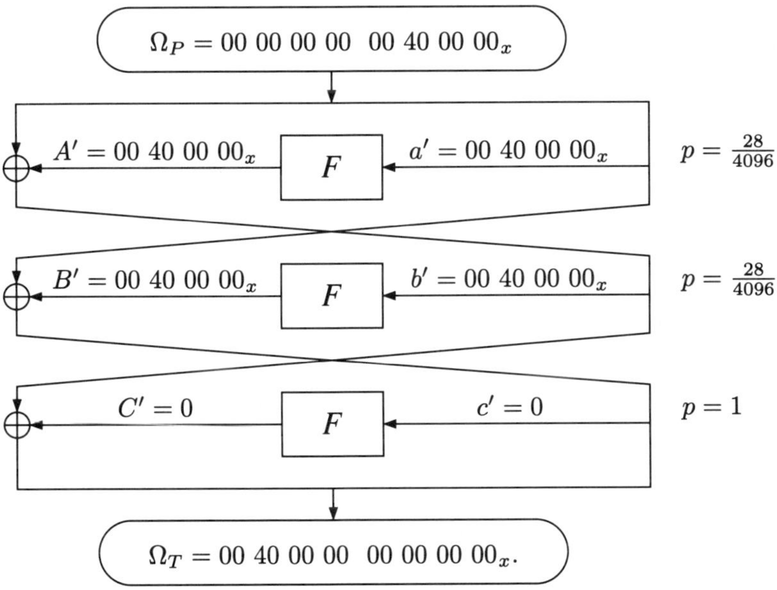

This characteristic can be used to break LOKI with up to 14 rounds, and requires up to 2^{60} chosen plaintexts. He also found many additional fixpoints of LOKI.

7.4 Cryptanalysis of Lucifer

Lucifer[15] is a substitution/permutation cryptosystem designed by IBM prior to the design of DES. In DES the output of the F function is XORed with the input of the previous round to form the input of the next round. This value is XORed (in turn) with a subkey to form the input of the S boxes. In Lucifer, the input of the S boxes is the permuted output of the S boxes of the previous round while the input of the S boxes of the first round is the plaintext itself. A key bit is used to choose the actual S box at each entry out of two possible S boxes. Figure 7.1 describes this structure. The other variant of Lucifer[37] is similar to DES, but is weaker than the variant attacked in this section. An attack on this other variant reduced to

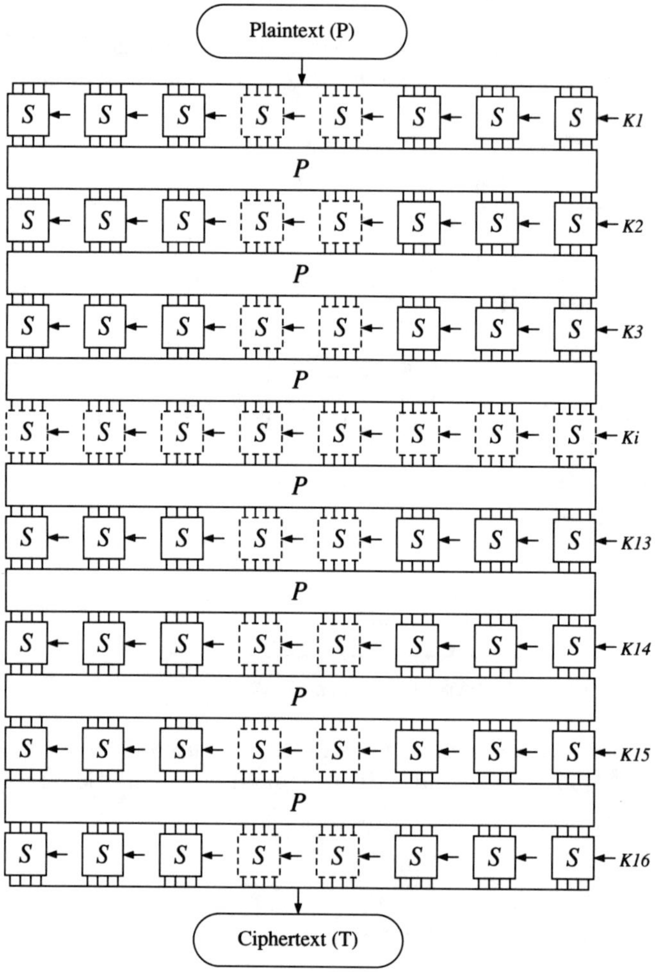

Figure 7.1. Lucifer.

eight rounds requires less than 256 chosen plaintexts and negligible time complexity.

Given an input of an S box, the outputs of the two possible S boxes are known. Each output bit may be the same in both S boxes or may differ. Usually only one or two output bits are the same in both S boxes. In few cases, one output bit is equal in all the four output values obtained when two input values differing by one bit (for example 8_x and A_x) enter the two

Input	Output of S_0	Output of S_1	Equal bits
0000	0100	1111	.1..
0001	0001	1100	..0.
0010	1110	1000	1..0
0011	1000	0010	.0.0
0100	1101	0100	.10.
0101	0110	1001	....
0110	0010	0001	00..
0111	1011	0111	..11
1000	1111	0101	.1.1
1001	1100	1011	1...
1010	1001	0011	.0.1
1011	0111	1110	.11.
1100	0011	1010	.01.
1101	1010	0000	.0.0
1110	0101	0110	01..
1111	0000	1101	..0.

Table 7.3. Output bits that are equal for both S boxes.

possible S boxes. There are pairs of inputs for which the same output bits stay fixed for both values and the same bits differ using either one of the two S boxes. In particular, there are pairs for which three output bits are equal although their fourth bit differ using either S box.

The published description of this variant of Lucifer does not specify the particular choice of the S boxes. For the sake of concreteness, we use the third and fourth lines of S1 of DES as the S boxes S_0 and S_1 of Lucifer. Other choices of the S boxes give similar results. Table 7.3 describes the S boxes and the equal bits of the outputs of the two S boxes. We see that 11 inputs have two equal bits in the outputs, four inputs have one equal bit and for one input all the output bits differ. Table 7.4 describes the equal bits of two input values that differ by one bit using both S boxes. A binary notation is used in these tables.

Table 7.5 describes pairs that have many equal bits, such that the replacement of one input with the other leaves those output bits unchanged using either S box. In this table '0' and '1' means that the output bit is '0' or '1' respectively at all the cases. '+' means that at either S box, the output bit is equal for both inputs of the pairs. '–' means the output bit value is different for the inputs of the pairs for either S box. '.' means that neither of the above cases holds.

By consulting these tables we can create many plaintexts whose partic-

Input	Equal bits
.000	.1..
0.00	.1..
001.	...0
.110	0...
10.0	...1
110.	.0..

Table 7.4. Output bits that are equal for both S boxes for two input values.

Input No. 1	Input No. 2	Common in S_0	Common in S_1	Common bits in Both S boxes
0001	1111	000-	110-	++0-
0010	1001	11-0	10--	1+-.
0011	1101	10-0	00-0	+0-0
1000	1010	1--1	0--1	+--1
1000	1101	1-1-	0-0-	+-+-
1010	1101	10--	00--	+0--
1011	1100	0-11	1-10	+-1+

Table 7.5. Output bits that are equal in pairs for either S box.

ular (chosen) bit at an interior round has a chosen fixed value, regardless of the choice of the key. We can also create pairs of plaintexts which differ in a later round only at a particular bit. Lucifer reduced to eight rounds can be attacked using the encryptions of such plaintexts.

Since Feistel did not fix the parameters of Lucifer in his paper[15], we show two attacks on variants with various choices of the blocksize and the P permutation, and with fixed S boxes derived from the S boxes of DES. Other choices of S boxes do not seems to strengthen the resultant ciphers.

7.4.1 First Attack

The following attack breaks eight-round Lucifer with 32-bit blocks, with the DES P permutation and with S boxes based on the third and fourth lines of S1 of DES. Most of the possible choices of the S boxes and the permutation are breakable with a similar complexity.

Table 7.6 describes 450 plaintexts as a Cartesian product of the specified inputs to the S boxes of the first round. These plaintexts cause bit 17 of

S box	Possible input values
S1	3_x, 6_x, A_x, C_x, D_x
S2	2_x
S3	A_x
S4	0_x, 4_x, 8_x, B_x, E_x
S5	6_x
S6	7_x, 8_x, A_x
S7	2_x, 3_x, D_x
S8	2_x, 9_x

Table 7.6. Input values that cause a bit in the fourth round to be zero.

Round	Common input and output values† (in binary)							
$\mathtt{I}_1$	0011	0010	1010	0000	0110	0111	0010	0010
$\mathtt{O}_1$	.0..	1..0	.0.1	.1..	00..	...1	...0	1...
$\mathtt{I}_2$	....	1100	....	10.0	0011	....	....	....
$\mathtt{O}_2$	....	.01.	....	...1	.0.0	....	....	....
$\mathtt{I}_3$	110.	....	....	.0..	....	....	...0	....
$\mathtt{O}_3$	.0..	....	....	....	....	....	....	....
$\mathtt{I}_4$	....	....	....	....	0...	....	....	....

† The first line of the table represents the first plaintext. The other lines represent values that are common to the encryptions of all the 450 plaintexts.

Table 7.7. Common input and output bits of the various rounds.

the input of the fourth round to be zero. The fixed input and output values in the various rounds are given in Table 7.7. $\mathtt{I}_1$ is the plaintext. $\mathtt{O}_i$ denotes the output of the S boxes for input $\mathtt{I}_i$. $\mathtt{I}_{i+1}$ is the input of round $i+1$ which is the permuted value of $\mathtt{O}_i$.

The key bits of the following rounds can be found by the following algorithm:

1. Try all the possible values of the key bits of the eighth, seventh and sixth rounds with the key bits of the four S boxes in the fifth round that are affected by the output of S5 in the fourth round, and the key bit of S5 in the fourth round (total of 29 bits).
2. For each of them, partially decrypt the ciphertexts to get the input bits of S5 in the fourth round. If for any one of them the bit number 17 is non-zero then the tried key is wrong.

3. Using 40 encryptions we get a probability of 2^{-40} for a wrong key to survive, i.e., there is a probability of about $2^{-40} \cdot 2^{29} = 2^{-11}$ that any wrong key remains. The real key must have zero for all the pairs and thus we find 29 key bits (out of $8 \times 8 = 64$).
4. Once these key bits are known, the other key bits can be found by a similar method with the same ciphertexts.

This algorithm has a time complexity of 2^{29} and needs about 29–35 chosen plaintexts.

There are similar attacks on Lucifer with 128-bit blocks with a chosen fixed bit in the fourth round (or possibly even the fifth round for some choices of the P permutation and the S boxes). In these attacks the above algorithm starts by finding 53 out of the $8 \times 32 = 256$ key bits, uses about 53–60 ciphertexts, and has a time complexity of about 2^{53}.

7.4.2 Second Attack

The following attack breaks eight-round Lucifer with 128-bit blocks. This attack is described in general terms to allow any choice of the P permutation.

In the preparation phase of the attack we choose an S box in the second round which will have inputs 8_x and A_x when the two members of each pair are encrypted. If its third bit (with value 2_x) comes from an S box in the first round from the output bit 1 (with value 8_x) then we try another S box (only about three quarters of the S boxes in the second round can be chosen using this particular choice of the S boxes). All the other inputs of the S boxes in the second round should be equal in the pair. At the first round we choose the following values for the bits of the two plaintexts:

1. One S box in the first round has an output bit which enters the third bit of the chosen S box in the second round. If this output bit is:

   bit 2: choose `1011` and `1100` as the input bits.
   bit 3: choose `0011` and `1101` as the input bits.
   bit 4: choose `0001` and `1111` as the input bits.

   These input bits are actual bits of the plaintexts. The outputs of this S box differ only by the bit which enters the chosen S box in the second round.
2. All the other plaintext bits are chosen identically for both members of each pair.

Rounds	Block size	Chosen plaintexts	Operations	Comments
8	128	53	2^{53}	First Attack
8	128	21	2^{21}	Second Attack
8	128	256	2^{9}	Other Variant[37]

Table 7.8. Summary of the attacks on Lucifer.

3. In particular, for the three other S boxes whose output bits enter the chosen S box in the second round, choose input values (using Table 7.3) which cause the output bit that enters the chosen S box in the second round to have identical value under S_0 and under S_1 and such that the value of these bits would be the constant derived from the chosen inputs 8_x and A_x of the S box in the second round.

After the first round the partially encrypted values differ only in one bit (the output of the S box from step 1). Thus, in the second round only one S box has different input values (1000 and 1010, respectively). In the output two bits differ. In the third round two S boxes have different inputs. Their outputs enter seven S boxes in the fourth round (they may enter eight S boxes, but with a proper choice they may enter seven S boxes). The output bits of the seven S boxes enter about 20–28 S boxes in the fifth round. Therefore, the outputs of at least four S boxes do not differ. In the sixth round we choose an S box with one of these bits as its input. We try all the possible values of the key bits of this S box, of the four affected S boxes in the seventh round and of the 16 affected S boxes in the eighth round. For each of their choices we verify the equality of the input bit in the sixth round. Since we try 2^{21} choices and each wrong pair has probability half to succeed, we need about 21–30 pairs to find the value of the 21 key bits. Once these key bits are found, the other key bits can be found with a similar method using the known key bits.

A summary of the results on Lucifer is given in Table 7.8.

8

Differential Cryptanalysis of Hash Functions

8.1 Cryptanalysis of Snefru

Snefru[21] is designed to be a cryptographically strong hash function which hashes messages of arbitrary length into m-bit values (typically 128 bits). The messages are divided into $(512 - m)$-bit chunks and each chunk is mixed with the hashed value computed so far by a randomizing function H. The function H takes a 512-bit input composed of the previous hashed value and the next chunk and calculates an m-bit output. The new hashed value is the output of H. More formally, for any $1 \leq i \leq \#c$:

$$h_i = \mathrm{H}(h_{i-1} \| c_i)$$

where $\#c$ is the number of chunks, '$\|$' is the concatenation operator of bit vectors, c_i is chuck number i and h_0 is an m-bit vector of zeroes. The final output is:

$$\text{output} = \mathrm{H}(h_{\#c} \| \text{length of message in bits}).$$

The process is outlined in Figure 8.1.

The function H is based on a (reversible) 512-bit to 512-bit function E and returns a XOR combination of the first m bits of the input and the last m bits of the output of E. The function E randomizes the data in several

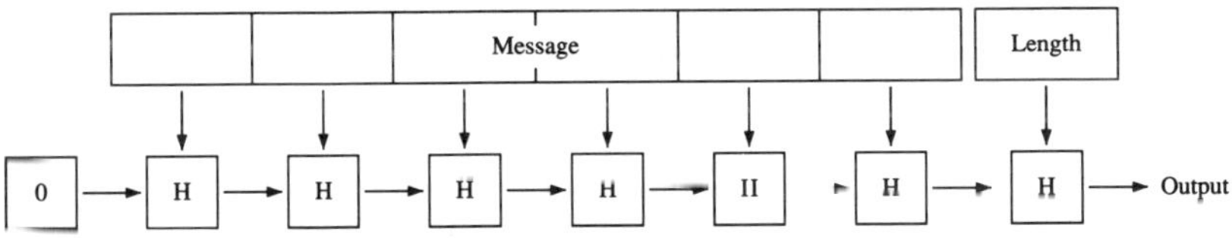

Figure 8.1. Outline of Snefru.

```
function H (int32 input[INPUT_BLOCK_SIZE])
        returns int32 output[OUTPUT_BLOCK_SIZE]
{
  int32 block[INPUT_BLOCK_SIZE];

  block = E(input);

  for i = 0 to OUTPUT_BLOCK_SIZE-1 do
    output[i] = input[i] ⊕ block[INPUT_BLOCK_SIZE-i-1];

  return(output);
}
```

Figure 8.2. The function H.

passes. Each pass is composed of 64 randomizing rounds, where in each one of them a different byte of the data is used as an input to an S box whose output word is XORed with the two neighboring words. The codes of the functions H and E are given by Figures 8.2 and 8.3. In the codes the block sizes are measured in units of 32-bit words and the values of the constants are:

INPUT_BLOCK_SIZE	=	16 (i.e., 512-bit block)
OUTPUT_BLOCK_SIZE	=	4 (for $m = 128$) or 8 (for $m = 256$)
NO_OF_PASSES	=	the number of passes (2, 3 or 4 passes).

A graphic description of the first 18 rounds of the function E is given in Figure 8.4. Each row represents a round. Each column represents a word of data, which is composed of four bytes. The input appears at the top of the figure, and the calculation is done downwards. The bytes used as inputs to the S boxes are surrounded by a thick rectangle. The words which are affected by the output of the S box in each round are painted in gray. After every group of 16 rounds the values of all the words are rotated.

A cryptographically strong hash function is broken if two different messages which hash to the same value are found. In particular, we break Snefru by finding two different chunk-sized messages which hash to the same value, or in other words, finding two inputs of the function H which differ only in the chunk part and have the same output. Unless specified otherwise, we concentrate in the following discussion on two-pass Snefru with $m = 128$ (whose chunks are 384-bit long).

A universal attack on hash functions is based on the birthday paradox. If we hash about $2^{m/2}$ random messages (2^{64} when $m = 128$) then with a high probability we can find among them a pair of messages which hash

```
function E (int32 input[INPUT_BLOCK_SIZE])
        returns int32 output[INPUT_BLOCK_SIZE]
{
  int32 block[INPUT_BLOCK_SIZE];
  int32 SBoxEntry;
  int shift, i, index, byteInWord;

  int shiftTable[4] = {16, 8, 16, 24};

  block = input;
  for index = 0 to NO_OF_PASSES-1 do {                    (for each pass)
    for byteInWord = 0 to 3 do {
      for i = 0 to INPUT_BLOCK_SIZE-1 do {                (for each round)
        SBoxEntry = {fetch entry number block[i] mod 256 of S box
              number 2 · index + (i/2) mod 2};
        block[(i + 1) mod INPUT_BLOCK_SIZE] ⊕= SBoxEntry;
        block[(i - 1) mod INPUT_BLOCK_SIZE] ⊕= SBoxEntry;
      }
      shift = shiftTable[byteInWord];
      for i = 0 to INPUT_BLOCK_SIZE-1 do
        block[i] = {rotate block[i] by shift bits to the right};
    }
  }

  return(output);
}
```

Figure 8.3. The function E.

to the same value. This attack is applicable to any hash function and is independent of its details.

For Snefru we designed a differential cryptanalytic attack which is also independent of the choice of S boxes. Its variants can be used even when the hash function is viewed as a black box with unknown S boxes.

The basic attack is as follows: choose a random chunk-sized message and prepend the 128-bit zero vector (or any previous hashed value calculated from previous chunks) to get the input of the function H. We create a second message from the first one by modifying the two bytes in the eighth and the ninth words which are used as inputs to the S boxes at rounds 56 and 57 (the fourth time we use these words). We hash both messages by the function H and compare the outputs of the two executions. A fraction of 2^{-40} of these pairs of messages are hashed to the same value. Therefore, by hashing about 2^{41} messages we can break Snefru. As described later in this section, the number can be greatly reduced by using more structured messages.

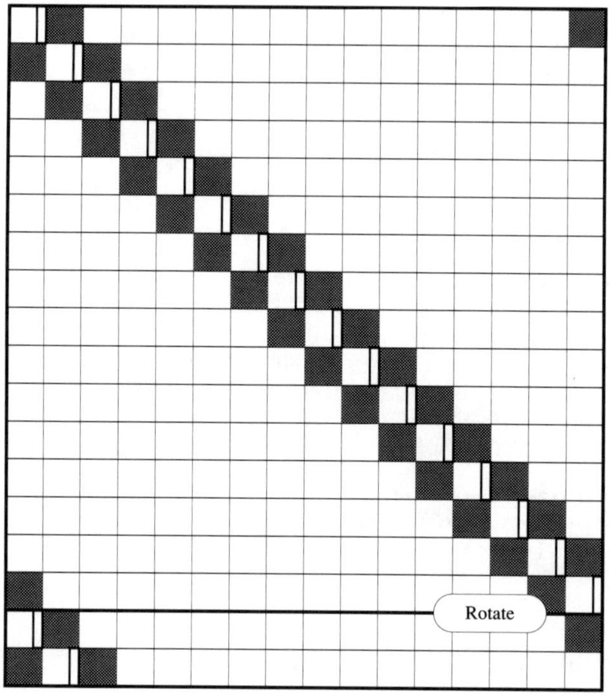

Figure 8.4. Graphic description of the first 18 rounds of the function E.

In the basic attack we use a characteristic which differentiates only zero XOR values from non-zero XOR values and does not a priori fix the values of the non-zero XORs. In round 56 the byte from word eight is used to garble words seven and nine. In a fraction of about 1/256 of the pairs the garbling cancels the differences in the byte in the ninth word. Therefore, for this fraction the XOR of this byte after round 56 is zero and the same values are XORed to the tenth word in both executions. The same values are used as inputs to the S boxes in both executions till the next time a byte of word seven is used at round 71. Round 71 garbles words six and eight by a different value for each execution and so does round 72 to words seven and nine. In a fraction of about 1/256 of the pairs the garbled version of the byte used as input to round 73 in the ninth word cancels its previous XOR value again. Therefore, for this fraction the XOR of this byte after round 72 is zero and the same values are XORed to the tenth word in both executions. The same values are used as inputs to the S boxes in both executions till the next time a byte of word six is used at round 86. The same cancellation should take place five times in rounds 56, 72, 88, 104 and 120. Therefore, the characteristic's probability is about $(1/256)^5 = 2^{-40}$. Each right pair with respect to this characteristic has

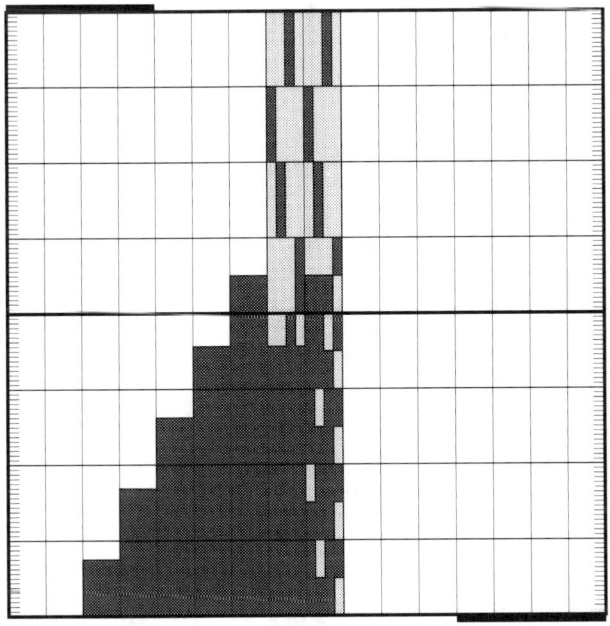

Figure 8.5. Graphic description of the characteristic.

zero XORs at the first m bits of the input and at the last m bits of the output and thus both messages are hashed to the same value. Figure 8.5 is a graphic description of the characteristic. In the figure each column represents a word of data and each row represents 16 rounds (represented by the thin lines along the edges). The gray area in the middle represents the modified words (non-zero XORs) in the characteristic. The brighter gray area represents the bytes with zero XORs in these words. The two black lines at the top-left and the bottom-right corners point to the words which are used in the calculation of the hash value by the function H (for $m = 128$). Since both of them occur in the white (unmodified) part of the block, the two messages hash to the same value. Figure 8.6 describes the modified bytes in intermediate rounds of the characteristic. In this figure each row represents a round. This same attack can break two-pass Snefru with any $m \leq 224$ bits. Similar attacks with modification of bytes of three to seven consecutive words of the input XOR of the characteristic are possible with the same characteristic's probability. Figure 8.7 describes a characteristic which modifies seven bytes.

This attack can be enhanced by using structures of messages. If we choose randomly about $2^{20.5}$ messages out of the 2^{24} messages which differ only in three bytes and hash them we get about $\frac{(2^{20.5})^2}{2} = 2^{40}$ legal pairs of messages which can be used by the attack. With high probability such a

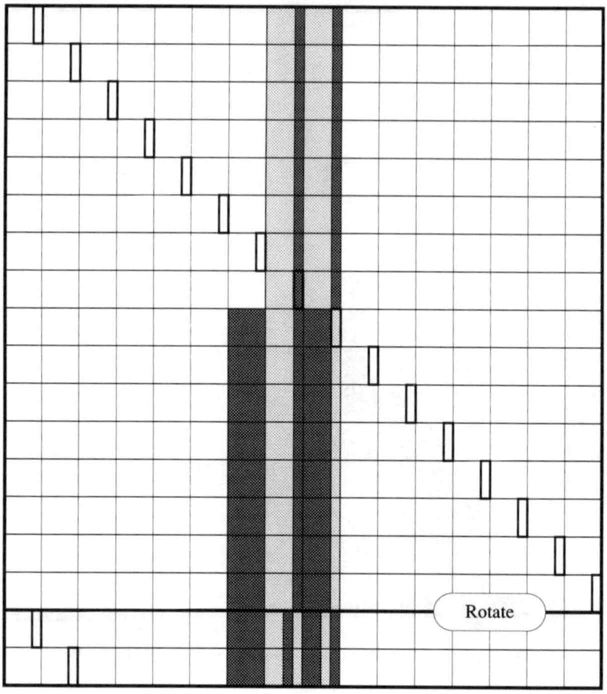

Figure 8.6. Zoomed part of the characteristic.

structure contains a right pair, i.e., a pair whose two messages hash to the same value, and such a pair can be easily found by sorting the $2^{20.5}$ hashed values. A variant of this attack can find a pair of messages composed only from ASCII letters or digits by hashing about $2^{20.5}$ messages which differ by the appropriate subset of bits in four bytes. By modifying up to seven bytes (which is the limit of this attack on two-pass Snefru) we can find pairs of messages hashing to the same value which are composed only from ASCII capital letters, only from ASCII digits or even from sets of eight different characters (for example octal digits) with the same complexity (since $\frac{(8^7)^2}{2} = 2^{41} > 2^{40}$). This attack can also be used when Snefru is considered as a black box which hides the choice of the S boxes.

In a black box attack on three-pass Snefru with $m = 128$ we can modify only three bytes and the characteristic's probability is 2^{-72}. Using structures of 2^{24} messages we obtain about $\frac{(2^{24})^2}{2} = 2^{47}$ pairs in each structure. Therefore, about $\frac{2^{72}}{2^{47}} \cdot 2^{24} = 2^{49}$ messages should be hashed. For three-pass Snefru with $m = 160$ only two bytes can be modified and the complexity of the attack becomes 2^{57}.

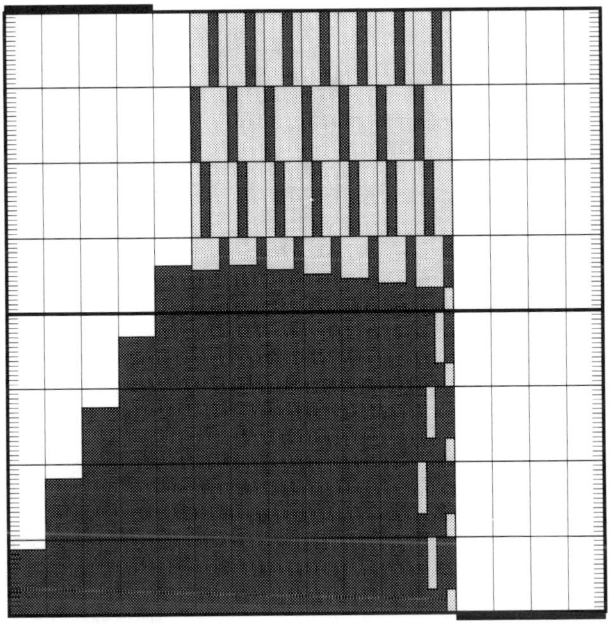

Figure 8.7. A characteristic with modification of seven bytes.

No. of passes	m	Char. prob.	No. mod bytes	Complexity of attack	Birthday complexity	Comments
2	128–192	2^{-40}	3	$2^{20.5}$	2^{64}–2^{96}	
	224		2	2^{25}	2^{112}	
	128–192	2^{-40}	4	$2^{20.5}$	2^{64}–2^{96}	Alphanumeric messages
	224		2	2^{29}	2^{112}	
3	128	2^{-72}	3	2^{49}	2^{64}	
	160		2	2^{57}	2^{80}	

Table 8.1. Summary of the black box attacks on Snefru.

The black box attacks are independent of the (unknown) S boxes. The attack is applicable even if different S boxes are used in different rounds. A summary of the black box attacks on Snefru is given in Table 8.1. Only one byte is modified in each word.

An important observation is that whenever the S boxes are known to the attacker, the modification of the bytes may be done at an intermediate round rather than in the message itself. In this case we choose a message

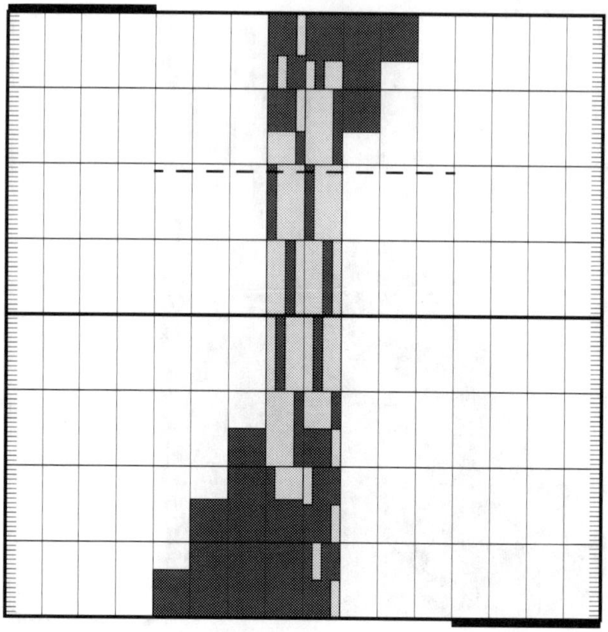

Figure 8.8. A characteristic with modification at an intermediate round.

and hash it, while recording the value of the data block at some intermediate round. We modify the value of bytes of consecutive words that are used in consecutive rounds in the computation. Then, the input of the function E is calculated backwards and its output is calculated forward. From the input and the output of E we calculate the output of H. Figure 8.8 describes a characteristic which modifies the data at the intermediate round denoted by the dashed line. Note that this technique can be applied to hash functions but not to encryption functions, since we cannot compute partially encrypted values without knowing the key.

Another observation is that the values of the last and the first modified bytes can be chosen directly. For each choice of the modifications of all the bytes except the last, there is exactly one possibility for the modified value of the last byte which cancels the difference from the previous word. This value can be easily calculated and thus we can save a factor of 2^8 relative to the characteristic's probability. The first modified bytes can also be chosen (with a small loop) to save another factor of 2^8. Therefore, a total factor of 2^{16} can be saved. Additional choices of bytes do not change the complexity.

An extension of these observations makes it possible to modify up to four bytes in each word and to choose up to twice the number of modified bytes in a word plus one (i.e., up to $2b+1$ bytes depending on the exact characteristic, where b is the number of modified bytes in a word). A characteristic which modifies only one byte in each word is called a *simple characteristic.* A characteristic which modifies more than one byte in a word is called a *complex characteristic.* Note that all the black box attacks described above use simple characteristics (although it is not necessary).

The probability of the simple characteristics of two-pass Snefru described earlier in this section is 2^{-40}. By modifying four bytes at an intermediate round and choosing directly the last and the first of them we get 2^{16} possible data blocks from which we choose and hash about $2^{12.5}$. The number of possible pairs is $\frac{(2^{12.5})^2}{2} = 2^{24}$. Each pair has probability of $2^{-40} \cdot 2^{16} = 2^{-24}$ to be a right pair. Therefore, by hashing $2^{12.5}$ messages we can find a right pair with a high probability. This attack can be used for any $m \leq 192$ bits. Using a complex characteristic we can attack the case of $m = 224$ with the same complexity.

The probability of the simple characteristics of three-pass Snefru is 2^{-72}. By modifying six bytes in an intermediate round and choosing directly the last and the first of them we get 2^{32} possible data blocks, from which we choose and hash about $2^{28.5}$. The number of possible pairs is about $\frac{(2^{28.5})^2}{2} = 2^{56}$. Each pair has a probability of $2^{-72} \cdot 2^{16} = 2^{-56}$ to be a right pair. Therefore, hashing $2^{28.5}$ messages we can find a right pair with a high probability. Modification of six bytes makes it possible to use this attack up to $m \leq 160$. The attacks on three-pass Snefru with $m = 192$ and $m = 224$ hash about $2^{28.5}$ and 2^{33} messages respectively using complex characteristics.

The probability of the simple characteristics of four-pass Snefru is 2^{-104}. Using simple characteristics we can only break the variants with $m = 192$ and $m = 224$ with complexities 2^{81} and 2^{89} respectively. Using the complex characteristic with probability 2^{-160} described in Figure 8.9 we can break four-pass Snefru with up to $m = 192$ with complexity $2^{44.5}$.

A summary of the attacks on Snefru with known S boxes is given in Table 8.2. The number of modified bytes is denoted by the number of modified words times the number of modified bytes in each modified word. The number in parentheses is the number of bytes chosen directly. The S boxes should be known but the attack is independent of their choice. The attack is applicable even if different S boxes are used in different rounds.

This attack can also find many partners which hash to the same value as a given message. For two-pass Snefru, given a message we create new messages by modifying the value of seven bytes by the characteristic in Figure 8.7. By trying about 2^{40} such messages we can find with a high probability a second message which hashes to the same value as the given

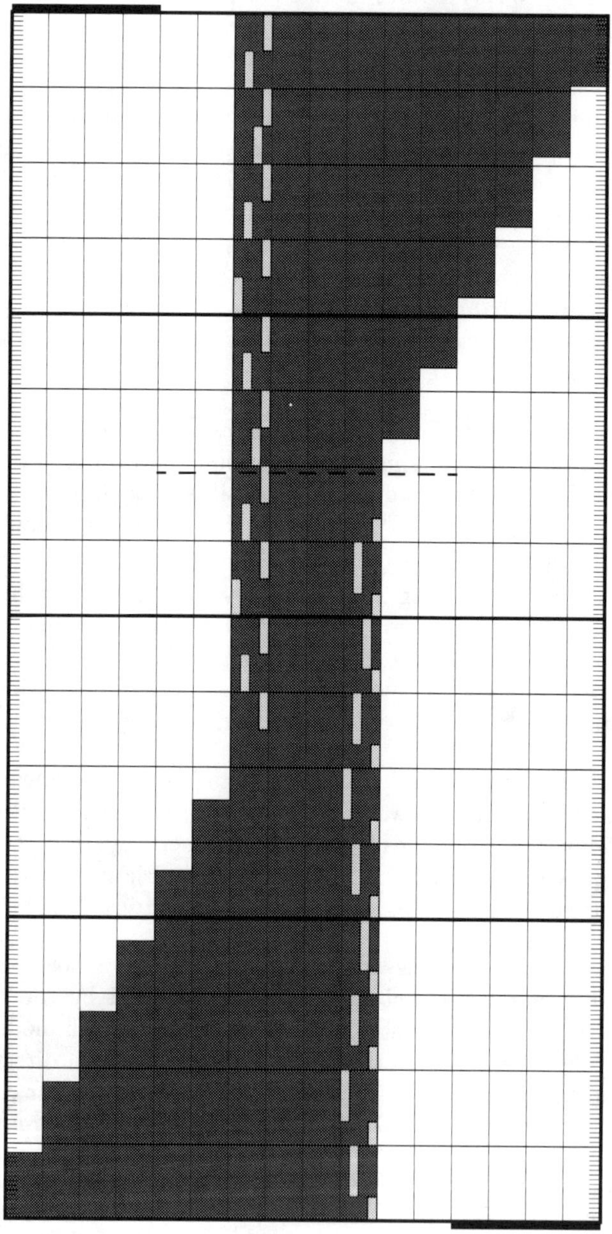

Figure 8.9. A complex four-pass characteristic.

No. of passes	m	Char. prob.	No. mod bytes	Complexity of attack	Birthday complexity	Comments
2	128–192	2^{-40}	4·1 (2)	$2^{12.5}$	2^{64}–2^{96}	
	224		2·1 (2)	2^{25}	2^{112}	
	224	2^{-56}	2·3 (4)	$2^{12.5}$	2^{112}	
	128–192	2^{-40}	4·1 (1)	2^{17}	2^{64}–2^{96}	Alphanumeric
	224		2·1 (1)	2^{29}	2^{112}	messages
3	128–160	2^{-72}	6·1 (2)	$2^{28.5}$	2^{64}–2^{80}	
	192	2^{-80}	4·2 (3)	$2^{28.5}$	2^{96}	
	224	2^{-96}	2·4 (5)	2^{33}	2^{112}	
4	128–192	2^{-160}	4·4 (9)	$2^{44.5}$	2^{64}–2^{96}	
	224	2^{-112}	2·2 (3)	2^{81}	2^{112}	

Table 8.2. Summary of the attacks on Snefru with known S boxes.

No. of passes	m	Char. prob.	No. mod bytes	Complexity of attack	Brute force	Comments
2	128–160	2^{-40}	6·1 (2)	2^{24}	2^{128}–2^{160}	
	128–160		6·1 (0)	2^{40}	2^{128}–2^{160}	Black box
	128–224	2^{-64}	2·4 (5)	2^{24}	2^{128}–2^{224}	
	128–160	2^{-40}	7·1 (1)	2^{32}	2^{128}–2^{160}	Alphanumeric
	128–160		7·1 (0)	2^{40}	2^{128}–2^{160}	Alphanumeric, black box
3	128–224	2^{-96}	2·4 (5)	2^{56}	2^{128}–2^{224}	
4	128–192	2^{-160}	4·4 (9)	2^{88}	2^{128}–2^{192}	

Table 8.3. Summary of the attacks which find partners of given messages.

message. Moreover, the modification of the last modified byte (typically in word 12) may be chosen after the garbling from the previous bytes is known. Therefore, the value of this modified byte can be chosen directly to cancel the garbling, and can decrease the complexity of this attack by a factor of 2^8. If the modification is in a middle round it is possible to verify the value of the first modified byte after choosing the last one directly and decrease the complexity by a total factor of 2^{16} to about 2^{24} hash calculations. This variant can be applied to three-pass and four-pass Snefru as well. A summary of the attacks on Snefru which can find many partners of given messages is given in Table 8.3.

A personal computer implementation of this attack on two-pass Snefru finds a pair of messages which hash to the same value within three minutes. It finds a partner of a given message in about an hour. Typical results of this implementation are:

1. The following two messages hash to the same value by two-pass Snefru. The messages are 48-byte long and are denoted as 12 words. The messages and the hashed value are given in hexadecimal.

- Message 1: `3fe15e26 23b7c030 c7089999 90efc48f a04d87ee 16493392 00046085 00003415 00000000 00000000 00000000 00000000`.
- Message 2: `3fe15e26 23b7c030 c7089999 90efc48f a9a09fee d74af7ae 096c7885 c19ef029 00000000 00000000 00000000 00000000`.
- Common hash value: `c8ff5e2c 8f9cf7c7 f08ddaa7 e4f9b44e`.

2. The following four messages hash to the same value as the (chosen) zero message:

- Message 1: `00000000 00000000 00000000 00000000 00000000 00000000 00000000 00000000 00000000 00000000 00000000 00000000`.
- Message 2: `00000000 f1301600 13dfc53e 4cc3b093 37461661 ccd8b94d 24d9d35f 71471fde 00000000 00000000 00000000 00000000`.
- Message 3: `00000000 1d197f00 2abd3f6f cf33f3d1 8674966a 816e5d51 acd9a905 53c1d180 00000000 00000000 00000000 00000000`.
- Message 4: `00000000 e98c8300 1e777a47 b5271f34 a04974bb 44cc8b62 be4b0efc 18131756 00000000 00000000 00000000 00000000`.
- Common hash value: `2e88e244 e9d4a208 b2d02fbb 72d0eee6`.

3. The following 36-byte messages hash to the same value by two-pass Snefru with $m = 224$:

- Message 1: `5bcc4d9b e1da3df2 a6fb6db0 002eef3f 00000007 00000000 00000000 00000000 00000000`.

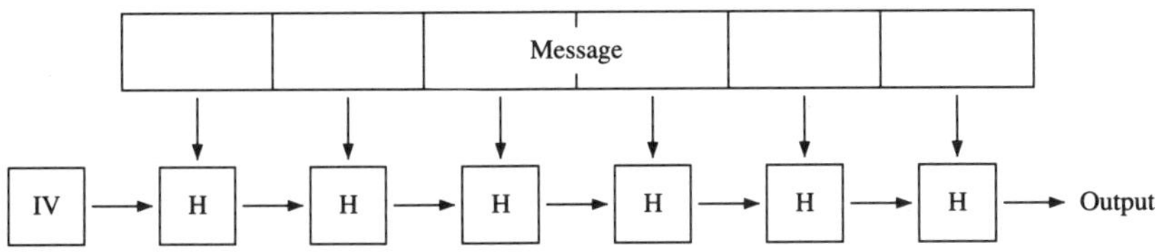

Figure 8.10. Outline of N-Hash.

- Message 2: `eb11879b e1da3d07 1626a76e 002eef3f 00000007 00000000 00000000 00000000 00000000`.
- Common hash value: `70c0577c 3feb6c47 42edcd49 a28241e3 b5e9fc88 1968f18f 1d712965`.

8.2 Cryptanalysis of N-Hash

N-Hash[25] is designed as a cryptographically strong hash function which hashes messages of arbitrary length into 128-bit values. The messages are divided into 128-bit blocks, and each block is mixed with the hashed value computed so far by a randomizing function g. The new hashed value is the XOR of the output of the g-function with the block itself and with the old hashed value. The g-function contains eight randomizing rounds, and each one of them calls an F function (which is similar to the one of FEAL) four times. A graphic description of N-Hash is given in Figures 8.10, 8.11, and 8.12.

We break N-Hash by finding two different 128-bit messages which are hashed to the same 128-bit value. Since the output of the g-function is XORed with its input in order to form the hashed value, it suffices to find a right pair for a characteristic of the g-function in which $\Omega_P = \Omega_T$. After XORing the input with the output of the g-function, the hashed value XOR becomes zero and thus the two messages have the same hashed value.

The following characteristic is a three-round iterative characteristic with probability 2^{-16} (N-Hash does not swap the two halves after each round since the swap operation is part of the round itself. Therefore, the concatenation of the characteristic Ω^1 with the characteristic Ω^2 is possible whenever $\Omega^1_T = \Omega^2_P$ without swapping). In the description of this characteristic we refer to the value $80\ 60\ 80\ 00_x$ as ψ and to the value $80\ E0\ 80\ 00_x$

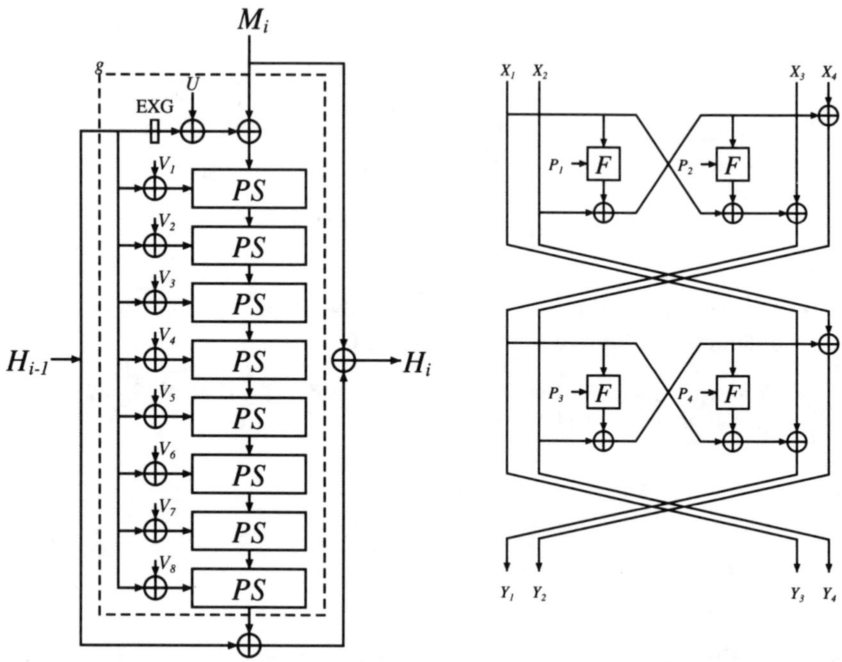

Figure 8.11. The function H and one round (PS) of N-Hash.

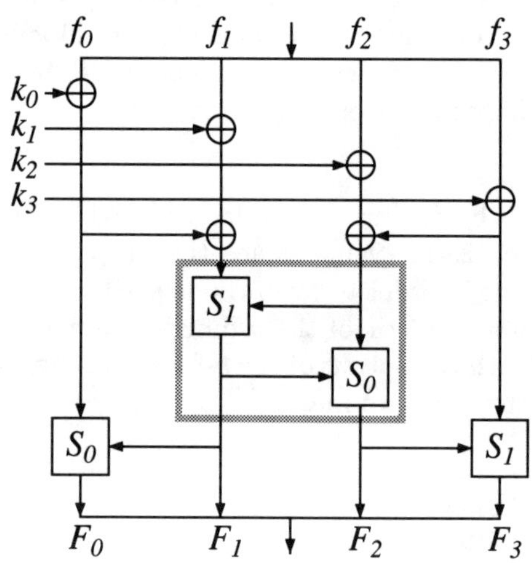

Figure 8.12. The F function of N-Hash.

as φ. Note that both $\psi \rightarrow (\psi \oplus \varphi)$ and $\varphi \rightarrow (\psi \oplus \varphi)$ with probability $\frac{1}{4}$ by the F function. The behavior of the XORs in the F function in this characteristic is similar to their behavior in the iterative characteristic of FEAL. The characteristic itself is based on the input difference:

$$\Omega_P = (\psi, \psi, 0, 0).$$

With probability $\frac{1}{256}$ the difference after the first round is

$$(0, 0, \varphi, \varphi).$$

With probability $\frac{1}{16}$ the difference after the second round is

$$(\psi, \psi, \varphi, \varphi).$$

And with probability $\frac{1}{16}$ the difference after the third round is

$$\Omega_T = \Omega_P = (\psi, \psi, 0, 0).$$

Therefore, the probability of the characteristic is 2^{-16}.

A pair of messages whose XOR equals Ω_P has probability $\left(2^{-16}\right)^2 = 2^{-32}$ to have Ω_T as its output XOR after the sixth round of the g-function, and thus to have the same hashed value after their inputs and outputs are XORed by the six-round variant of N-Hash. Instead of trying about 2^{32} random pairs of messages we can choose only pairs from a smaller set in which the characteristic is guaranteed to be satisfied in the four F functions of the first round. The pairs in this set are chosen by the following algorithm. For each F function in the first round we search a priori a list of input pairs for which the input XOR and the output XOR are as expected by the characteristic. To get a new pair we choose a random input pair for each F function and from the four input pairs and their corresponding outputs we deduce the two messages backwards. Therefore, the probability in this set is increased by a factor of 256, and only about 2^{24} such pairs have to be tested in order to find a pair of messages which hash to the same value.

Since we use a three-round iterative characteristic, this specific attack works only for variants of N-Hash whose number of rounds is divisible by three. Table 8.4 describes the results of this attack. We can see from the table that this attack is faster than the birthday attack (whose complexity is 2^{64}) for variants of N-Hash with up to 12 rounds.

The attack on N-Hash with six rounds was implemented on a personal computer and the following pairs of messages (as well as many others) were found within about two hours:

- – `CAECE595 127ABF3C 1ADE09C8 1F9AD8C2`

Number of Rounds	Complexity
3	2^{8}
6	2^{24}
9	2^{40}
12	2^{56}
15	2^{72}

Table 8.4. Summary of the attack on N-Hash.

  - 4A8C6595 921A3F3C 1ADE09C8 1F9AD8C2
  - Common hash value: 12B931A6 399776B7 640B9289 36C2EF1D

-
  - 5878BE49 F2962D67 30661E17 0C38F35E
  - D8183E49 72F6AD67 30661E17 0C38F35E
  - Common hash value: 29B0FE97 3D179E0E 5B147598 137D28CF.

9

Non-Differential Cryptanalysis of DES with a Small Number of Rounds

In this chapter we describe several novel attacks on DES reduced to 3–6 rounds which are not based on the ciphertext pair paradigm. These attacks are of three kinds: ciphertext only attacks, known plaintext attacks and statistical known plaintext attacks. Compared to differential attacks, they analyze fewer ciphertexts but require more time.

9.1 Ciphertext Only Attacks

9.1.1 A Three-Round Attack

This attack assumes that the eight plaintext bytes are ASCII characters whose most significant bits are zeroes, and crucially depends on the fact that the initial permutation (IP) moves the most significant bits of all these bytes into a single byte. This byte is the fifth byte of the permuted plaintext which is the first byte of the right half. Given a ciphertext $T = (T_L, T_R)$ we can easily calculate eight bits of the output of the second round by $B = a \oplus c = P_R \oplus T_R$. From Table A.4 we see that these eight bits are the output of seven S boxes in the second round (two of them are outputs of S5). The attack is as follows:

1. We try all the possibilities of the key bits entering S5 in the second round and all the key bits entering the six S boxes S1, S2, S3, S4, S6 and S8 in the third round whose output bits are XORed into the data bits entering S5 in the second round. Three of these bits are counted twice (in both rounds) and thus only 39 bits are exhaustively tried.
2. Using the tried key bits and any ciphertext we can calculate the output of the six S boxes in the third round and the input and the

output of S5 in the second round.

3. We compare the two computed output bits of S5 in the second round to their expected value. If they are different then the value of the 39 key bits is wrong. A quarter of the tried keys have the expected value. By trying additional ciphertexts we can discard additional key values. We stop when only one candidate remains.

Since we start with 2^{39} possible keys and only $\frac{1}{4}$ of them survive each test, we need about $\log_4 2^{39} = 19.5$ ciphertexts. When the correct 39 key bits are determined, we can exhaustively try all the possible values of the remaining 17 bits by checking whether the decoded plaintexts are ASCII characters. This ciphertext only attack requires a total of 2^{39} steps and 20 ciphertexts to break DES reduced to three rounds.

9.1.2 Another Three-Round Attack

In this attack we assume that the plaintext bytes belong to a smaller set in which the three most significant bits are constant. Such sets are the ASCII capital letters, the ASCII lower case letters and the ASCII digits. The three most significant bits of all the eight plaintext bytes are packed into three bytes by the initial permutation. These three bytes are the first byte of the left half and the first and second bytes of the right half. Since the first and second bytes of the right half are constant in all the plaintext blocks, the inputs of S2 and S3 in the first round are constant and thus their outputs are constant as well. We can calculate the output of the third round by $C = P_L \oplus A \oplus T_L$. Two bits of the eight constant bits in P_L have corresponding constant bits in A: one of them is an output of S2 and the other is an output of S3 (see Table A.4). Since T_L is known, the two bits in C are known up to a XOR with a constant. These bits are outputs of S2 and S3. Trying all the 64 possibilities of the key bits entering S2 in the third round, we can check that in any pair of ciphertexts the output bit of S2 satisfies $C_1 \oplus T_{L1} = C_2 \oplus T_{L2}$. Since half the keys satisfy this condition, we need about $1 + \log_2 64 = 7$ ciphertexts to find the six key bits entering S2 in the third round. The same ciphertexts can be used to find the six key bits entering S3 in the third round. This leaves 44 unknown key bits which can be found later.

9.1.3 A Four-Round Attack

This attack is an extension of the previous three-round attack and assumes (as before) that the three most significant bits of each plaintext byte are constant. In this attack two bits of C are found by $C = A \oplus P_L \oplus T_R$. Then two output bits (one in S2 and one in S3 in the third round) are known up to a constant. We try all the possible key values of the six key bits of S2 (or similarly S3) in the third round and all the possible key values of the six S boxes in the fourth round whose output bits are XORed with the data bits entering S2 (or S3) in the third round. We try a total of 36 key bits entering the fourth round and six key bits entering the third round, but five bits are common (six when using S3) and thus we have to try 2^{37} possible key values. We need about $1 + \log_2 2^{37} = 1 + 37 = 38$ ciphertexts to make the computed key unique.

9.2 Known Plaintext Attacks

9.2.1 A Three-Round Attack

The DES key scheduling algorithm divides the 56 key bits into two 28-bit key registers (called the C register and the D register, see Appendix A.1). Each register supplies the key bits to the same four S boxes in all the rounds. The following attack exploits this particular aspect of DES.

Consider DES reduced to three rounds with a single known plaintext and its corresponding ciphertext. The exclusive-or value of the output of the first round and the third round is known by $A \oplus C = P_L \oplus T_L$.

We first try all the 2^{28} possibilities of one key register. Each candidate makes it possible to compute the output of four S boxes in the first round and the output of the same S boxes in the third round. We know their expected exclusive-or value. Since the value has 16 bits, only about 2^{-16} of the candidates survive this test. Thus we get about 2^{12} possibilities for the first 28 bits of the key. In a similar way we get about 2^{12} possibilities for the other 28 bits of the key. Therefore we find about $2^{12} \cdot 2^{12} = 2^{24}$ possibilities for the full key, which can be exhaustively searched. The complexity of this algorithm is about 2^{29}, and can be reduced to about 2^{21} by choosing the key bits entering each S box sequentially rather than in parallel, and discarding partial keys as soon as they lead to a contradiction. Using several known plaintexts, the complexity of this attack can be reduced to 2^8.

9.3 Statistical Known Plaintext Attacks

9.3.1 A Three-Round Attack

In this attack we use the fact that in a difference distribution table, if we know that the output XOR is zero then the input XOR is zero with probability $\frac{1}{4}$. Given the plaintext and the ciphertext of an encryption, we can easily calculate $A \oplus C = P_L \oplus T_L$. Then the following algorithm is used for each S box. Choose only the encryptions whose output XOR from this S box is zero ($\frac{1}{16}$ of the encryptions): $S_{Oa} \oplus S_{Oc} = 0$. If $S_{Ia} \oplus S_{Ic} = 0$ then the corresponding bits of $a \oplus c = P_R \oplus T_R$ equal $S_{Ka} \oplus S_{Kc}$. We count the number of occurrences of each such value. The right value is suggested by about $\frac{1}{4}$ of the encryptions. Each incorrect value is suggested by about $\frac{3}{4} \cdot \frac{1}{63}$ of the encryptions. The value that appears most frequently is likely to be the value of $S_{Ka} \oplus S_{Kc}$. This algorithm is used for each S box and thus we find $8 \cdot 6 = 48$ bits that are XORs of the actual key bits. Then trying 2^8 possibilities we can find the full 56 bit key. We need about four occurrences of the right value of the key XOR for each S box, i.e., a total of about $4 \cdot 4 \cdot 16 = 256$ random plaintext/ciphertext pairs.

9.3.2 A Four-Round Attack

In this attack we use the fact that for all the S boxes there is a weak correlation between the value of the XOR of the four output bits and the value of bit number 2 of the input (this phenomenon was pointed out by Shamir[34], but at the time it did not seen to make cryptanalysis easier). In particular, for every two inputs of an S box, if the XOR of the four output bits of the first input equals the corresponding value of the second input then both bits 2 of the input are equal with a certain probability. This probability is different for each S box and varies between 0.56 and 0.70.

Given a plaintext and its corresponding ciphertext, we can easily calculate $S_{Oa} \oplus S_{Oc}$ by $A \oplus C = P_L \oplus T_R$. Then the following algorithm can be used separately for each S box. For every encryption calculate the (single bit) XOR of the four output bits of the first round and the four output bits of the third round by the above equation. This value is likely to be equal to the XOR of bits number 2 of the inputs of the S box in these two rounds. S_{Ia} is known up to a XOR with the key (by the plaintext) and thus bit number 2 of the input in the third round is known up to a XOR with a constant with a high probability. This constant is the XOR of the corresponding bit number 2 in $S_{Ka} \oplus S_{Kc}$. Thus by $D = T_L \oplus c$ we find the corresponding output bit in the fourth round up to that constant with

By	Finding	Average	Best tradeoff	
S box	Bits of	Probability	Values	Encryptions
S1	S4	66%	16	75
S2	S8	57%	8	195
S3	S1	58%	7	240
S4	S2	56%	9	370
S5	S1	70%	16	50
S6	S8	61%	8	135
S7	S5	60%	14	210
S8	S6	63%	12	120

Table 9.1. Number of encryptions needed to find S_{Kd} for each S box.

a high probability. We try all the 64 possibilities of the key bits entering the corresponding S box in the fourth round and the two possibilities of the constant and verify that the specific output bit of the S box equals its expected value. The right key value is counted in about 56%–70% of the encryptions, depending on the exact S box. Any wrong key value is counted in about half of the encryptions. The key value which is counted most frequently is likely to be the right value. For each tried S box, this attack finds a total of seven bits: six of them are actual key bits and the seventh is an XOR of two key bits.

The attack obtains the best results when the probability is as high as possible. To increase the probability we use only encryptions with specific values of $S_{Oa} \oplus S_{Oc}$ which maximize this probability. For instance, when $S5_{Oa} \oplus S5_{Oc} = 0$ this probability is about 0.81. There is a tradeoff between the number of allowed values and the corresponding probability. As the number of allowed values increases, the probability decreases so we need more data to carry out the attack. However, as the number of allowed values decreases we need more data to make the occurrence of these values sufficiently probable. Table 9.1 describes the best tradeoff achievable by this attack. To make the best use of this attack it is advisable to use about 200 plaintext/ciphertext pairs, from which we can find almost 28 key bits, and search exhaustively for the (about 2^{28}) remaining possibilities of the key. Using about 370 plaintext/ciphertext pairs we can find almost 42 key bits and search exhaustively for the (about 2^{14}) remaining possibilities of the key.

9.3.3 A Five-Round Attack

This five-round attack is similar to the previous algorithm. We can calculate $B \oplus D = P_R \oplus T_R$. Then an input XOR bit of the S box in the second and fourth round is known with probability between 0.56 and 0.70. As a result, an output bit of $A \oplus E$ is known up to a XOR with a constant by $P_L \oplus A = b$ and $d \oplus E = T_L$ and thus $A \oplus E = b \oplus d \oplus P_L \oplus T_L$. Using a counting method that counts on the key bits entering the same S box in the first round, the key bits entering the corresponding S box in the fifth round, and the constant, we can find 13 bits of the key: six of them are actual key bits from the first round, six are actual key bits from the fifth round, and the thirteenth bit is an XOR of two key bits. The amount of data needed to find these 13 key bits is about the same as in the previous attack.

9.3.4 A Six-Round Attack

This attack is again similar to the attack on five rounds, but we also have to count all the possibilities of the 36 subkey bits of the sixth round which enter S boxes whose output bits enter the counted S box in the fifth round by the P permutation. In total we count on 49 bits. The total complexity of this attack is about 2^{55}–2^{56} but the basic operation (which is similar to a single application of the F function) is simpler than an encryption, and thus the time needed is marginally faster than exhaustive search.

Appendix A

Description of DES

The Data Encryption Standard (DES)[28] is a blockcipher which encrypts 64-bit plaintexts into 64-bit ciphertexts under 56-bit keys. In the description of DES, the bit locations are numbered from 1 to 64 for 64-bit values, and similarly for shorter values. Bit number 1 is the most significant bit of the first byte, and bit number 64 is the least significant bit of the eighth byte. The 56-bit key is represented as a 64-bit value, in which 56 bits are the key bits, while all the bits whose numbers are multiples of eight are used as parity bits, and are ignored by the algorithm.

The first part of the algorithm permutes the plaintext by an *initial permutation* IP while the final part of the algorithm permutes the bits by the inverse of the initial permutation, called *final permutation*. The body of the algorithm, which is executed between these two permutations, divides the block of the data into two 32-bit halves: the *right half* of the data and the *left half* of the data. The basic step of the algorithm is called a *round*, in which two new halves are calculated using the previous two halves and a 48-bit *subkey*, which is calculated by a *key scheduling algorithm* from the key. In DES, the body of the algorithm is composed of 16 rounds, which use 16 different subkeys K1, K2, ..., K16, where K1 is used in the first round, K2 in used in the second round, and so on. In the round itself, an F *function* is calculated with the right half of the data and the subkey as inputs. The left half of the data is XORed with the output of the F function. Between any two rounds, the two halves are exchanged (but not before the first round nor after the last round). Figure A.1 describes this structure of DES.

The F function expands the 32-bit right half to 48 bits by an E *expansion* which duplicates 16 bits, and the result is XORed with the 48-bit subkey. Then, the resultant 48-bit value is subjected to eight S *boxes*, called S1, S2, ..., S8, each one of which maps six bits into four bits using a particular lookup table. The 32 output bits of the S boxes are concatenated and permuted by a P *permutation*, whose output is the final output of the F function. The F function of DES is outlined in Figure 3.2.

The particular choices of the initial permutation, of the P permutation

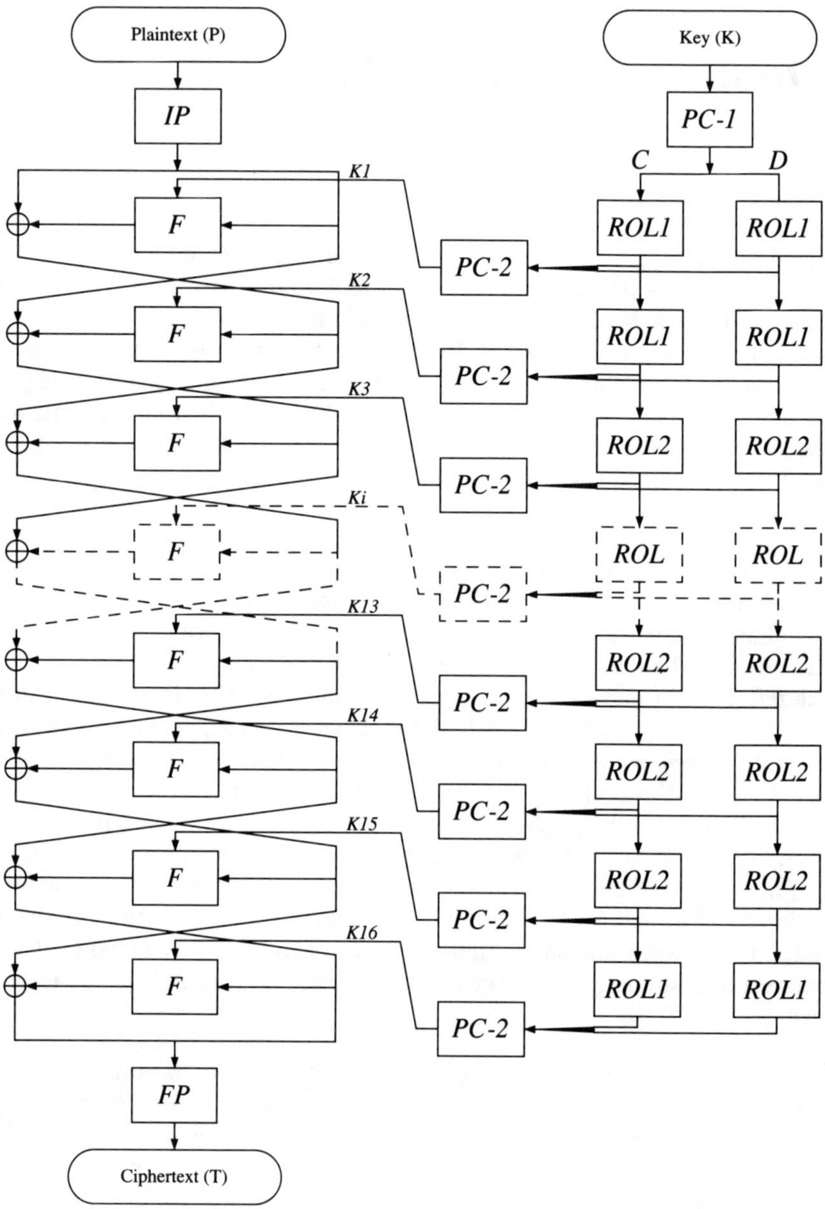

Figure A.1. Outline of DES and of its key scheduling algorithm.

58	50	42	34	26	18	10	2
60	52	44	36	28	20	12	4
62	54	46	38	30	22	14	6
64	56	48	40	32	24	16	8
57	49	41	33	25	17	9	1
59	51	43	35	27	19	11	3
61	53	45	37	29	21	13	5
63	55	47	39	31	23	15	7

Table A.1. The initial permutation.

16	7	20	21
29	12	28	17
1	15	23	26
5	18	31	10
2	8	24	14
32	27	3	9
19	13	30	6
22	11	4	25

Table A.2. The P permutation.

and of the E expansion of DES are given in Tables A.1, A.2 and A.3 respectively. These tables are arranged as bit selection tables. Each location corresponds to an output bit, and contains the number of the input bit which is copied into that location. For example, the first bit in the output of the P permutation has the same value as bit number 16 of its input. For easy reference, we also include Table A.4 which describes how the output bits of each S box in any particular round are permuted and expanded towards the S boxes in the following round.

32	1	2	3	4	5
4	5	6	7	8	9
8	9	10	11	12	13
12	13	14	15	16	17
16	17	18	19	20	21
20	21	22	23	24	25
24	25	26	27	28	29
28	29	30	31	32	1

Table A.3. The E expansion.

From				To			
Bit no.	S box and bit		Bit Mask (hex)	Bit no.	S box and bit	Bit Mask (hex)	Missing S box
1	S1	1	80 00 00 00	9	S2.6 S3.2	00 80 00 00	S7
2		2	40 00 00 00	17	S4.6 S5.2	00 00 80 00	
3		3	20 00 00 00	23	S6.4	00 00 02 00	
4		4	10 00 00 00	31	S8.4	00 00 00 02	
5	S2	1	08 00 00 00	13	S3.6 S4.2	00 08 00 00	S6
6		2	04 00 00 00	28	S7.5 S8.1	00 00 00 10	
7		3	02 00 00 00	2	S1.3	40 00 00 00	
8		4	01 00 00 00	18	S5.3	00 00 40 00	
9	S3	1	00 80 00 00	24	S6.5 S7.1	00 00 01 00	S1
10		2	00 40 00 00	16	S4.5 S5.1	00 01 00 00	
11		3	00 20 00 00	30	S8.3	00 00 00 04	
12		4	00 10 00 00	6	S2.3	04 00 00 00	
13	S4	1	00 08 00 00	26	S7.3	00 00 00 40	S2
14		2	00 04 00 00	20	S5.5 S6.1	00 00 10 00	
15		3	00 02 00 00	10	S3.3	00 40 00 00	
16		4	00 01 00 00	1	S8.6 S1.2	80 00 00 00	
17	S5	1	00 00 80 00	8	S2.5 S3.1	01 00 00 00	S8
18		2	00 00 40 00	14	S4.3	00 04 00 00	
19		3	00 00 20 00	25	S6.6 S7.2	00 00 00 80	
20		4	00 00 10 00	3	S1.4	20 00 00 00	
21	S6	1	00 00 08 00	4	S1.5 S2.1	10 00 00 00	S4
22		2	00 00 04 00	29	S7.6 S8.2	00 00 00 08	
23		3	00 00 02 00	11	S3.4	00 20 00 00	
24		4	00 00 01 00	19	S5.4	00 00 20 00	
25	S7	1	00 00 00 80	32	S8.5 S1.1	00 00 00 01	S5
26		2	00 00 00 40	12	S3.5 S4.1	00 10 00 00	
27		3	00 00 00 20	22	S6.3	00 00 04 00	
28		4	00 00 00 10	7	S2.4	02 00 00 00	
29	S8	1	00 00 00 08	5	S1.6 S2.2	08 00 00 00	S3
30		2	00 00 00 04	27	S7.4	00 00 00 20	
31		3	00 00 00 02	15	S4.4	00 02 00 00	
32		4	00 00 00 01	21	S5.6 S6.2	00 00 08 00	

Table A.4. Expanded P permutation.

The S boxes of DES are six-bit to four-bit lookup tables. Each S box maps 64 possible input values into 16 output values. In the standard description of DES, the S boxes are described as four permutations of the numbers 0,. . . ,15. In this description, the middle four bits of the six input bits denote the value to be permuted, while the outer two bits (bit 1 and bit 6) choose the permutation. The standard choice of the S boxes of DES is described in Tables A.5–A.12. Table A.13 describes the input values which correspond

14	4	13	1	2	15	11	8	3	10	6	12	5	9	0	7
0	15	7	4	14	2	13	1	10	6	12	11	9	5	3	8
4	1	14	8	13	6	2	11	15	12	9	7	3	10	5	0
15	12	8	2	4	9	1	7	5	11	3	14	10	0	6	13

Table A.5. S box S1.

15	1	8	14	6	11	3	4	9	7	2	13	12	0	5	10
3	13	4	7	15	2	8	14	12	0	1	10	6	9	11	5
0	14	7	11	10	4	13	1	5	8	12	6	9	3	2	15
13	8	10	1	3	15	4	2	11	6	7	12	0	5	14	9

Table A.6. S box S2.

to each entry in the standard description of the S boxes.

A.1 The Key Scheduling Algorithm

The key scheduling algorithm calculates the values of the 16 48-bit subkeys K1, K2, ..., K16 from the 56-bit key. These subkeys are later used as inputs to the F functions in the various rounds of the encryption algorithm. The first part of the key scheduling algorithm permutes the 56 key bits by a permutation called PC-1 which is described in Table A.14 and divides them into two 28-bit key registers called the C register and the D register. The key bits are numbered from 1 to 64, while the eight bits whose numbers are multiples of eight (8, 16, 24, ..., 64) are parity bits, and thus only 56 bits are participating in the algorithm itself. The bits of the C register are

10	0	9	14	6	3	15	5	1	13	12	7	11	4	2	8
13	7	0	9	3	4	6	10	2	8	5	14	12	11	15	1
13	6	4	9	8	15	3	0	11	1	2	12	5	10	14	7
1	10	13	0	6	9	8	7	4	15	14	3	11	5	2	12

Table A.7. S box S3.

7	13	14	3	0	6	9	10	1	2	8	5	11	12	4	15
13	8	11	5	6	15	0	3	4	7	2	12	1	10	14	9
10	6	9	0	12	11	7	13	15	1	3	14	5	2	8	4
3	15	0	6	10	1	13	8	9	4	5	11	12	7	2	14

Table A.8. S box S4.

2	12	4	1	7	10	11	6	8	5	3	15	13	0	14	9
14	11	2	12	4	7	13	1	5	0	15	10	3	9	8	6
4	2	1	11	10	13	7	8	15	9	12	5	6	3	0	14
11	8	12	7	1	14	2	13	6	15	0	9	10	4	5	3

Table A.9. S box S5.

12	1	10	15	9	2	6	8	0	13	3	4	14	7	5	11
10	15	4	2	7	12	9	5	6	1	13	14	0	11	3	8
9	14	15	5	2	8	12	3	7	0	4	10	1	13	11	6
4	3	2	12	9	5	15	10	11	14	1	7	6	0	8	13

Table A.10. S box S6.

4	11	2	14	15	0	8	13	3	12	9	7	5	10	6	1
13	0	11	7	4	9	1	10	14	3	5	12	2	15	8	6
1	4	11	13	12	3	7	14	10	15	6	8	0	5	9	2
6	11	13	8	1	4	10	7	9	5	0	15	14	2	3	12

Table A.11. S box S7.

13	2	8	4	6	15	11	1	10	9	3	14	5	0	12	7
1	15	13	8	10	3	7	4	12	5	6	11	0	14	9	2
7	11	4	1	9	12	14	2	0	6	10	13	15	3	5	8
2	1	14	7	4	10	8	13	15	12	9	0	3	5	6	11

Table A.12. S box S8.

0	2	4	6	8	10	12	14	16	18	20	22	24	26	28	30
1	3	5	7	9	11	13	15	17	19	21	23	25	27	29	31
32	34	36	38	40	42	44	46	48	50	52	54	56	58	60	62
33	35	37	39	41	43	45	47	49	51	53	55	57	59	61	63

Table A.13. The input values which correspond to the standard description of the S boxes.

57	49	41	33	25	17	9
1	58	50	42	34	26	18
10	2	59	51	43	35	27
19	11	3	60	52	44	36
63	55	47	39	31	23	15
7	62	54	46	38	30	22
14	6	61	53	45	37	29
21	13	5	28	20	12	4

Table A.14. PC-1.

57, 49, ..., 36 of the key and the bits of the D register are 63, 55, ..., 4 of the key. In each round the registers C and D are rotated one or two bits to the left, as is defined in Table A.15. Then, PC-2 takes the concatenated value of the C and the D registers, selects 48 bits (24 bits from each key register) and permutes them to form the 48-bit subkey of the corresponding round. PC-2 is described in Table A.16. The outline of the key scheduling algorithm is given in Figure A.1.

Round	1	2	3	4	5	6	7	8	9	10	11	12	13	14	15	16
Rotations	1	1	2	2	2	2	2	2	1	2	2	2	2	2	2	1

Table A.15. Number of rotations in the key scheduling algorithm.

14	17	11	24	1	5
3	28	15	6	21	10
23	19	12	4	26	8
16	7	27	20	13	2
41	52	31	37	47	55
30	40	51	45	33	48
44	49	39	56	34	53
46	42	50	36	29	32

Table A.16. PC-2.

A.2 DES Modes of Operation

The standard includes several modes of operation in which DES can be used[29].

The simplest mode of operation is the Electronic Code Book (ECB) mode. In this mode, any plaintext P is divided into 64-bit blocks $P = P_1P_2P_3\ldots P_m$, and all the plaintext blocks are encrypted under a key K into ciphertext blocks by $T_i = \mathrm{DES}(P_i, K)$. The ciphertext is the concatenated value of the ciphertext blocks $T = T_1T_2T_3\ldots T_m$.

A more complicated mode of operation is the Cipher Block Chaining (CBC) mode. In this mode, each plaintext block is encrypted after it is mixed with the previous ciphertext block by $T_i = \mathrm{DES}(P_i \oplus T_{i-1}, K)$. Again, the ciphertext is the concatenated value of the ciphertext blocks $T = T_1T_2T_3\ldots T_m$. This mode requires an initial value T_0 (which is also called IV).

The other two modes of operation are feedback modes which generate long pseudo-random bit streams by repeatedly encrypting an initial value. The ith block of pseudo-random bits V_i is then XORed with the ith plaintext block P_i to form the ith ciphertext block $T_i = P_i \oplus V_i$.

In the Output Feedback (OFB) mode, V_i is calculated by encrypting V_{i-1} by $V_i = \mathrm{DES}(V_{i-1}, K)$, and an initial value V_0 (which is also called IV) is required.

In the Cipher Feedback (CFB) mode, V_i is calculated by encrypting the previous ciphertext block T_{i-1} by $V_i = \mathrm{DES}(T_{i-1}, K)$, and an initial value T_0 (which is also called IV) is required.

Both feedback modes have variants with shift-registers which use fewer than 64 bits from V_{i-1} or T_{i-1} as feedback. However, these variants are slower than the 64-bit variants, and the OFB variants with less than 64 bits of feedback have short cycles[10].

Appendix B

The Difference Distribution Tables of DES

The difference distribution table of an S box shows how many input pairs have each combination of the input XOR and output XOR values. In the table, each row corresponds to one input XOR value and each column corresponds to one output XOR value (both in hexadecimal notation). The value in each entry counts the number of pairs (in decimal notation, among all the $64 \cdot 64 = 4096$ possible pairs) whose input XORs and output XORs are as specified by the row and by the column of the entry. Since there are only $64 \cdot 16 = 1024$ entries in the table, the average value of the number of pairs in each entry is four.

The first row in the table is special. Since in the first row the input XOR is zero, the output XOR must be zero as well. Therefore, the entry with zero output XOR counts all the 64 pairs whose input XOR is zero and the other entries in this row do not count any pair at all. In other rows, many possible values arise. For example, for the input XOR 1_x, eleven output XORs are possible. For the input XOR 34_x and the output XOR 2_x the number of possible pairs is 16, and thus a quarter of the pairs with this input XOR lead to the output XOR 2_x.

Input XOR	Output XOR															
	0_x	1_x	2_x	3_x	4_x	5_x	6_x	7_x	8_x	9_x	A_x	B_x	C_x	D_x	E_x	F_x
0_x	64	0	0	0	0	0	0	0	0	0	0	0	0	0	0	0
1_x	0	0	0	6	0	2	4	4	0	10	12	4	10	6	2	4
2_x	0	0	0	8	0	4	4	4	0	6	8	6	12	6	4	2
3_x	14	4	2	2	10	6	4	2	6	4	4	0	2	2	2	0
4_x	0	0	0	6	0	10	10	6	0	4	6	4	2	8	6	2
5_x	4	8	6	2	2	4	4	2	0	4	4	0	12	2	4	6
6_x	0	4	2	4	8	2	6	2	8	4	4	2	4	2	0	12
7_x	2	4	10	4	0	4	8	4	2	4	8	2	2	2	4	4
8_x	0	0	0	12	0	8	8	4	0	6	2	8	8	2	2	4
9_x	10	2	4	0	2	4	6	0	2	2	8	0	10	0	2	12
A_x	0	8	6	2	2	8	6	0	6	4	6	0	4	0	2	10
B_x	2	4	0	10	2	2	4	0	2	6	2	6	6	4	2	12
C_x	0	0	0	8	0	6	6	0	0	6	6	4	6	6	14	2
D_x	6	6	4	8	4	8	2	6	0	6	4	6	0	2	0	2
E_x	0	4	8	8	6	6	4	0	6	6	4	0	0	4	0	8
F_x	2	0	2	4	4	6	4	2	4	8	2	2	2	6	8	8
10_x	0	0	0	0	0	0	2	14	0	6	6	12	4	6	8	6
11_x	6	8	2	4	6	4	8	6	4	0	6	6	0	4	0	0
12_x	0	8	4	2	6	6	4	6	6	4	2	6	6	0	4	0
13_x	2	4	4	6	2	0	4	6	2	0	6	8	4	6	4	6
14_x	0	8	8	0	10	0	4	2	8	2	2	4	4	8	4	0
15_x	0	4	6	4	2	2	4	10	6	2	0	10	0	4	6	4
16_x	0	8	10	8	0	2	2	6	10	2	0	2	0	6	2	6
17_x	4	4	6	0	10	6	0	2	4	4	4	6	6	6	2	0
18_x	0	6	6	0	8	4	2	2	2	4	6	8	6	6	2	2
19_x	2	6	2	4	0	8	4	6	10	4	0	4	2	8	4	0
$1A_x$	0	6	4	0	4	6	6	6	6	2	2	0	4	4	6	8
$1B_x$	4	4	2	4	10	6	6	4	6	2	2	4	2	2	4	2
$1C_x$	0	10	10	6	6	0	0	12	6	4	0	0	2	4	4	0
$1D_x$	4	2	4	0	8	0	0	2	10	0	2	6	6	6	14	0
$1E_x$	0	2	6	0	14	2	0	0	6	4	10	8	2	2	6	2
$1F_x$	2	4	10	6	2	2	2	8	6	8	0	0	0	4	6	4
20_x	0	0	0	10	0	12	8	2	0	6	4	4	4	2	0	12
21_x	0	4	2	4	4	8	10	0	4	4	10	0	4	0	2	8
22_x	10	4	6	2	2	8	2	2	2	2	6	0	4	0	4	10
23_x	0	4	4	8	0	2	6	0	6	6	2	10	2	4	0	10
24_x	12	0	0	2	2	2	2	0	14	14	2	0	2	6	2	4
25_x	6	4	4	12	4	4	4	10	2	2	2	0	4	2	2	2
26_x	0	0	4	10	10	10	2	4	0	4	6	4	4	4	2	0
27_x	10	4	2	0	2	4	2	0	4	8	0	4	8	8	4	4
28_x	12	2	2	8	2	6	12	0	0	2	6	0	4	0	6	2
29_x	4	2	2	10	0	2	4	0	0	14	10	2	4	6	0	4
$2A_x$	4	2	4	6	0	2	8	2	2	14	2	6	2	6	2	2
$2B_x$	12	2	2	2	4	6	6	2	0	2	6	2	6	0	8	4
$2C_x$	4	2	2	4	0	2	10	4	2	2	4	8	8	4	2	6
$2D_x$	6	2	6	2	8	4	4	4	2	4	6	0	8	2	0	6
$2E_x$	6	6	2	2	0	2	4	6	4	0	6	2	12	2	6	4
$2F_x$	2	2	2	2	2	6	8	8	2	4	4	6	8	2	4	2
30_x	0	4	6	0	12	6	2	2	8	2	4	4	6	2	2	4
31_x	4	8	2	10	2	2	2	2	6	0	0	2	2	4	10	8
32_x	4	2	6	4	4	2	2	4	6	6	4	8	2	2	8	0
33_x	4	4	6	2	10	8	4	2	4	0	2	2	4	6	2	4
34_x	0	8	16	6	2	0	0	12	6	0	0	0	0	8	0	6
35_x	2	2	4	0	8	0	0	0	14	4	6	8	0	2	14	0
36_x	2	6	2	2	8	0	2	2	4	2	6	8	6	4	10	0
37_x	2	2	12	4	2	4	4	10	4	4	2	6	0	2	2	4
38_x	0	6	2	2	2	0	2	2	4	6	4	4	4	6	10	10
39_x	6	2	2	4	12	6	4	8	4	0	2	4	2	4	4	0
$3A_x$	6	4	6	4	6	8	0	6	2	2	6	2	2	6	4	0
$3B_x$	2	6	4	0	0	2	4	6	4	6	8	6	4	4	6	2
$3C_x$	0	10	4	0	12	0	4	2	6	0	4	12	4	4	2	0
$3D_x$	0	8	6	2	2	6	0	8	4	4	0	4	0	12	4	4
$3E_x$	4	8	2	2	2	4	4	14	4	2	0	2	0	8	4	4
$3F_x$	4	8	4	2	4	0	2	4	4	2	4	8	8	6	2	2

Table B.1. The difference distribution table of S1.

Input	Output XOR															
XOR	0_x	1_x	2_x	3_x	4_x	5_x	6_x	7_x	8_x	9_x	A_x	B_x	C_x	D_x	E_x	F_x
0_x	64	0	0	0	0	0	0	0	0	0	0	0	0	0	0	0
1_x	0	0	0	4	0	2	6	4	0	14	8	6	8	4	6	2
2_x	0	0	0	2	0	4	6	4	0	0	4	6	10	10	12	6
3_x	4	8	4	8	4	6	4	2	4	2	2	4	6	2	0	4
4_x	0	0	0	0	0	6	0	14	0	6	10	4	10	6	4	4
5_x	2	0	4	8	2	4	6	6	2	0	8	4	2	4	10	2
6_x	0	12	6	4	6	4	6	2	2	10	2	8	2	0	0	0
7_x	4	6	6	4	2	4	4	2	6	4	2	4	4	6	0	6
8_x	0	0	0	4	0	4	0	8	0	10	16	6	6	0	6	4
9_x	14	2	4	10	2	8	2	6	2	4	0	0	2	2	2	4
A_x	0	6	6	2	10	4	10	2	6	2	2	4	2	2	4	2
B_x	6	2	2	0	2	4	6	2	10	2	0	6	6	4	4	8
C_x	0	0	0	4	0	14	0	10	0	6	2	4	4	8	6	6
D_x	6	2	6	2	10	2	0	4	0	10	4	2	8	2	2	4
E_x	0	6	12	8	0	4	2	0	8	2	4	4	6	2	0	6
F_x	0	8	2	0	6	6	8	2	4	4	4	6	8	0	4	2
10_x	0	0	0	8	0	4	10	2	0	2	8	10	0	10	6	4
11_x	6	6	4	6	4	0	6	4	8	2	10	2	2	4	0	0
12_x	0	6	2	6	2	4	12	4	6	4	0	4	4	6	2	2
13_x	4	0	4	0	8	6	6	0	0	2	0	6	4	8	2	14
14_x	0	6	6	4	10	0	2	12	6	2	2	2	4	4	2	2
15_x	6	8	2	0	8	2	0	2	2	2	2	2	2	14	10	2
16_x	0	8	6	4	2	2	4	2	6	4	6	2	6	0	6	6
17_x	6	4	8	6	4	4	0	4	6	2	4	4	4	2	4	2
18_x	0	6	4	6	10	4	0	2	4	8	0	0	4	8	2	6
19_x	2	4	6	4	4	2	4	2	6	4	6	8	0	6	4	2
$1A_x$	0	6	8	4	2	4	2	2	8	2	2	6	2	4	4	8
$1B_x$	0	6	4	4	0	12	6	4	2	2	2	4	4	2	10	2
$1C_x$	0	4	6	6	12	0	4	0	10	2	6	2	0	0	10	2
$1D_x$	0	6	2	2	6	0	4	16	4	4	2	0	0	4	6	8
$1E_x$	0	1	8	2	10	0	6	0	8	4	0	2	4	4	0	6
$1F_x$	4	2	6	6	2	2	2	4	8	6	10	6	4	0	0	2
20_x	0	0	0	2	0	12	10	4	0	0	0	2	14	2	8	10
21_x	0	4	6	8	2	10	4	2	2	6	4	2	6	2	0	6
22_x	4	12	8	4	2	2	0	0	2	8	8	6	0	6	0	2
23_x	8	2	0	2	8	4	2	6	4	8	2	2	6	4	2	4
24_x	10	4	0	0	0	4	0	2	6	8	6	10	8	0	2	4
25_x	6	0	12	2	8	6	10	0	0	8	2	6	0	0	2	2
26_x	2	2	4	4	2	2	10	14	2	0	4	2	2	4	6	4
27_x	6	0	0	2	6	4	2	4	4	4	8	4	8	0	6	6
28_x	8	0	8	2	4	12	2	0	2	6	2	0	6	2	0	10
29_x	0	2	4	10	2	8	6	4	0	10	0	2	10	0	2	4
$2A_x$	4	0	4	8	6	2	4	4	6	6	2	6	2	2	4	4
$2B_x$	2	2	6	4	0	2	2	6	2	8	8	4	4	4	8	2
$2C_x$	10	6	8	6	0	6	4	4	4	2	4	4	0	0	2	4
$2D_x$	2	2	2	4	0	0	0	2	8	4	4	6	10	2	14	4
$2E_x$	2	4	0	2	10	4	2	0	2	2	6	2	8	8	10	2
$2F_x$	12	4	6	8	2	6	2	8	0	4	0	2	0	8	2	0
30_x	0	4	0	2	4	4	8	6	10	6	2	12	0	0	0	6
31_x	0	10	2	0	6	2	10	2	6	0	2	0	6	6	4	8
32_x	8	4	6	0	6	4	4	8	4	6	8	0	2	2	2	0
33_x	2	2	6	10	2	0	0	6	4	4	12	8	4	2	2	0
34_x	0	12	6	4	6	0	4	4	4	0	4	6	4	2	4	4
35_x	0	12	4	6	2	4	4	0	10	0	0	8	0	8	0	6
36_x	8	2	4	0	4	0	4	2	0	8	4	2	6	16	2	2
37_x	6	2	2	2	6	6	4	8	2	2	6	2	2	2	4	8
38_x	0	8	8	10	6	2	2	0	4	0	4	2	4	0	4	10
39_x	0	2	0	0	8	0	10	4	10	0	8	4	4	4	4	6
$3A_x$	4	0	2	8	4	2	2	2	4	8	2	0	4	10	10	2
$3B_x$	16	4	4	2	8	2	2	6	4	4	4	2	0	2	2	2
$3C_x$	0	2	6	2	8	4	6	0	10	2	2	4	4	10	4	0
$3D_x$	0	16	10	2	4	2	4	2	8	0	0	8	0	6	2	0
$3E_x$	4	4	0	10	2	4	2	14	4	2	6	6	0	0	6	0
$3F_x$	4	0	0	2	0	8	2	4	0	2	4	4	4	14	10	6

Table B.2. The difference distribution table of S2.

Input	Output XOR															
XOR	0_x	1_x	2_x	3_x	4_x	5_x	6_x	7_x	8_x	9_x	A_x	B_x	C_x	D_x	E_x	F_x
0_x	64	0	0	0	0	0	0	0	0	0	0	0	0	0	0	0
1_x	0	0	0	2	0	4	2	12	0	14	0	4	8	2	6	10
2_x	0	0	0	2	0	2	0	8	0	4	12	10	4	6	8	8
3_x	8	6	10	4	8	6	0	6	4	4	0	0	0	4	2	2
4_x	0	0	0	4	0	2	4	2	0	12	8	4	6	8	10	4
5_x	6	2	4	8	6	10	6	2	2	8	2	0	2	0	4	2
6_x	0	10	6	6	10	0	4	12	2	4	0	0	6	4	0	0
7_x	2	0	0	4	4	4	4	2	10	4	4	8	4	4	4	6
8_x	0	0	0	10	0	4	4	6	0	6	6	6	6	0	8	8
9_x	10	2	0	2	10	4	6	2	0	6	0	4	6	2	4	6
A_x	0	10	6	0	14	6	4	0	4	6	6	0	4	0	2	2
B_x	2	6	2	10	2	2	4	0	4	2	6	0	2	8	14	0
C_x	0	0	0	8	0	12	12	4	0	8	0	4	2	10	2	2
D_x	8	2	8	0	0	4	2	0	2	8	14	2	6	2	4	2
E_x	0	4	4	2	4	2	4	4	10	4	4	4	4	4	2	8
F_x	4	6	4	6	2	2	4	8	6	2	6	2	0	6	2	4
10_x	0	0	0	4	0	12	4	8	0	4	2	6	2	14	0	8
11_x	8	2	2	6	4	0	2	0	8	4	12	2	10	0	2	2
12_x	0	2	8	2	4	8	0	8	8	0	2	2	4	2	14	0
13_x	4	4	12	0	2	2	2	10	2	2	2	2	4	4	4	8
14_x	0	6	4	4	6	4	6	2	8	6	6	2	2	0	0	8
15_x	4	8	2	8	2	4	8	0	4	2	2	2	2	6	8	2
16_x	0	6	10	2	8	4	2	0	2	2	2	8	4	6	4	4
17_x	0	6	6	0	6	2	4	4	6	2	2	10	6	8	2	0
18_x	0	8	4	6	6	0	6	2	4	0	4	2	10	0	6	6
19_x	4	2	4	8	4	2	10	2	2	2	6	8	2	6	0	2
$1A_x$	0	8	6	4	4	0	6	4	4	8	0	10	2	2	2	4
$1B_x$	4	10	2	0	2	4	2	4	8	2	2	8	4	2	8	2
$1C_x$	0	6	8	8	4	2	8	0	12	0	10	0	4	0	2	0
$1D_x$	0	2	0	6	2	8	4	6	2	0	4	2	4	10	0	14
$1E_x$	0	4	8	2	4	6	0	4	10	0	2	6	4	8	4	2
$1F_x$	0	6	8	0	10	6	4	6	4	2	2	10	4	0	0	2
20_x	0	0	0	0	0	4	4	8	0	2	2	4	10	16	12	2
21_x	10	8	8	0	8	4	2	4	0	6	6	6	0	0	2	0
22_x	12	6	4	4	2	4	10	2	0	4	4	2	4	4	0	2
23_x	2	2	0	6	0	2	4	0	4	12	4	2	6	4	8	8
24_x	4	8	2	12	6	4	2	10	2	2	2	4	2	0	4	0
25_x	6	0	2	0	8	2	0	2	8	8	2	2	4	4	10	6
26_x	6	2	0	4	4	0	4	0	4	2	14	0	8	10	0	6
27_x	0	2	4	16	8	6	6	6	0	2	4	4	0	2	2	2
28_x	6	2	10	0	6	4	0	4	4	2	4	8	2	2	8	2
29_x	0	2	8	4	0	4	0	6	4	10	4	8	4	4	4	2
$2A_x$	2	6	0	4	2	4	4	6	4	8	4	4	4	2	4	6
$2B_x$	10	2	6	6	4	4	8	0	4	2	2	0	2	4	4	6
$2C_x$	10	4	6	2	4	2	2	2	4	10	4	4	0	2	6	2
$2D_x$	4	2	4	4	4	2	4	16	2	0	0	4	4	2	6	6
$2E_x$	4	0	2	10	0	6	10	4	2	6	6	2	2	0	2	8
$2F_x$	8	2	0	0	4	4	4	2	6	4	6	2	4	8	4	6
30_x	0	10	8	6	2	0	4	2	10	4	4	6	2	0	6	0
31_x	2	6	2	0	4	2	8	8	2	2	2	0	2	12	6	6
32_x	2	0	4	8	2	8	4	4	8	4	2	8	6	2	0	2
33_x	4	4	6	8	6	6	0	2	2	2	6	4	12	0	0	2
34_x	0	6	2	2	16	2	2	2	12	2	4	0	4	2	0	8
35_x	4	6	0	10	8	0	2	2	6	0	0	6	2	10	2	6
36_x	4	4	4	4	0	6	6	4	4	4	4	4	0	6	2	8
37_x	4	8	2	4	2	2	6	0	2	4	8	4	10	0	6	2
38_x	0	8	12	0	2	2	6	6	2	10	2	2	0	8	0	4
39_x	2	6	4	0	6	4	6	4	8	0	4	4	2	4	8	2
$3A_x$	6	0	2	2	4	6	4	4	4	2	2	6	12	2	6	2
$3B_x$	2	2	6	0	0	10	4	8	4	2	4	8	4	4	0	6
$3C_x$	0	2	4	2	12	2	0	6	2	0	2	8	4	6	4	10
$3D_x$	4	6	8	6	2	2	2	2	10	2	6	6	2	4	2	0
$3E_x$	8	6	4	4	2	10	2	0	2	2	4	2	4	2	10	2
$3F_x$	2	6	4	0	0	10	8	2	2	8	6	4	6	2	0	4

Table B.3. The difference distribution table of S3.

Input XOR	Output XOR															
	0_x	1_x	2_x	3_x	4_x	5_x	6_x	7_x	8_x	9_x	A_x	B_x	C_x	D_x	E_x	F_x
0_x	64	0	0	0	0	0	0	0	0	0	0	0	0	0	0	0
1_x	0	0	0	0	0	16	16	0	0	16	16	0	0	0	0	0
2_x	0	0	0	8	0	4	4	8	0	4	4	8	8	8	8	0
3_x	8	6	2	0	2	4	8	2	6	0	4	6	0	6	2	8
4_x	0	0	0	8	0	0	12	4	0	12	0	4	8	4	4	8
5_x	4	2	2	8	2	12	0	2	2	0	12	2	8	2	2	4
6_x	0	8	8	4	8	8	0	0	8	0	8	0	4	0	0	8
7_x	4	2	6	4	6	0	16	6	2	0	0	2	4	2	6	4
8_x	0	0	0	4	0	8	4	8	0	4	8	8	4	8	8	0
9_x	8	4	4	4	4	0	8	4	4	0	0	4	4	4	4	8
A_x	0	6	6	0	6	4	4	6	6	4	4	6	0	6	6	0
B_x	0	12	0	8	0	0	0	0	12	0	0	12	8	12	0	0
C_x	0	0	0	4	0	8	4	8	0	4	8	8	4	8	8	0
D_x	8	4	4	4	4	0	0	4	4	8	0	4	4	4	4	8
E_x	0	6	6	4	6	0	4	6	6	4	0	6	4	6	6	0
F_x	0	6	6	4	6	4	0	6	6	0	4	6	4	6	6	0
10_x	0	0	0	0	0	8	12	4	0	12	8	4	0	4	4	8
11_x	4	2	2	16	2	4	0	2	2	0	4	2	16	2	2	4
12_x	0	0	0	8	0	4	4	8	0	4	4	8	8	8	8	0
13_x	8	2	6	0	6	4	0	6	2	8	4	2	0	2	6	8
14_x	0	8	8	0	8	0	8	0	8	8	0	0	0	0	0	16
15_x	8	4	4	0	4	8	0	4	4	0	8	4	0	4	4	8
16_x	0	8	8	4	8	8	0	0	8	0	8	0	4	0	0	8
17_x	4	6	2	4	2	0	0	2	6	16	0	6	4	6	2	4
18_x	0	8	8	8	8	4	0	0	8	0	4	0	8	0	0	8
19_x	4	4	4	0	4	4	16	4	4	0	4	4	0	4	4	4
$1A_x$	0	6	6	4	6	0	4	6	6	4	0	6	4	6	6	0
$1B_x$	0	6	6	4	6	4	0	6	6	0	4	6	4	6	6	0
$1C_x$	0	8	8	8	8	4	0	0	8	0	4	0	8	0	0	8
$1D_x$	4	4	4	0	4	4	0	4	4	16	4	4	0	4	4	4
$1E_x$	0	6	6	0	6	4	4	6	6	4	4	6	0	6	6	0
$1F_x$	0	0	12	8	12	0	0	12	0	0	0	0	8	0	12	0
20_x	0	0	0	8	0	0	0	12	0	0	0	12	8	12	12	0
21_x	0	4	8	0	8	4	8	8	4	0	4	4	0	4	8	0
22_x	8	2	2	0	2	4	8	6	2	8	4	6	0	6	6	0
23_x	4	6	2	8	2	4	0	2	6	0	4	6	8	6	2	4
24_x	0	6	6	4	6	4	0	6	6	0	4	6	4	6	6	0
25_x	0	8	4	4	4	0	0	4	8	8	0	8	4	8	4	0
26_x	0	6	6	0	6	4	8	2	6	8	4	2	0	2	2	8
27_x	4	6	2	8	2	4	0	2	6	0	4	6	8	6	2	4
28_x	16	4	4	0	4	4	4	4	4	4	4	4	0	4	4	0
29_x	0	6	2	8	2	4	0	2	6	8	4	6	8	6	2	0
$2A_x$	0	2	2	16	2	4	4	2	2	4	4	2	16	2	2	0
$2B_x$	8	0	4	0	4	8	16	4	0	0	8	0	0	0	4	8
$2C_x$	8	4	4	4	4	0	8	4	4	8	0	4	4	4	4	0
$2D_x$	4	2	6	4	6	8	0	6	2	0	8	2	4	2	6	4
$2E_x$	16	0	0	0	0	16	0	0	0	0	16	0	0	0	0	16
$2F_x$	16	0	0	0	0	0	16	0	0	16	0	0	0	0	0	16
30_x	0	6	6	4	6	4	0	6	6	0	4	6	4	6	6	0
31_x	0	8	4	4	4	0	0	4	8	8	0	8	4	8	4	0
32_x	16	6	6	4	6	0	4	2	6	4	0	2	4	2	2	0
33_x	0	2	6	4	6	8	8	6	2	0	8	2	4	2	6	0
34_x	0	12	12	8	12	0	0	0	12	0	0	0	8	0	0	0
35_x	0	4	8	0	8	4	8	8	4	0	4	4	0	4	8	0
36_x	0	2	2	4	2	0	4	6	2	4	0	6	4	6	6	16
37_x	0	2	6	4	6	8	8	6	2	0	8	2	4	2	6	0
38_x	0	4	4	0	4	4	4	4	4	4	4	4	0	4	4	16
39_x	0	6	2	8	2	4	0	2	6	8	4	6	8	6	2	0
$3A_x$	0	4	4	0	4	8	8	4	4	8	8	4	0	4	4	0
$3B_x$	16	4	4	0	4	0	0	4	4	0	0	4	0	4	4	16
$3C_x$	0	4	4	4	4	0	8	4	4	8	0	4	4	4	4	8
$3D_x$	4	2	6	4	6	8	0	6	2	0	8	2	4	2	6	4
$3E_x$	0	2	2	8	2	12	4	2	2	4	12	2	8	2	2	0
$3F_x$	8	4	0	8	0	0	0	0	4	16	0	4	8	4	0	8

Table B.4. The difference distribution table of S4.

Input	Output XOR															
XOR	0_x	1_x	2_x	3_x	4_x	5_x	6_x	7_x	8_x	9_x	A_x	B_x	C_x	D_x	E_x	F_x
0_x	64	0	0	0	0	0	0	0	0	0	0	0	0	0	0	0
1_x	0	0	0	4	0	10	8	6	0	4	2	2	12	10	2	4
2_x	0	0	0	4	0	10	6	4	0	6	4	2	4	8	10	6
3_x	8	2	4	6	4	4	2	2	6	8	6	4	4	0	2	2
4_x	0	0	0	8	0	4	10	6	0	6	6	4	8	6	0	6
5_x	12	2	0	4	0	4	8	2	4	0	16	2	0	2	0	8
6_x	0	8	4	6	4	6	2	2	4	4	6	0	6	0	2	10
7_x	2	0	4	8	4	2	6	6	2	8	6	2	2	0	6	6
8_x	0	0	0	2	0	8	10	4	0	4	10	4	8	4	4	6
9_x	8	6	0	4	0	6	6	2	2	10	2	8	6	2	0	2
A_x	0	6	8	6	0	8	0	0	8	10	4	2	8	0	0	4
B_x	4	2	2	4	8	10	6	4	2	6	2	2	6	2	2	2
C_x	0	0	0	10	0	2	10	2	0	6	10	6	6	6	2	4
D_x	10	4	2	2	0	6	16	0	0	2	10	2	2	4	0	4
E_x	0	6	4	8	4	6	10	2	4	4	4	2	4	0	2	4
F_x	4	4	0	8	0	2	0	2	8	2	4	2	8	4	4	12
10_x	0	0	0	0	0	4	4	12	0	2	8	10	4	6	12	2
11_x	6	6	10	10	4	0	2	6	2	4	0	6	2	4	2	0
12_x	0	2	4	2	10	4	0	10	8	6	0	6	0	6	6	0
13_x	0	0	6	2	8	0	0	4	4	6	2	8	2	8	10	4
14_x	0	12	2	6	4	0	4	4	8	4	4	4	6	2	4	0
15_x	4	8	0	2	8	0	2	4	2	2	4	2	4	8	8	6
16_x	0	6	10	2	14	0	2	2	4	4	0	6	0	4	6	4
17_x	0	6	8	4	8	4	0	2	8	4	0	2	2	8	6	2
18_x	0	10	8	0	6	4	0	4	4	4	6	4	4	4	0	6
19_x	0	4	6	2	4	4	2	6	4	2	2	4	12	2	10	0
$1A_x$	0	2	16	2	12	2	0	6	4	0	0	4	0	4	4	8
$1B_x$	2	8	12	0	0	2	2	6	8	4	0	6	0	0	8	6
$1C_x$	0	10	2	6	6	6	6	4	8	2	0	4	4	4	2	0
$1D_x$	4	6	2	0	8	2	4	6	6	0	8	6	2	4	2	4
$1E_x$	0	2	6	2	4	0	0	2	12	2	2	6	2	10	10	4
$1F_x$	0	6	8	4	8	8	0	6	6	2	0	6	0	6	2	2
20_x	0	0	0	8	0	8	2	6	0	4	4	4	6	6	8	8
21_x	0	0	0	6	6	2	6	4	6	10	14	4	0	0	4	2
22_x	14	4	0	10	0	2	12	2	2	2	10	2	0	0	2	2
23_x	2	0	0	4	2	2	10	4	0	8	8	2	6	8	0	8
24_x	6	2	8	4	4	4	6	2	2	6	6	2	6	2	2	2
25_x	6	0	0	8	2	8	2	6	6	4	2	2	4	2	6	6
26_x	12	0	0	4	0	4	4	4	0	8	4	0	12	8	0	4
27_x	12	2	0	2	0	12	2	2	4	4	8	4	8	2	2	0
28_x	2	8	4	6	2	4	6	0	6	6	4	0	2	2	2	10
29_x	6	4	6	8	8	4	6	2	0	0	2	2	10	0	2	4
$2A_x$	4	4	0	2	2	4	6	2	0	0	6	4	10	4	4	12
$2B_x$	4	6	2	6	0	0	12	2	0	4	12	2	6	4	0	4
$2C_x$	8	6	2	6	4	8	6	0	4	4	0	2	6	0	6	2
$2D_x$	4	4	0	4	0	6	4	2	4	12	0	4	4	6	4	6
$2E_x$	6	0	2	4	0	6	6	4	2	10	6	10	6	2	0	0
$2F_x$	10	4	0	2	2	6	10	2	0	2	2	4	6	2	2	10
30_x	0	4	8	4	6	4	0	6	10	4	2	4	2	6	4	0
31_x	0	6	6	4	10	2	0	0	4	4	0	0	4	6	12	6
32_x	4	6	0	2	6	4	6	0	6	0	4	6	4	10	6	0
33_x	8	10	0	14	8	0	0	8	2	0	2	4	0	4	4	0
34_x	0	4	4	2	14	4	0	8	6	8	2	2	0	4	6	0
35_x	0	4	16	0	8	4	0	4	4	4	0	8	0	4	4	4
36_x	4	4	4	6	2	2	2	12	2	4	4	8	2	4	4	0
37_x	4	2	2	2	4	2	0	8	2	2	2	12	6	2	8	6
38_x	0	4	8	4	12	0	0	8	10	2	0	0	0	4	2	10
39_x	0	8	12	0	2	2	2	2	12	4	0	8	0	4	4	4
$3A_x$	0	14	4	0	4	6	0	0	6	2	10	8	0	0	4	6
$3B_x$	0	2	2	2	4	4	8	6	8	2	2	2	6	14	2	0
$3C_x$	0	0	10	2	6	0	0	2	6	2	2	10	2	4	10	8
$3D_x$	0	6	12	2	4	8	0	8	8	2	2	0	2	2	4	4
$3E_x$	4	4	10	0	2	4	8	8	2	2	0	2	6	8	4	0
$3F_x$	8	6	6	0	4	2	2	4	4	2	8	6	2	4	6	0

Table B.5. The difference distribution table of S5.

Input	Output XOR															
XOR	0_x	1_x	2_x	3_x	4_x	5_x	6_x	7_x	8_x	9_x	A_x	B_x	C_x	D_x	E_x	F_x
0_x	64	0	0	0	0	0	0	0	0	0	0	0	0	0	0	0
1_x	0	0	0	6	0	2	6	2	0	4	2	4	6	16	14	2
2_x	0	0	0	2	0	10	6	10	0	2	4	8	6	6	8	2
3_x	0	8	0	8	0	6	4	6	4	4	4	12	2	4	2	0
4_x	0	0	0	8	0	0	8	0	0	6	8	10	2	4	10	8
5_x	10	2	4	4	4	8	8	4	2	2	0	4	0	8	0	4
6_x	0	8	4	4	8	4	2	2	12	0	2	6	6	2	2	2
7_x	6	6	4	0	2	10	2	2	2	2	6	6	8	0	6	2
8_x	0	0	0	6	0	2	16	4	0	2	6	2	4	12	6	4
9_x	10	4	2	6	0	2	6	2	4	0	8	6	4	4	2	4
A_x	0	14	4	4	0	2	2	2	10	4	4	4	6	4	2	2
B_x	4	6	2	0	2	2	12	8	2	2	2	6	8	2	0	6
C_x	0	0	0	12	0	10	4	6	0	8	4	4	2	12	2	0
D_x	12	0	2	10	6	4	4	2	4	2	6	0	2	6	0	4
E_x	0	6	4	0	4	4	10	8	6	2	4	6	2	0	6	2
F_x	2	2	2	2	6	2	6	2	10	4	8	2	6	4	4	2
10_x	0	0	0	8	0	8	0	12	0	4	2	6	8	4	6	6
11_x	6	2	6	4	6	2	6	4	6	6	4	2	4	0	6	0
12_x	0	8	4	2	0	4	2	0	4	10	6	2	8	6	4	4
13_x	6	6	12	0	12	2	0	6	6	2	0	4	0	2	4	2
14_x	0	4	6	2	8	6	0	2	6	10	4	0	2	4	6	4
15_x	2	2	6	6	4	4	2	6	2	6	8	4	4	0	4	4
16_x	0	4	14	6	8	4	2	6	2	0	2	0	4	2	0	10
17_x	2	6	8	0	0	2	0	2	2	6	0	8	8	2	12	6
18_x	0	4	6	6	8	4	2	2	6	4	6	4	2	4	2	4
19_x	2	6	0	2	4	4	4	6	4	8	6	4	2	2	6	4
$1A_x$	0	6	6	0	8	2	4	6	4	2	4	6	2	0	4	10
$1B_x$	0	4	10	2	4	4	2	6	6	6	2	2	6	6	2	2
$1C_x$	0	0	8	2	12	2	6	2	8	6	6	2	4	0	4	2
$1D_x$	2	4	0	6	8	6	0	2	6	8	6	0	2	4	0	10
$1E_x$	0	10	8	2	8	2	0	2	6	4	2	4	6	4	2	4
$1F_x$	0	6	6	8	6	4	2	4	4	2	2	0	2	4	2	12
20_x	0	0	0	0	0	6	6	4	0	4	8	8	4	6	10	8
21_x	2	8	6	8	4	4	6	6	8	4	0	4	0	2	2	0
22_x	16	2	4	6	2	4	2	0	6	4	8	2	0	2	2	4
23_x	0	4	0	4	4	6	10	4	2	2	6	2	4	6	6	4
24_x	10	8	0	6	12	6	10	4	8	0	0	0	0	0	0	0
25_x	0	2	4	2	0	4	4	0	4	0	10	10	4	10	6	4
26_x	2	2	0	12	2	2	6	2	4	4	8	0	6	6	8	0
27_x	8	4	0	8	2	4	2	4	0	6	2	4	4	8	2	6
28_x	6	8	4	6	0	4	2	2	4	8	2	6	4	2	2	4
29_x	2	4	4	0	8	8	6	8	6	4	0	4	4	4	2	0
$2A_x$	6	0	0	6	6	4	6	8	2	4	0	2	2	4	6	8
$2B_x$	12	0	4	0	0	4	2	2	2	6	10	6	10	2	4	0
$2C_x$	4	2	6	0	0	6	8	6	4	2	2	8	4	6	4	2
$2D_x$	6	2	2	6	6	4	4	2	6	2	4	8	4	2	4	2
$2E_x$	4	6	2	4	2	4	4	2	4	2	4	6	4	10	4	2
$2F_x$	10	0	4	8	0	6	6	2	0	4	4	2	6	2	2	8
30_x	0	12	8	2	0	6	0	0	6	6	0	2	8	2	6	6
31_x	2	6	10	4	2	2	2	4	6	0	2	6	0	2	4	12
32_x	4	2	2	8	10	8	8	6	0	2	2	4	4	2	2	0
33_x	4	2	2	2	6	0	4	0	10	6	6	4	0	4	8	6
34_x	0	4	4	2	6	4	0	4	6	2	6	4	2	8	0	12
35_x	6	12	4	2	4	2	2	4	8	2	2	0	6	4	4	2
36_x	0	2	2	4	4	4	4	0	2	10	12	4	0	10	4	2
37_x	10	2	2	6	14	2	2	6	2	0	4	6	2	0	4	2
38_x	0	4	14	0	8	2	0	4	4	4	2	0	8	2	4	8
39_x	2	4	8	0	6	2	0	6	2	6	4	2	8	6	2	6
$3A_x$	8	4	0	4	6	2	0	4	6	8	6	0	6	0	4	6
$3B_x$	0	4	6	6	2	2	2	14	0	12	0	4	2	2	8	0
$3C_x$	0	6	16	0	2	2	2	8	4	2	0	12	6	2	2	0
$3D_x$	0	6	2	2	2	6	8	2	4	2	6	2	6	2	4	10
$3E_x$	4	2	2	4	4	0	6	10	4	2	4	6	6	2	6	2
$3F_x$	0	4	6	6	4	8	4	0	4	8	4	0	4	8	2	2

Table B.6. The difference distribution table of S6.

Input XOR	Output XOR															
	0_x	1_x	2_x	3_x	4_x	5_x	6_x	7_x	8_x	9_x	A_x	B_x	C_x	D_x	E_x	F_x
0_x	64	0	0	0	0	0	0	0	0	0	0	0	0	0	0	0
1_x	0	0	0	2	0	4	4	14	0	12	4	6	2	6	6	4
2_x	0	0	0	0	0	12	2	2	0	4	0	4	8	12	6	14
3_x	8	2	12	2	6	8	6	0	6	4	4	2	2	0	0	2
4_x	0	0	0	8	0	4	4	8	0	8	8	12	2	6	2	2
5_x	6	0	0	2	8	0	8	4	0	2	6	0	10	6	6	6
6_x	0	2	12	0	8	4	8	2	4	4	4	2	6	0	6	2
7_x	4	6	4	12	0	4	2	0	0	14	2	6	4	0	0	6
8_x	0	0	0	8	0	0	6	10	0	4	12	4	6	6	0	8
9_x	10	8	4	8	6	2	2	0	2	6	8	2	0	6	0	0
A_x	0	10	6	2	12	2	4	0	4	4	6	4	4	0	0	6
B_x	0	2	2	2	4	8	6	4	4	0	4	2	6	4	2	14
C_x	0	0	0	4	0	4	8	4	0	2	6	0	14	12	8	2
D_x	6	6	2	4	2	6	4	6	6	4	8	8	0	2	0	0
E_x	0	12	10	10	0	2	4	2	8	6	4	2	0	0	2	2
F_x	2	0	0	0	6	8	8	0	6	2	4	6	8	0	6	8
10_x	0	0	0	4	0	2	8	6	0	6	4	10	8	4	8	4
11_x	6	10	10	4	4	2	0	4	4	0	2	8	4	2	2	2
12_x	0	0	8	8	2	8	2	8	6	4	2	8	0	0	8	0
13_x	4	4	2	2	8	6	0	2	2	2	0	4	6	8	14	0
14_x	0	8	6	2	8	8	2	6	4	2	0	2	8	6	0	2
15_x	4	4	8	2	4	0	4	10	8	2	4	4	4	2	0	4
16_x	0	6	10	2	2	2	2	4	10	8	2	2	0	4	10	0
17_x	8	2	4	2	6	4	0	6	4	4	2	2	0	4	8	8
18_x	0	16	2	2	6	0	6	0	6	2	8	0	6	0	2	8
19_x	0	8	0	2	4	4	10	4	8	0	6	4	2	6	2	4
$1A_x$	0	2	4	8	12	4	0	6	4	4	0	2	0	6	4	8
$1B_x$	0	6	2	6	4	2	4	4	6	4	8	4	2	0	10	2
$1C_x$	0	8	4	4	2	6	6	6	6	4	6	8	0	2	0	2
$1D_x$	4	4	4	0	0	2	4	2	4	2	2	4	10	10	8	4
$1E_x$	0	0	2	2	12	6	2	0	12	2	2	4	2	6	8	4
$1F_x$	2	2	10	14	2	4	2	4	4	6	0	2	4	8	0	0
20_x	0	0	0	14	0	8	4	2	0	4	2	8	2	6	0	14
21_x	4	2	6	2	12	2	4	0	6	4	10	2	4	2	2	2
22_x	10	6	0	2	4	4	10	0	4	0	12	2	8	0	0	2
23_x	0	6	2	2	2	4	6	10	0	4	8	2	2	6	0	10
24_x	4	2	0	6	8	2	6	0	8	2	2	0	8	2	12	2
25_x	2	0	2	16	2	4	6	4	6	8	2	4	0	6	0	2
26_x	6	10	0	10	0	6	4	4	2	2	4	6	2	4	2	2
27_x	4	0	2	0	2	2	14	0	4	6	6	2	12	2	4	4
28_x	14	4	6	4	4	6	2	0	6	6	2	2	4	0	2	2
29_x	2	2	0	2	0	8	4	2	4	6	4	4	6	4	12	4
$2A_x$	2	4	0	0	0	2	8	12	0	8	2	4	8	4	4	6
$2B_x$	16	6	2	4	6	10	2	2	2	2	2	2	4	2	2	0
$2C_x$	2	6	6	8	2	2	0	6	0	8	4	2	2	6	8	2
$2D_x$	6	2	4	2	8	8	2	8	2	4	4	0	2	0	8	4
$2E_x$	2	4	8	0	2	2	2	4	0	2	8	4	14	6	0	6
$2F_x$	2	2	2	8	0	2	2	6	4	6	8	8	6	2	0	6
30_x	0	6	8	2	8	4	4	0	10	4	4	6	0	0	2	6
31_x	0	8	4	0	6	2	2	6	6	0	0	2	6	4	8	10
32_x	2	4	0	0	6	4	10	6	6	4	6	2	4	6	2	2
33_x	0	16	6	8	2	0	2	2	4	2	8	4	0	4	6	0
34_x	0	4	14	8	2	2	2	4	16	2	2	2	0	2	0	4
35_x	0	6	0	0	10	8	2	2	6	0	0	8	6	4	4	8
36_x	2	0	2	2	4	6	4	4	2	2	4	2	4	16	10	0
37_x	6	6	6	8	4	2	4	4	4	0	6	8	2	4	0	0
38_x	0	2	2	2	8	8	0	2	2	2	0	6	6	4	10	10
39_x	4	4	16	8	0	6	4	2	4	4	2	6	0	2	2	0
$3A_x$	16	6	4	0	2	0	2	6	0	4	8	10	0	0	4	2
$3B_x$	2	0	0	2	0	4	4	4	2	6	2	6	6	12	12	2
$3C_x$	0	0	8	0	12	8	2	6	6	4	0	2	2	4	6	4
$3D_x$	2	4	12	2	2	2	0	4	6	10	2	6	4	2	0	6
$3E_x$	4	6	6	6	2	0	4	8	2	10	4	6	0	4	2	0
$3F_x$	14	0	0	0	8	0	6	8	4	2	0	0	4	8	4	6

Table B.7. The difference distribution table of S7.

Input	Output XOR															
XOR	0_x	1_x	2_x	3_x	4_x	5_x	6_x	7_x	8_x	9_x	A_x	B_x	C_x	D_x	E_x	F_x
0_x	64	0	0	0	0	0	0	0	0	0	0	0	0	0	0	0
1_x	0	0	0	6	0	16	10	0	0	0	6	0	14	6	2	4
2_x	0	0	0	8	0	10	4	2	0	10	2	4	8	8	6	2
3_x	6	0	2	8	2	6	4	0	6	6	6	2	2	0	8	6
4_x	0	0	0	2	0	4	6	12	0	6	8	4	10	4	8	0
5_x	4	10	6	0	0	2	6	0	4	10	4	6	8	2	0	2
6_x	0	0	10	4	6	4	4	8	2	6	4	2	4	2	2	6
7_x	6	2	8	2	8	10	6	6	4	2	0	4	0	0	0	6
8_x	0	0	0	4	0	6	4	2	0	8	6	10	8	2	2	12
9_x	8	4	0	6	0	4	4	6	2	4	6	2	12	2	0	4
A_x	0	0	16	4	6	6	4	0	4	6	4	2	2	0	0	10
B_x	2	8	0	6	2	6	0	4	4	10	0	2	10	2	6	2
C_x	0	0	0	2	0	10	10	6	0	6	6	6	2	6	10	0
D_x	6	0	4	10	2	0	8	6	2	2	6	10	2	2	2	2
E_x	0	0	6	8	4	8	0	2	10	6	2	4	6	2	4	2
F_x	8	0	4	2	2	4	2	2	2	6	4	6	0	2	14	6
10_x	0	0	0	4	0	0	8	12	0	0	8	8	2	10	6	6
11_x	0	6	4	6	2	2	6	6	4	6	4	6	0	4	4	4
12_x	0	4	0	8	6	2	8	4	2	4	4	6	2	4	10	0
13_x	4	2	2	6	8	6	2	2	14	2	2	4	2	2	2	4
14_x	0	16	4	2	6	0	2	6	4	0	4	6	4	6	4	0
15_x	0	10	6	0	6	0	2	8	2	2	0	8	2	6	6	6
16_x	0	12	6	4	6	0	0	0	8	6	6	2	2	6	4	2
17_x	0	6	8	0	6	2	4	6	6	0	2	6	4	4	2	8
18_x	0	12	2	2	8	0	8	0	10	4	4	2	4	2	0	6
19_x	6	4	8	0	8	0	4	2	0	0	12	2	4	6	2	6
$1A_x$	0	4	0	2	8	8	0	4	8	0	0	0	6	2	0	16
$1B_x$	2	4	8	10	2	4	2	8	2	4	8	2	0	2	4	2
$1C_x$	0	12	6	4	6	4	2	2	6	0	4	4	2	10	2	0
$1D_x$	8	6	0	0	10	0	0	8	10	4	2	2	2	8	4	0
$1E_x$	0	4	8	6	8	2	4	4	10	2	2	4	2	0	6	2
$1F_x$	4	2	4	2	6	2	4	0	2	6	2	2	2	16	8	2
20_x	0	0	0	16	0	4	0	0	0	14	6	4	2	0	4	14
21_x	0	0	2	10	2	8	10	0	0	6	6	0	10	2	2	6
22_x	8	0	6	0	6	4	10	2	0	6	8	0	4	4	2	4
23_x	4	8	0	6	0	4	8	6	2	2	10	4	8	0	0	2
24_x	4	0	4	8	4	6	2	4	8	6	2	0	0	4	4	8
25_x	0	4	6	8	2	8	8	0	4	2	4	4	2	2	6	4
26_x	2	6	0	6	4	4	4	6	6	0	4	4	10	4	2	2
27_x	6	6	0	0	2	2	6	2	4	4	6	10	2	6	2	6
28_x	10	2	6	2	4	12	12	0	2	2	4	0	0	0	2	6
29_x	4	0	0	14	2	10	4	2	8	6	4	0	4	2	2	2
$2A_x$	8	8	0	2	0	2	4	0	2	6	8	14	2	8	0	0
$2B_x$	2	2	0	0	4	2	10	4	6	2	4	0	6	4	8	10
$2C_x$	2	6	6	2	4	6	2	0	2	6	4	0	6	4	10	4
$2D_x$	8	0	4	4	6	2	0	0	6	8	2	4	6	4	4	6
$2E_x$	6	2	2	4	2	2	6	12	4	0	4	2	8	8	0	2
$2F_x$	8	12	4	6	6	4	2	2	2	2	4	2	2	4	0	4
30_x	0	4	6	2	10	2	2	2	4	8	0	0	8	4	6	6
31_x	4	6	8	0	4	6	0	4	4	6	10	2	2	4	4	0
32_x	6	6	6	2	4	6	0	2	0	6	8	2	2	6	6	2
33_x	6	6	4	2	4	0	0	10	2	2	0	6	8	4	0	10
34_x	0	2	12	4	10	4	0	4	12	0	2	4	2	2	2	4
35_x	6	4	4	0	10	0	0	4	10	0	0	4	2	8	8	4
36_x	4	6	2	2	2	2	6	8	6	4	2	6	0	4	10	0
37_x	2	2	8	2	4	4	4	2	6	2	0	10	6	10	2	0
38_x	0	4	8	4	2	6	6	2	4	2	2	4	6	4	4	6
39_x	4	4	4	8	0	6	0	6	4	8	2	2	2	4	8	2
$3A_x$	8	8	0	4	2	0	10	4	0	0	0	4	8	6	8	2
$3B_x$	8	2	6	4	4	4	4	0	6	4	4	6	4	4	4	0
$3C_x$	0	6	6	6	6	0	0	8	8	2	4	8	4	2	4	0
$3D_x$	2	2	8	0	10	0	2	12	0	4	0	8	0	2	6	8
$3E_x$	6	4	0	0	4	4	0	10	6	2	6	12	2	4	0	4
$3F_x$	0	6	6	0	4	4	6	10	0	6	8	2	0	4	8	0

Table B.8. The difference distribution table of S8.

Glossary

The purpose of this glossary is to provide informal (and often imprecise) definitions for commonly used terms and phrases. Formal definitions can be found either in the text or in the cited references.

0R-attack: A differential cryptanalytic attack in which the characteristic has the same number of rounds as the cryptosystem.

1R-attack: A differential cryptanalytic attack in which the characteristic is shorter by one round than the cryptosystem.

2R-attack: A differential cryptanalytic attack in which the characteristic is shorter by two rounds than the cryptosystem.

3R-attack: A differential cryptanalytic attack in which the characteristic is shorter by three rounds than the cryptosystem.

Actual Subkey: The subkeys of the equivalent description of FEAL, in which the XOR of the data with a subkey in the final transformation is eliminated. Differential cryptanalytic attacks find the actual subkeys, rather than the subkeys.

Adaptive Attack: A cryptanalytic attack in which the attacker is able to choose each new plaintexts to be encrypted under the secret key (or each new ciphertexts to be decrypted) as a function of all the previous plaintexts and ciphertexts. The attack uses the knowledge of both the plaintexts and the ciphertexts in order to find the key.

Birthday Attack: An attack on hash functions which is based on the birthday paradox. Its complexity is about the square-root of the number of possible hash values.

Birthday Paradox: There is probability of about one half that in a class of 23 children, there are two with the same birthday. The extension of this paradox states that when more than $\sqrt{n}$ elements are chosen at random from n possible elements, at least one element is likely to be chosen twice.

CBC mode: See *Cipher Block Chaining (CBC) mode.*

CFB mode: See *Cipher Feedback (CFB) mode.*

Characteristic: An n-round characteristic describes a possible evolution of the differences in the various rounds of an iterated cryptosystem and estimates the probability that a random pair with the specified plaintext difference would have the specified differences in the various rounds when it is encrypted under a random key. Characteristics can be concatenated with other characteristics under certain circumstances. Characteristics which can be concatenated with themselves are called iterative characteristics.

Chosen Ciphertext Attack: A cryptanalytic attack in which the attacker chooses the ciphertexts to be decrypted under the secret key. The attack uses the knowledge of both the plaintexts and the ciphertexts in order to find the key.

Chosen Plaintext Attack: A cryptanalytic attack in which the attacker chooses the plaintexts to be encrypted under the secret key. The attack uses the knowledge of both the plaintexts and the ciphertexts in order to find the key.

Cipher Block Chaining (CBC) mode: An operation mode in which each plaintext block is XORed with the previous ciphertext block before the encryption algorithm is applied. In this mode, two equal plaintext blocks may be encrypted to different ciphertext blocks, even if the same key is used, if the previous ciphertext blocks are different.

Cipher Feedback (CFB) mode: An operation mode similar to the output feedback mode which uses the previous ciphertext as input to the encryption process, rather than the previous output of the blockcipher. Each plaintext block is XORed with the resulting output block to form the ciphertext block. Variants of this mode with blocks shorter than 64 bits are also defined.

Ciphertext: The encrypted form of the plaintext, which is supposed to hide the information from anybody who does not know the key.

Ciphertext Only Attack: A cryptanalytic attack which uses only the ciphertexts (whose plaintexts are unknown to the attacker) in order to find the plaintexts or the key.

Complementation Property: For certain cryptosystems, complementation of particular bits in the plaintext and of particular bits in the key causes complementation of particular bits the ciphertext. Such a property can be used to reduce the complexity of exhaustive search under a chosen plaintext attack, and in some circumstances even under a known plaintext attack. DES has such a complementation property that reduces the complexity of exhaustive search from 2^{56} to 2^{55}.

Counting Scheme: Differential cryptanalytic attacks locate the most probable keys from a sufficiently large pool of pairs. Each pair suggests several keys, and the key suggested by the maximal number of pairs is likely to be the real key. All counting schemes count the number of pairs suggesting each possible key value, but they differ by the characteristic they use, the number of key bits they count on and the signal to noise ratio.

Cryptanalytic Attack: An algorithm in which an attacker can uncover the plaintexts of given ciphertexts without knowing the key, or even find the key itself. The four major types of cryptanalytic attacks are: ciphertext only attacks, known plaintext attacks, chosen plaintext attacks and adaptive attacks.

Cryptosystem: A tool for making data unintelligible to unauthorized parties. Cryptosystems use keys to encrypt plaintexts to ciphertexts. When the key is known, transforming plaintexts to ciphertexts should be easy. When the key is unknown, extracting any information about the key or the plaintexts should be very difficult.

Data Analysis Phase: Differential cryptanalytic attacks on cryptosystems are divided into two phases. In the data collection phase many plaintexts are encrypted on the target machine with the unknown key. In the data analysis phase the resultant ciphertexts are analyzed by the attacker in order to find the key.

Data Collection Phase: See the description of the *Data Analysis Phase.*

Data Encryption Standard: See *DES.*

Dependent Key: A key from which subkeys are derived via some key scheduling algorithm. This is the standard type of key for iterated cryptosystems. In this book, dependent keys are viewed as a special type of independent keys.

DES: A cryptosystem which was developed by IBM[28] and adopted by the NBS in 1977 as the standard cryptosystem for securing civilian applications dealing with sensitive but unclassified data. See Appendix A for technical description.

DES-like Cryptosystem: An iterated cryptosystem whose structure is similar to DES: In each round the data is divided into two halves, an F function operates on the right half, its output is XORed into the left half, and the halves are exchanged.

Design rules: The design rules of DES were never published due to national security reasons. Recently, Don Coppersmith who was one of the designers of DES announced that the design team at IBM was aware of differential cryptanalysis in 1974 and that DES was specifically designed to defeat it.

Difference Distribution Table: A table that shows the distribution of the input XORs and output XORs of all the possible pairs of mappings by an S box. In a difference distribution table each row corresponds to a particular input XOR, each column corresponds to a particular output XOR and the entries contain the number of possible pairs with such an input XOR and an output XOR.

Differential Cryptanalysis: A method which studies the evolution of differences during the encryption of pairs of plaintexts, and derives the most likely keys from a pool of many pairs. Differential cryptanalysis can also be used to find collisions in hash functions. For DES-like cryptosystems the differences are usually in terms of exclusive-or of the intermediate data in the pair.

ECB mode: See *Electronic Code Book (ECB) mode.*

Electronic Code Book (ECB) mode: An operation mode in which each plaintext block is encrypted separately. In this mode, two equal plaintext blocks are always encrypted to the same ciphertext blocks, if the same key is used.

Exhaustive Search: Under a known plaintext attack, it is possible to search the whole key space and locate the key which encrypts a known plaintext to its corresponding known ciphertext. The complexity of exhaustive search (which is the size of the key space) is an obvious upper bound on the strength of cryptosystems.

F function: The main operation in a round of a DES-like cryptosystem is called the F function. The role of the F function is to mix the data with the subkeys. The F function of DES uses S boxes, XORs and permutations. The F function of FEAL use addition operations, XORs and byte rotations.

FEAL: A family of DES-like cryptosystems which is designed to be easily and efficiently implementable on microprocessors. The F function of FEAL is based on the addition operation and byte rotation (rather than S boxes and permutations). The original four-round variant of FEAL, called FEAL-4[36], was broken by Den-Boer[12]. Then, the eight-round variant FEAL-8[35,26] was suggested. Later, FEAL-N[23] with an arbitrary number of rounds and FEAL-NX[24] with a longer 128-bit key were also suggested. In this book we cryptanalyze all the variants of FEAL with up to 31 rounds.

GDES: See *Generalized DES Scheme (GDES).*

Generalized DES Scheme (GDES): GDES[31,33] is an attempt to speed up DES without weakening its security. In GDES the blocksize is extended and the block is divided into more than two 32-bit parts.

In each round the F function of DES is applied on one part and its output is XORed into all the other parts. In the recommended variant, the F function is applied 16 times (as in DES) but the blocksize is 256 bits.

Hash Function: Cryptographic functions which hash arbitrarily long messages into fixed length values (usually 128-bit long) with the following two criteria: (a) It is hard to find a message which hashes to any particular value. (b) It is hard to find a pair of messages which hash to the same value. Implementations of digital signatures use hash functions to speed up the signature process by hashing long messages and signing only the fixed length result.

IBM: IBM has developed the Lucifer cryptosystem in the 1970's. DES evolved from the Lucifer project.

Independent Key: A list of subkeys which is not necessarily derivable from some key via the key scheduling algorithm.

Initial Permutation (IP): The first operation during the encryption by DES is to permute the order of the plaintext bits. After the initial permutation, the 16 rounds are applied.

Iterated Cryptosystem: A cryptosystem based on iterating a relatively weak round-function many times. In many iterated cryptosystems the round-function is based on an F function which mixes half of the data with a subkey, and the output of the F function is XORed to the other half of the data.

Iterative Characteristic: A characteristic which can be concatenated with itself.

Key: A secret random value which is used to control the encryption of a plaintext into its secure ciphertext form. Decryption should be easy when the key is known, but very difficult when the key is unknown.

Key Processing Algorithm: The particular algorithm which calculates the subkeys from the key in the FEAL cryptosystem. This algorithm is more complex than the key scheduling algorithm of DES, and it calculates the subkeys in a non-linear way.

Key Scheduling Algorithm: The algorithm which calculates the subkeys from the key in iterated cryptosystems. In DES, the key scheduling algorithm copies each key bit into various positions in about 14 subkeys.

Khafre: A fast software oriented cryptosystem[22] whose round-function is based on fixed eight bit to 32-bit S boxes.

Khufu: A fast software oriented cryptosystem[22] whose round-function is based on key-dependent eight-bit to 32-bit S boxes.

Known Plaintext Attack: A cryptanalytic attack which uses given plaintexts as well as their corresponding ciphertexts in order to find the key.

LOKI: A DES-like cryptosystem[6] whose F function uses one twelve-bit to eight-bit S box (based on irreducible polynomials) replicated four times in each round.

Lucifer: A 128-bit substitution/permutation cryptosystem designed by IBM prior to the design of DES. Lucifer has two variants: In the first variant[15] the data is divided in each round into groups of four bits, an S box chosen by a key bit from two possible S boxes is applied on each group, and the output bits of the S boxes are permuted. The ciphertexts are decrypted by applying the rounds in a reverse order and using the inverse of the S boxes. The second variant[37] is a direct predecessor of DES, whose F function uses only two four-bit to four-bit S boxes replicated eight times.

Meet in the Middle Attack: An attack in which the evolution of the data is studied from both directions: from the plaintext forwards towards an intermediate round and from the ciphertext backwards towards the same intermediate round. If the results at the intermediate round are not the same in both directions, then the tested value of the key is not the real value. If both results are the same in several encryptions, then the tested value of the key is the real value with high probability.

Method of Formal Coding: A method in which the formal expression of each bit in the ciphertext is found as a XOR sum of products of the bits of the plaintext and the key. The formal manipulations of these expressions may decrease the key search effort. The application of this method to DES requires an enormous amount of computer memory which makes the whole approach impractical[31,32].

Modes of Operation: Methods in which cryptosystems can be used to encrypt multi-block plaintexts. The simplest mode is the electronic code book (ECB) mode in which all the plaintext blocks in a message are encrypted separately using the same key. A more complex mode is the cipher block chaining (CBC) mode in which each plaintext block is XORed with the previous ciphertext block before the encryption. Additional modes of operation are the output feedback (OFB) mode and the cipher feedback (CFB) mode. They are described in Appendix A.2.

N-Hash: A hash function[25] which was suggested by the designers of FEAL and which uses an F function similar to the one of FEAL. N-Hash hashes messages of arbitrary length into 128-bit values.

National Bureau of Standards (NBS): The U.S. institute that standardized DES. Its name was later changed to National Institute for Standards and Technology (NIST).

Octet: A structure of eight plaintexts which consists of four pairs motivated by each one of three different characteristics. In total, there are 12 pairs in each octet.

OFB mode: See *Output Feedback (OFB) mode.*

Output Feedback (OFB) mode: An operation mode which generates a pseudo-random bit string by repeatedly encrypting a 64-bit block (initially set to an initial value) under a fixed key. Each plaintext block is XORed with the pseudo-random block to form the ciphertext block. Variants of this mode with blocks shorter than 64 bits are also defined.

Pair: Differential cryptanalytic attacks analyze the evolution of the differences between intermediate values when two related plaintexts are encrypted. The two plaintexts of a pair are chosen to have a particular initial difference. A pair whose differences during the various rounds are as expected by the corresponding characteristic is called a right pair, and any other pair is called a wrong pair.

Plaintext: The original (clear) form of the encrypted data, which is transformed into a ciphertext form by using a cryptosystem and a key.

Quartet: A structure of four plaintexts which consists of two pairs motivated by each one of two different characteristics. In total, there are four pairs in each quartet.

REDOC-II: A ten-round 70-bit block software oriented cryptosystem[38,8] whose round-function is relatively complex, and thus it is claimed to be secure even with a small number of rounds.

Right Pair: A pair in which the differences during the encryption of the two plaintexts are as predicted in the corresponding characteristic.

Round: Iterated cryptosystems iterate weak functions many times. Each iteration of the weak function is called a round, and the weak function itself is called a round-function. In many iterated cryptosystems, the round-function is based on an F function.

Round-Function: See the description of *Round.*

S Box: A lookup table which maps short input strings into short output strings. In many iterated cryptosystems (like DES) the S boxes are the only non-linear operations, and thus the strength of the cryptosystem crucially depends on the choice of the S boxes.

Signal to Noise Ratio: The expected ratio between the number of times the correct key value is counted by right pairs and the number of times an incorrect key value is counted (by right or wrong pairs) in a particular counting scheme. The number of pairs required by the counting scheme can be approximated by using the signal to noise ratio. A counting scheme whose signal to noise ratio is high requires relatively few pairs (with relatively few right pairs among them). A counting scheme whose signal to noise ratio is too low may require an unrealistic number of pairs. The signal to noise ratio is denoted by S/N.

Snefru: A hash function[21] which uses fixed eight-bit to 32-bit S boxes. Snefru hashes messages of arbitrary length into 128-bit values.

Structure: A structure groups together many related plaintexts in a way which saves data by allowing many pairs to exist in a relatively small group of plaintexts. Typical examples of structures are quartets and octets.

Subkey: A key dependent value used in one round of an iterated cryptosystem. DES has 16 rounds and uses 16 subkeys derived from the key by placing each key bit in about 14 subkeys via the key scheduling algorithm. In other iterated cryptosystems the subkeys are derived by more complex procedures. In FEAL, this procedure is called key processing algorithm.

Wrong Pair: Any pair of plaintexts which is not a right pair.

Bibliography

[1] Carlisle M. Adams, *On Immunity against Biham and Shamir's "Differential Cryptanalysis"*, Information Processing Letters, Vol. 41, No. 2, pp. 77–80, 1992.

[2] Thomas A. Berson, *Long Key Variants of DES*, Advances in Cryptology, proceedings of CRYPTO'82, pp. 311–313, 1982.

[3] Eli Biham, Adi Shamir, *Differential Cryptanalysis of FEAL and N-Hash*, technical report CS91-17, Department of Applied Mathematics and Computer Science, The Weizmann Institute of Science, 1991. The extended abstract appears in Lecture Notes in Computer Science, Advances in Cryptology, proceedings of EUROCRYPT'91, pp. 1–16, 1991.

[4] E. F. Brickell, J. H. Moore, M. R. Purtill, *Structure in the S-Boxes of the DES*, Lecture Notes in Computer Science, Advances in Cryptology, proceedings of CRYPTO'86, pp. 3–7, 1986.

[5] Lawrence Brown, Matthew Kwan, Josef Pieprzyk, Jennifer Seberry, *Improving Resistance to Differential Cryptanalysis and the Redesign of LOKI*, Lecture Notes in Computer Science, Advances in Cryptology, proceedings of ASIACRYPT'91, 1991, to appear.

[6] Lawrence Brown, Josef Pieprzyk, Jennifer Seberry, *LOKI - A Cryptographic Primitive for Authentication and Secrecy Applications*, Lecture Notes in Computer Science, Advances in Cryptology, proceedings of AUSCRYPT'90, pp. 229–236, 1990.

[7] David Chaum, Jan-Hendrik Evertse, *Cryptanalysis of DES with a reduced number of rounds, Sequences of linear factors in block ciphers*, Lecture Notes in Computer Science, Advances in Cryptology, proceedings of CRYPTO'85, pp. 192–211, 1985.

[8] Thomas W. Cusick, Michael C. Wood, *The REDOC-II Cryptosystem*, Lecture Notes in Computer Science, Advances in Cryptology, proceedings of CRYPTO'90, pp. 545–563, 1990.

[9] D. W. Davies, private communication.

[10] D. W. Davies, G. I. P. Parkin, *The average Cycle Size of the Key Stream in Output Feedback Encipherment*, Lecture Notes in Computer Science, Cryptography, proceedings of the Workshop on Cryptography, Burg Feuerstein, Germany, March 29–April 2 1982, pp. 263–279, 1982. Also in Advances in Cryptology, proceedings of CRYPTO'82, pp. 97–98, 1982.

[11] M. H. Dawson, S. E. Tavares, *An Expanded Set of S-box Design Criteria Based On Information Theory and its Relation to Differential-Like Attacks*, Lecture Notes in Computer Science, Advances in Cryptology, proceedings of EUROCRYPT'91, pp. 352–367, 1991.

[12] Bert Den-Boer, *Cryptanalysis of F.E.A.L.*, Lecture Notes in Computer Science, Advances in Cryptology, proceedings of EUROCRYPT'88, pp. 293–300, 1988.

[13] Yvo Desmedt, Jean-Jacque Quisquater, Marc Davio, *Dependence of Output on Input in DES: Small Avalanche Characteristics*, Lecture Notes in Computer Science, Advances in Cryptology, proceedings of CRYPTO'84, pp. 359–376, 1984.

[14] W. Diffie, M. E. Hellman, *Exhaustive Cryptanalysis of the NBS Data Encryption Standard*, Computer, Vol. 10, No. 6, pp. 74–84, June 1977.

[15] H. Feistel, *Cryptography and Data Security*, Scientific American, Vol. 228, No. 5, pp. 15–23, May 1973.

[16] Henry Gilbert, Guy Chasse, *A Statistical Attack on the FEAL-8 Cryptosystem*, Lecture Notes in Computer Science, Advances in Cryptology, proceedings of CRYPTO'90, pp. 22–33, 1990.

[17] M. E. Hellman, *A Cryptanalytic Time-Memory Tradeoff*, IEEE Trans. Inform. Theory, Vol. 26, No. 4, pp. 401–406, July 1980.

[18] M. E. Hellman, R. Merkle, R. Schroppel, L. Washington, W. Diffie, S. Pohlig and P. Schweitzer, *Results of an Initial Attempt to Cryptanalyze the NBS Data Encryption Standard*, Stanford University, September 1976.

[19] Matthew Kwan, private communications.

[20] M. Matsui, *A New Method for Known Plaintext Attack of FEAL Cipher*, Abstracts of EUROCRYPT'92, May 1992.

[21] Ralph C. Merkle, *A Fast Software One-Way Hash Function*, Journal of Cryptology, Vol. 3, No. 1, pp. 43-58, 1990.

[22] Ralph C. Merkle, *Fast Software Encryption Functions*, Lecture Notes in Computer Science, Advances in Cryptology, proceedings of CRYPTO'90, pp. 476–501, 1990.

[23] Shoji Miyaguchi, *FEAL-N specifications*, technical note, NTT, 1989.

[24] Shoji Miyaguchi, *The FEAL cipher family*, Lecture Notes in Computer Science, Advances in Cryptology, proceedings of CRYPTO'90, pp. 627–638, 1990.

[25] S. Miyaguchi, K. Ohta, M. Iwata, *128-bit hash function (N-Hash)*, proceedings of SECURICOM'90, pp. 123–137, March 1990.

[26] Shoji Miyaguchi, Akira Shiraishi, Akihiro Shimizu, *Fast Data Encryption Algorithm FEAL-8*, Review of electrical communications laboratories, Vol. 36, No. 4, pp. 433–437, 1988.

[27] Sean Murphy, *The Cryptanalysis of FEAL-4 with 20 Chosen Plaintexts*, The Journal of Cryptology, Vol. 2, No. 3, pp. 145–154, 1990.

[28] National Bureau of Standards, *Data Encryption Standard*, U.S. Department of Commerce, FIPS pub. 46, January 1977.

[29] National Bureau of Standards, *DES Modes of Operation*, U.S. Department of Commerce, FIPS pub. 81, December 1980.

[30] Kaisa Nyberg, *Perfect nonlinear S-boxes*, Lecture Notes in Computer Science, Advances in Cryptology, proceedings of EUROCRYPT'91, pp. 378–386, 1991.

[31] Ingrid Schaumuller-Bichl, *Zur Analyse des Data Encryption Standard und Synthese Verwandter Chiffriersysteme*, Ph.D. Thesis, Linz University, May 1981.

[32] Ingrid Schaumuller-Bichl, *Cryptanalysis of the Data Encryption Standard by the Method of Formal Coding*, Lecture Notes in Computer Science, Cryptography, proceedings of the Workshop on Cryptography, Burg Feuerstein, Germany, March 29–April 2 1982, pp. 235–255, 1982.

[33] Ingrid Schaumuller-Bichl, *On the Design and Analysis of New Cipher Systems Related to the DES*, technical report, Linz University, 1983.

[34] Adi Shamir, *On the Security of DES*, Lecture Notes in Computer Science, Advances in Cryptology, proceedings of CRYPTO'85, pp. 280–281, 1985.

[35] Akihiro Shimizu, Shoji Miyaguchi, *Fast Data Encryption Algorithm FEAL*, Lecture Notes in Computer Science, Advances in Cryptology, proceedings of EUROCRYPT'87, pp. 267–278, 1987.

[36] Akihiro Shimizu, Shoji Miyaguchi, *Fast Data Encryption Algorithm FEAL*, Abstracts of EUROCRYPT'87, pp. VII-11–VII-14, April 1987.

[37] Arthur Sorkin, *Lucifer, a Cryptographic Algorithm*, Cryptologia, Vol. 8, No. 1, pp. 22–41, January 1984.

[38] Michael C. Wood, technical report, Cryptech Inc., Jamestown, NY, July 1990.

Index